LANDMARKS

Robert Macfarlane

PENGUIN BOOKS

PENGUIN BOOKS

UK | USA | Canada | Ireland | Australia
India | New Zealand | South Africa

Penguin Books is part of the Penguin Random House group of companies
whose addresses can be found at global.penguinrandomhouse.com.

First published by Hamish Hamilton 2015
Published with an additional glossary in Penguin Books 2016
001

Copyright © Robert Macfarlane, 2015, 2016

The moral right of the author has been asserted

The permissions on page 423 constitute an extension of this copyright page

Interior wood engravings by Jonathan Gibbs

Set in 11.13/14.28 pt Fournier MT Std
Typeset by Jouve (UK), Milton Keynes
Printed in Great Britain by Clays Ltd, St Ives plc

A CIP catalogue record for this book is available from the British Library

ISBN: 978-0-241-96787-4

*For Anne Campbell, Will Macfarlane
and Finlay MacLeod*

Where lies your landmark, seamark, or soul's star?
Gerard Manley Hopkins (1886)

Scholars, I plead with you,
Where are your dictionaries of the wind, the grasses?
Norman MacCaig (1983)

CONTENTS

Contents

I

The Word-Hoard

This is a book about the power of language – strong style, single words – to shape our sense of place. It is a field guide to literature I love, and it is a word-hoard of the astonishing lexis for landscape that exists in the comprision of islands, rivers, strands, fells, lochs, cities, towns, corries, hedgerows, fields and edgelands uneasily known as Britain and Ireland. The ten following chapters explore writing so fierce in its focus that it can change the vision of its readers for good, in both senses. Their nine glossaries gather thousands of words from dozens of languages and dialects for specific aspects of landscape, nature and weather. The writers collected here come from Essex to the Cairngorms, Connemara to Northumbria and Suffolk to Surbiton. The words collected here come from Unst to the Lizard, from Pembrokeshire to Norfolk; from Norn and Old English, Anglo-Romani, Cornish, Welsh, Irish, Gaelic, the Orcadian, Shetlandic and Doric dialects of Scots, and numerous regional versions of English, through to the last vestiges of living Norman still spoken on the Channel Islands.

Landmarks has been years in the making. For as long as I can remember, I have been drawn to the work of writers who use words exactly and exactingly when describing landscape and natural life. 'The hardest thing of all to see is what is really there,' wrote J. A. Baker in *The Peregrine* (1967), a book that brilliantly shows how such seeing might occur in language, written as it is in prose that has 'the quivering intensity of an arrow thudding into a tree'. And for over a decade I have been collecting place-words as I have found them: gleaned singly from conversations, correspondences or books, and jotted down in journals or on slips of paper. Now and then I have hit buried treasure in the form of vernacular dictionaries or extraordinary people – troves that have held gleaming handfuls of coinages. The word-lists of *Landmarks* have their origin in one such trove, turned up on the moors of the Outer Hebridean island of Lewis in 2007. There, as you will read in the next chapter, I was shown a 'Peat Glossary': a list of the hundreds of Gaelic terms for the moorland that stretches over much of Lewis's interior. The glossary had been compiled by Hebridean friends of mine through archival research and oral history. Some of the language it recorded was still spoken – but much had fallen into disuse. The remarkable referential exactitude of that glossary, and the poetry of so many of its terms, set my head a-whirr with words.

Although I knew Gaelic to be richly responsive to the sites in which it was spoken, it was my guess that other tongues in these islands also possessed wealths of words for features of place – words that together constituted a vast vanished, or vanishing, language for landscape. It seemed to me then that although we have our compendia of flora, fauna, birds, reptiles and insects, we lack a *Terra Britannica*, as it were: a gathering of terms for the land and its specificities – terms used by fishermen, farmers, sailors, scientists, crofters, mountaineers, soldiers, shepherds, walkers and unrecorded ordinary others for whom specialized ways of indicating aspects of place have been vital to everyday practice and perception. It seemed, too, that it might be worthwhile assembling some of this fine-grained and fabulously diverse vocabulary, and releasing its poetry back into imaginative circulation.

The same year I first saw the Peat Glossary, a new edition of the *Oxford Junior Dictionary* was published. A sharp-eyed reader noticed that there had been a culling of words concerning nature. Under pressure, Oxford University Press revealed a list of the entries it no longer felt to be relevant to a modern-day childhood. The deletions included *acorn, adder, ash, beech, bluebell, buttercup, catkin, conker, cowslip, cygnet, dandelion, fern, hazel, heather, heron, ivy, kingfisher, lark, mistletoe, nectar, newt, otter, pasture* and *willow*. The words introduced to the new edition included *attachment, block-graph, blog, broadband, bullet-point, celebrity, chatroom, committee, cut-and-paste, MP3 player* and *voice-mail*.

When the head of children's dictionaries at OUP was asked why the decision had been taken to delete those 'nature words', she explained that the dictionary needed to reflect the consensus experience of modern-day childhood. 'When you look back at older versions of dictionaries, there were lots of examples of flowers for instance,' she said; 'that was because many children lived in semi-rural environments and saw the seasons. Nowadays, the environment has changed.' There is a realism to her response – but also an alarming acceptance of the idea that children might no longer see the seasons, or that the rural environment might be so unproblematically disposable.

The substitutions made in the dictionary – the outdoor and the natural being displaced by the indoor and the virtual – are a small but significant symptom of the simulated life we increasingly live. Children are now (and valuably) adept ecologists of the technoscape, with numerous terms for file types but few for different trees and creatures. For *blackberry*, read *BlackBerry*. A basic literacy of landscape is falling away up and down the ages. A common language – a language *of* the commons – is getting rarer. And what is lost along with this literacy is something precious: a kind of word magic, the power that certain terms possess to enchant our relations with nature and place. As the writer Henry Porter observed, the OUP deletions removed the 'euphonious vocabulary of the natural world – words which do not simply label an object or action but in some mysterious and beautiful way become part of it'.

Landmarks is a celebration and defence of such language. Over the years, and especially over the past two years, thousands of place-terms have reached me. They have come by letter, email and telephone, scribbled on postcards or yellowed pre-war foolscap, transcribed from cassette recordings of Suffolk longshoremen made half a century ago, or taken from hand-drawn maps of hill country and coastline, and delved with delight from lexicons and archives around the country and the Web. I have had such pleasure meeting them, these words: migrant birds, arriving from distant places with story and metaphor caught in their feathers; or strangers coming into the home, stamping the snow from their feet, fresh from the blizzard and a long journey.

Many of these terms have mingled oddness and familiarity in the manner that Freud calls uncanny: peculiar in their particularity, but recognizable in that they name something conceivable, if not instantly locatable. *Ammil* is a Devon term for the fine film of silver ice that coats leaves, twigs and grass when freeze follows thaw, a beautifully exact word for a fugitive phenomenon I have several times seen but never before been able to name. Shetlandic has a word, *af'rug*, for 'the reflex of a wave after it has struck the shore'; another, *pirr*, meaning 'a light breath of wind, such as will make a cat's paw on the water'; and another, *klett*, for 'a low-lying earth-fast rock on the seashore'. On Exmoor, *zwer* is the onomatopoeic term for the sound made by a covey of partridges taking flight. *Smeuse* is a Sussex dialect noun for 'the gap in the base of a hedge made by the regular passage of a small animal'; now I know the word *smeuse*, I will notice these signs of creaturely movement more often.

Most fascinating to me are those terms for which no counterpart of comparable concision exists in another language. Such scalpel-sharp words are untranslatable without remainder. The need for precise discrimination of this kind has occurred most often where landscape is the venue of work. The Icelandic novelist Jón Kalman Stefánsson writes of fishermen speaking 'coddish' far out into the North Atlantic; the miners working the Great Northern Coalfield in England's north-east developed a dialect known as 'Pitmatical' or 'yakka', so dense it proved incomprehensible to Victorian parliamentary commissioners seeking to improve conditions in the mines in the 1840s. The name 'Pitmatical' was originally chosen to echo 'mathematical', and thereby emphasize the craft and skilful precision of the colliers. Such super-specific argots are born of lives lived long – and laboured hard – on land and at sea. The terms they contain allow us glimpses through other eyes, permit brief access to distant habits of perception. The poet Norman MacCaig commended the 'seagull voice' of his Aunt Julia, who lived her long life on the Isle of Harris, so embedded in her terrain that she came to think *with* and speak *in* its creatures and climate.

As well as these untranslatable terms, I have gathered synonyms – especially those that bring new energies to familiar phenomena. The variant English terms for 'icicle' – *aquabob* (Kent), *clinkerbell* and *daggler* (Wessex), *cancervell* (Exmoor), *ickle* (Yorkshire), *tankle* (Durham), *shuckle* (Cumbria) – form a tinkling poem of their own. In Northamptonshire dialect 'to thaw' is *to ungive*. The beauty of this variant I find hard to articulate, but it surely has to do with the paradox of thaw figured as restraint or retention, and the wintry notion that cold, frost and snow might themselves be a form of gift – an addition to the landscape that will in time be subtracted by warmth.

~

'Language is fossil poetry,' wrote Ralph Waldo Emerson in 1844, '[a]s the limestone of the continent consists of infinite masses of the shells of animalcules, so language is made up of images, or tropes, which now, in their secondary use, have long ceased to remind us of their poetic origin.' Emerson, as essayist, sought to reverse this petrification and restore the 'poetic origin' of words, thereby revealing the originary role of 'nature' in language. Considering the verb *to consider*, he reminds us that it comes from the Latin *con-siderare*, and thus carries a meaning of 'to study or see with the stars'. Etymology illuminates – a mundane verb is suddenly starlit. Many of the terms in the glossaries that follow seem, at least to me, as yet unpetrified and still vivid with poetry. They function as topograms – tiny poems that conjure scenes. *Blinter* is a northern Scots word meaning 'a cold dazzle', connoting especially 'the radiance of winter stars on a clear night', or 'ice-splinters catching low light'. Instantly the word opens prospects: walking sunwards through snow late on a midwinter day, with the wind shifting spindrift into the air such that the ice-dust acts as a prismatic mist, refracting sunshine into its pale and separate colours; or out on a crisp November night in a city garden, with the lit windows of houses and the orange glow of street light around, while the stars *blinter* above in the cold high air.

By no means are all place-words poetic or innocent. Take the familiar word *forest*, which can designate not a wooded region, but an area of land set aside for deer-hunting – as those who have walked through the treeless 'forests' of Fisherfield, Applecross and Corrour in the Highlands of Scotland will know. *Forest* – like numerous wood-words – is complicatedly tangled up in political histories of access and landownership. Nature is not now, nor has ever been, a pure category. We inhabit a post-pastoral terrain, full of modification and compromise: this is why the glossaries contain plenty of unnatural language, such as terms from coastal sea-defences (*pillbox*, *bulwark*, *rock-armour*) that register threats both from the sea and of the sea, or *soft estate*, the Highways Agency term for those natural habitats that exist along the verges of motorways and trunk roads.

Some of the words collected here are eldritch, acknowledging a sense of our landscapes not as settled but as unsettling – the terror in the terroir, the spectred isle. Some are funny, and some ripely rude. Before beginning this work, I would not have guessed at the existence of quite so many terms for animal dung, from *crottle* (a foresters' term for hare excrement) to *doofers* (Scots for horse shit) to the expressive *ujller* (Shetlandic for the unctuous filth that runs from a dunghill) and *turdstool* (West Country for a very substantial cowpat). Nor did I know that a dialect name for the kestrel, alongside such felicities as *windhover* and *bell-hawk*, is *wind-fucker*. Once learnt, never forgotten – it is hard now not to see in the pose of the hovering kestrel a certain lustful quiver. Often I have been reminded of Douglas Adams and John Lloyd's genius catalogue of nonce words, *The Meaning of Liff* (1983), in which British place-names are used as nouns for the 'hundreds of common experiences, feelings, situations and even objects which we all know and recognize, but for which no words exist'. Thus '*Kimmeridge* (n.): The light breeze which blows through your armpit hair when you are stretched out sunbathing'; or '*Glassel* (n.): A seaside pebble which was shiny and interesting when wet, and which is now a lump of rock, but which children nevertheless insist on filling their suitcases with after a holiday'. When I mentioned to my then seven-year-old son that there was no word for the shining hump of water that rises above a submerged boulder in a stream, he quickly suggested *currentbum*.

The makers and users of the words in the glossaries range from such canonical writers as Gerard Manley Hopkins and John Clare, through to the anonymous workers, watchers and farmers who have added to the prosperity of place-language in these islands over the millennia. This prosperity is by no means the exclusive product of literacy or high culture. Margaret Gelling, the great scholar of English place-names, notes that 'the Anglo-Saxon peasant farmer' had a vast range of words for 'hill' and 'valley', and that the Anglo-Saxons generally were 'a people in possession of a vast and subtle topographical vocabulary', with little tolerance for synonyms. The huge richness of place-language is also, of course, a function of miscellany. The culture of these islands has been formed by waves of invasion, settlement and immigration, and for this reason the lexicons seek to reflect the diversity of languages of arrival, as well as those of staying put. You will find terms here from Old English and Norn; harder to find and reach have been the place-words used by modern minority communities to describe aspects of, say, the Peak District tors and moors or the estuaries of Essex. 'British Bengalis, Gujaratis and Punjabis often . . . move from one language to another,' the poet Debjani Chatterjee told me, 'and frequently sprinkle in words from one when speaking the other. So we may be speaking in Bengali but referring to certain landscape features in English – and vice versa. But,' she added, 'it is a slow creeping process for such vocabulary to get established.' Because of this slow creep, among other reasons, these glossaries do not (could never) aspire to completion. They contain only a fraction of an impossible whole. They are intended not as closed archives but glorious galli-maufries, relishing the awesome range and vigour of place-languages in this archipelago, and the taste of their words on the tongue.

~

In *The History of the Countryside* (1986), the great botanist Oliver Rackham describes four ways in which 'landscape is lost': through the loss of beauty, the loss of freedom, the loss of wildlife and vege-tation, and the loss of meaning. I admire the way that aesthetics, human experience, ecology and semantics are given parity in his list. Of these losses the last is hardest to measure. But it is clear that there is now less need to know in detail the terrains beyond our towns and cities, unless our relationships with them are in some way profes-sionally or recreationally specialized.

It is my hope (but not my presumption) that the words grouped here might in small measure re-wild our contemporary language for landscape. I do not, of course, believe that these words will magic-ally summon us into a pure realm of harmony and communion with nature. Rather that they might offer a vocabulary which is 'conviv-ial' as the philosopher Ivan Illich intended the word – meaning enriching of life, stimulating to the imagination and 'encouraging creative relations between people, and people and nature'. And, per-haps, that the vibrancy of perception evoked in these glossaries may irrigate the dry meta-languages of modern policy-making (the DEFRA glossary, for instance, which offers such tautological arid-ities as '*Land use*: the use to which a piece of land is put'). For there is no single mountain language, but a range of mountain languages; no one coastal language, but a fractal of coastal languages; no lone tree language, but a forest of tree languages. To celebrate the lexis of landscape is not nostalgic, but urgent. 'People *exploit* what they have merely concluded to be of value, but they *defend* what they love,' writes the American essayist and farmer Wendell Berry, 'and to defend what we love we need a particularizing language, for we love what we particularly know.'

I am wary of the dangers of fetishizing dialect and archaism – all that *mollocking* and *sukebinding* Stella Gibbons spoofed so brilliantly in *Cold Comfort Farm* (1932). Wary, too, of being seen to advocate a tyranny of the nominal – a taxonomic need to point and name, with the intent of citing and owning – when in fact I perceive no opposition between precision and mystery, or between naming and not-knowing. There are experiences of landscape that will always resist articulation, and of which words offer only a remote echo – or to which silence is by far the best response. Nature does not name itself. Granite does not self-identify as igneous. Light has no grammar. Language is always late for its subject. Sometimes on the top of a mountain I just say, 'Wow.'

But we are and always have been name-callers, christeners. Words are grained into our landscapes, and landscapes grained into our words. 'Every language is an old-growth forest of the mind,' in Wade Davis's memorable phrase. We see in words: in webs of words, wefts of words, woods of words. The roots of individual words reach out and intermesh, their stems lean and criss-cross, and their outgrowths branch and clasp.

~

'I want my writing to bring people not just to think of "trees" as they mostly do now,' wrote Roger Deakin in a notebook that was discovered after his early death, 'but of each individual tree, and each kind of tree.' John Muir, spending his first summer working as a shepherd among the pines of the Sierra Nevada in California, reflected in his journal that 'Every tree calls for special admiration. I have been making many sketches and regret that I cannot draw every needle.' The chapters of *Landmarks* all concern writers who are particularizers, and who seek in some way to 'draw every needle'. Deakin, Muir, Baker, Nan Shepherd, Jacquetta Hawkes, Richard Skelton, Autumn Richardson, Peter Davidson, Barry Lopez, Richard Jefferies: all have sought, in Emerson's phrase, to 'pierce . . . rotten diction and fasten words again to visible things'. All have written with committing intensity about their chosen territories. And for all of them, to use language well is to use it particularly: precision of utterance as both a form of lyricism and a species of attention.

Before you become a writer you must first become a reader. Every hour spent reading is an hour spent learning to write; this continues to be true throughout a writer's life. *The Living Mountain*, *Waterlog*, *The Peregrine*, *Arctic Dreams*, *My First Summer in the Sierra*: these are among the books that have taught me to write, but also the books that have taught me to see. In that respect, *Landmarks* is a record of my own pupillage, if the word may be allowed to carry its senses both of 'tuition' and (in that ocular flicker) of 'gaining vision'. Thus the book is filled with noticers and noticings. 'The surface of the ground, so dull and forbidding at first sight,' wrote Muir of the Sierra Nevada, in fact 'shines and sparkles with crystals: mica, hornblende, feldspar, quartz, tourmaline . . . the radiance in some places is so great as to be fairly dazzling'. How typical of Muir to see dazzle where most would see dullness! Again and again in the chapters that follow you will encounter similar acts of 'dazzling' perception: Finlay MacLeod and Anne Campbell detailing the intricacies of the

Lewisian moor; Shepherd finding a micro-forest of lichens and heathers on the Cairngorm plateau; Baker scrying a skyful of birds; and Richard Jefferies pacing out a humble roadside verge in a London suburb, counting off sixty different wild flowers, from agrimony to yellow vetch.

Books, like landscapes, leave their marks in us. Sometimes these traces are so faint as to be imperceptible – tiny shifts in the weather of the spirit that do not register on the usual instruments. Mostly, these marks are temporary: we close a book, and for the next hour or two the world seems oddly brighter at its edges; or we are moved to a kindness or a meanness that would otherwise have gone unexpressed. Certain books, though, like certain landscapes, stay with us even when we have left them, changing not just our weathers but our climates. The word *landmark* is from the Old English *landmearc*, meaning 'an object in the landscape which, by its conspicuousness, serves as a guide in the direction of one's course'. John Smith, writing in his 1627 *Sea Grammar*, gives us this definition: 'A Land-marke is any Mountaine, Rocke, Church, Wind-mill or the like, that the Pilot can now by comparing one by another see how they beare by the compasse.' Strong books and strong words can be landmarks in Smith's sense – offering us a means both of establishing our location and of knowing how we 'beare by the compasse'. Taken in sum, the chapters of *Landmarks* explore how reading can change minds, revise behaviour and shape perception. All of the writers here have altered their readers in some way. Some of these alterations are conspicuous and public: Muir's essays convinced Theodore Roosevelt of the need to protect Yosemite and its sequoias, and massively to extend the National Park regions of America; Deakin's *Waterlog* revolutionized open-water swimming in twenty-first-century Britain. Others are private and unmappable, manifesting in ways that are unmistakable to experience, but difficult to express – leaving our attention re-focused, our sight freshly scintillated.

Strange events occurred in the course of my travels for *Landmarks* – convergences that pressed at the limits of coincidence and tended to the eerie. You will read about them here: the discovery of the tunnel of swords and axes in Cumbria; the appearance of the Cambridge peregrines (first at sillion, then at sill); the experience of walking *into* the pages of Nan Shepherd's *The Living Mountain* in the Cairngorms; the widening ripples of a forgotten word, found in a folder in Suffolk that had been left behind by a friend who had died; and then the discovery – told in the Postscript – on the day before I finished *Landmarks* that its originating dream had, almost, come true. In all of these incidents, life and language collapsed curiously into one another. I have tried to account for these collapses, but such events – like many of the subjects of this book – are often best represented not by proposition but by pattern, such that unexpected constellations of relation light up. Metamorphosis and shape-shifting, magnification, miniaturization, cabinets of curiosity, crystallization, hollows and dens, archives, wonder, views from above: these are among the images and tropes that recur. The chapters here do not together tell the story of a single journey or quest, but all are fascinated by the same questions concerning the mutual relations of place, language and spirit – how we landmark, and how we are landmarked.

I have come to understand that although place-words are being lost, they are also being created. Nature is dynamic, and so is language. Loanwords from Chinese, Urdu, Korean, Portuguese and Yiddish are right now being used to describe the landscapes of Britain and Ireland; portmanteaus and neologisms are constantly in manufacture. As I travelled I met new words as well as salvaging old ones: a painter in the Hebrides who used *landskein* to refer to the braid of blue horizon lines in hill country on a hazy day; a five-year-old girl who concocted *honeyfur* to describe the soft seeds of grasses held in the fingers. When Clare and Hopkins could not find words for natural phenomena, they just made them up: *sutering* for the cranky action of a rising heron (Clare), *wolfsnow* for a dangerous sea-blizzard, and *slogger* for the sucking sound made by waves against a ship's side (both Hopkins). John Constable invented the verb *to sky*, meaning 'to lie on one's back and study the clouds'. We have forgotten 10,000 words for our landscapes, but we will make 10,000 more, given time. This is why *Landmarks* moves over its course from the peat-deep word-hoard of Hebridean Gaelic, through to the fresh-minted terms and stories of young children at play on the outskirts of a Cambridgeshire town. And this is why the penultimate glossary of the book is left blank, for you to fill in – there to hold the place-words that have yet to be coined.

2

A Counter-Desecration Phrasebook

I

In Which Nothing Is Seen

Five thousand feet below us, the Minch was in an ugly mood. Grey Atlantic water, arrowed with white wave-tops. Our twin-prop plane reached the east coast of the Isle of Lewis and banked north towards Stornoway, bucking as it picked up the cross-buffets of a stiff westerly. The air was clear, though, and I could see the tawny expanse of Mòinteach riabhach, the Brindled Moor: several hundred square miles of bog, hag, crag, heather, loch and lochan that make up the interior of Lewis.

Across the aisle from me, two people looked out of the window at the moor. One of them laughed.

'We're flying over nothing!' she said.

'Remind me why we've come here?' the other asked.

'We've come to see nothing!'

'Then we have come to the *right* place!'

They pressed their shoulders together, both laughing now. *Whirr. Thunk.* The landing gear lowered, engaged.

'We're about to land on nothing!'

'Hold on tight!'

II

In Which Names Are Spoken

It is true that, seen for the first time, and especially when seen from altitude, the moor of Lewis resembles a *terra nullius*, a nothing-place, distinguished only by its self-similarity. Peat, moor and more moor. It is vast, flat, repetitive in form, and its colours are motley and subtle. This is a region whose breadth seems either to return the eye's enquiries unanswered, or to swallow all attempts at interpretation. Like other extensive lateral landscapes – desert, ice cap, prairie, tundra – it confronts us with difficulties of purchase (how to anchor perception in a context of immensity) and evaluation (how to structure significance in a context of uniformity). Or, to borrow the acronym that Welsh farmers fondly use to describe the hills of the Elan range in mid-Wales, the Brindled Moor can easily be mistaken for MAMBA country: Miles And Miles of Bugger All.

I had come to Lewis to visit a friend of mine, Finlay MacLeod, who loves the moor, and who lives on its western brink in a coastal township called Shawbost. Finlay is known to almost everyone on Lewis and Harris. Even those who have not met him are aware of 'Doctor Finlay of Shawbost'. His fame is born of his remarkable range of expertises (he is, among other things, a teacher, naturalist, novelist, broadcaster, oral historian, archivist and map-collector) and his rare combination of intellectual curiosity, gentle generosity of spirit, and eloquence as a communicator in both Gaelic and English.

Finlay met me at Stornoway, and we drove across the island to Shawbost. The journey was slow and digressive. Often Finlay pulled over to greet people out on the moor (walkers, peat-cutters), or to point out moor features I would otherwise have missed (the start of shieling paths; cairned islands in the centre of lochans). We took two detours, one to a beehive shieling hard by a sheep-fank, and one to a huge Iron Age broch, whose inner stones of gneiss were cold as steel to the touch.

That evening, after we'd eaten, we sat in Finlay's living room and he played me a crackly recording of Gaelic psalm-singing, made on the remote skerry of Sula Sgeir in the early 1950s. It set my scalp tingling. Then he passed me a stapled sheaf of paper. 'I've been working on this recently,' he said, 'and I thought it might interest you.'

Oh, it did. The document was a word-list entitled 'Some Lewis Moorland Terms: A Peat Glossary'. Together with his friends Anne Campbell, Catriona Campbell and Donald Morrison, Finlay explained, he had been carrying out a survey of the language used in three Lewisian townships – Shawbost, Bragar and Shader – to denote aspects of the moor. The Peat Glossary ran to several pages and more than 120 terms – and as that modest 'Some' in its title acknowledged, it was incomplete. 'There's so much more to be added to it,' Anne told me later. 'It represents only three villages' worth of words. I have a friend from South Uist who said that her grandmother would add dozens to it. Every village in the upper islands would have its different phrases to contribute.' I thought of Norman MacCaig's great Hebridean poem 'By the Graveyard, Luskentyre', where he imagines creating a dictionary out of the language of Donnie, a lobster fisherman from the Isle of Harris. It would be an impossible book, MacCaig concludes:

A volume thick as the height of the Clisham,
A volume big as the whole of Harris,
A volume beyond the wit of scholars.

I sat and read the glossary that evening by the fire in Finlay's house, fascinated and moved. Many of the terms it contains are notable for their compressive precision. *Bugha* is 'a green bow-shaped area of moor grass or moss, formed by the winding of a stream'. *Mòine dhubh* are 'the heavier and darker peats which lie deeper and older into the moor'. *Teine biorach* means 'the flame or will-o'-the-wisp that runs on top of heather when the moor is burnt during the summer'. A *rùdhan* is 'a set of four peat blocks leaned up against one another such that wind and sun hasten their drying'. Groups of words carefully distinguish between comparable phenomena: *lèig-chruthaich* is 'quivering bog with water trapped beneath it, and an intact surface', whereas *breunloch* is 'dangerous sinking bog that may be bright green and grassy', and *botann* is 'a hole in the moor, often wet, where an animal might get stuck'. Other terms are distinctive for their poetry. *Rionnach maoim*, for instance, means 'the shadows cast on the moorland by clouds moving across the sky on a bright and windy day'. *Èit* refers to 'the practice of placing quartz stones in moorland streams so that they would sparkle in moonlight and thereby attract salmon to them in the late summer and autumn'.

The existence of a moorland lexis of such scope and exactitude is testimony to the long relationship of labour between the Hebrideans and their land: this is, dominantly, a use-language – its development a function of the need to name that which is being done, and done to. That this lexis should also admit the poetic and metaphorical to its designations is testimony to the long aesthetic relationship between the Hebrideans and their land. For this is also a language of looking, touching and appreciation – and its development is partly a function of the need to love that which is being done, and done to.

I take the Peat Glossary to be a prose-poem, and a document that gives the lie to any idea of the moor as *terra nullius*. 'Glossary' – with its hints both of tongue and of gleam – is just the right term for this text's eloquence, and also for the substance to which its description is devoted: peat being gleamy as tar when wet, and as dark in its pools as Japanese lacquer. The glossary reveals the moor to be a terrain of immense intricacy. A slow capillary creep of knowledge has occurred on Lewis, up out of landscape's details and into language's. The result is a lexis so supply suited to the place being described that it fits it like a skin. Precision and poetry co-exist: the denotative and the figurative are paired as accomplices rather than as antagonists.

Ultra-fine discrimination operates in Hebridean Gaelic place-names, as well as in descriptive nouns. In the 1990s an English linguist called Richard Cox moved to northern Lewis, taught himself Gaelic, and spent several years retrieving and recording the place-names in the Carloway district of Lewis's west coast. Carloway contains thirteen townships and around 500 people; it is fewer than sixty square miles in area. But Cox's magnificent resulting work, *The Gaelic Place-Names of Carloway, Isle of Lewis: Their Structure and Significance* (2002), runs to almost 500 pages and details more than 3,000 place-names. Its eleventh section, titled 'The Onomasticon', lists the hundreds of toponyms identifying 'natural features' of the landscape. Unsurprisingly for such a maritime culture, there is a proliferation of names for coastal features – narrows, currents, indentations, projections, ledges, reefs – often of exceptional specificity. *Beirgh*, for instance, a loanword from the Old Norse, refers to 'a promontory or point with a bare, usually vertical rock face and sometimes with a narrow neck to land', while *corran* has the sense of 'rounded point', deriving from its common meaning of 'sickle'. There are more than twenty different terms for eminences and precipices, depending on the sharpness of the summit and the aspects of the slope. *Sìthean*, for instance, deriving from *sìth*, 'a fairy hill or mound', is a knoll or hillock possessing the qualities which were thought to constitute desirable real estate for fairies – being well drained, for instance, with a distinctive rise, and crowned by green grass. Such qualities also fulfilled the requirements for a good shieling site, and so almost all toponyms including the word *sìthean* indicate shieling locations. Characterful personifications of places also abound: A' Ghnùig, for instance, means 'the steep slope of the scowling expression'.

Reading 'The Onomasticon', you realize that Gaelic speakers of this landscape inhabit a terrain which is, in Proust's phrase, 'magnificently surcharged with names'. For centuries, these place-names have spilled their poetry into everyday Hebridean life. They have anthologized local history, anecdote and myth, binding story to place. They have been functional – operating as territory markers and ownership designators – and they have also served as navigational aids. Until well into the twentieth century, most inhabitants of the Western Isles did not use conventional paper maps, but relied instead on memory maps, learnt on the land and carried in the skull. These memory maps were facilitated by first-hand experience and were also – as Finlay put it – 'lit by the mnemonics of words'. For their users, these place-names were necessary for getting from location to location, and for the purpose of guiding others to where they needed to go. It is for this reason that so many toponyms incorporate what is known in psychology and design as 'affordance' – the quality of an environment or object that allows an individual to perform an action on, to or with it. So a *bealach* is a gap in a ridge or cliff which may be walked through, but the element *beàrn* or *beul* in a place-name suggests an opening that is unlikely to admit human passage, as in

Am Beul Uisg, 'the gap from which the water gushes'. Blàr a' Chlachain means 'the plain of the stepping stones', while Clach an Linc means 'the rock of the link', indicating a place where boats can safely be tied up. To speak out a run of these names is therefore to create a story of travel – an act of naming that is also an act of wayfinding. Angus MacMillan, a Lewisian, remembers being sent by his father seven miles across the Brindled Moor to fetch a missing sheep spotted by someone the night before: 'Cùl Leac Ghlas ri taobh Sloc an Fhithich fos cionn Loch na Muilne' – 'just behind the Grey Ledge by the Raven's Hollow above the Mill Loch'. 'Think of it,' writes MacMillan drily, 'as an early form of GPS: the Gaelic Positioning System.'

One of the most influential ethnographic works concerning landscape and language is Keith Basso's *Wisdom Sits in Places* (1996), an investigation into the extreme situatedness of thought in the Apache people of Western Arizona. Basso spent a decade living and working alongside the Apache inhabitants of a town called Cibecue. He became especially interested in the interconnections of story, place-name, historical sense and the ethical relationships of person to person and person to place. Early in the book, Basso despatches what he calls the 'widely accepted' fallacy in anthropology that place-names operate only as referents. To the Apache, place-names do refer, indispensably, but they are used and valued for other reasons as well: aesthetically, ethically, musically. The Apache understand how powerfully language constructs the human relation to place, and as such they possess, Basso writes, 'a modest capacity for wonder and delight at the large tasks that small words can be made to perform'. In their imagination geography and history are consubstantial. Placeless events are inconceivable, in that everything that happens must happen somewhere.

Basso writes of the 'bold, visual, evocative' imagery of Apache place-names, which hold 'ear and eye jointly enthralled':

Tséé Dotł'ʐh Ténaahijaahá, which translates as Green Rocks Side by Side Jut Down Into Water (designating a group of mossy boulders on the bank of a stream)
Tséé Ditł'ige Naaditiné, which translates as Trail Extends Across Scorched Rocks (designating a crossing at the bottom of a canyon).

Like their Gaelic counterparts, these place-names are distinctive for their descriptive precision. They often imply the position from which a place is being viewed – an optimal or actual vantage point – such that when the name is spoken, it 'requires that one imagine it as if standing or sitting at a particular spot'. Basso records that this 'precision' is a quality openly appreciated by their Apache users, in that it invites and permits imaginative journeying within a known landscape. At one point, labouring on a fence-building project with two cowboys from Cibecue, he listens to one of the men reciting lists of place-names to himself as he strings and then tightens barbed wire between posts. When Basso asks him why he is doing so, the cowboy answers, 'I like to. I ride that way in my mind.'

In both Lewis and Arizona, language is used not only to navigate but also to charm the land. Words act as compass; place-speech serves literally to en-chant the land – to sing it back into being, and to sing one's being back into it.

III

In Which Language Is Lost

The extraordinary language of the Outer Hebrides is currently being lost. Gaelic itself is in danger of withering on the tongue: the total number of those speaking or learning to speak Gaelic in Scotland is now around 58,000. Of those, many are understandably less interested in the intricacies of toponymy, or the exactitudes of which the language is capable with regard to landscape. Tim Robinson – the great writer, mathematician and deep-mapper of the Irish Atlantic seaboard – notes how with each generation in the west of Ireland 'some of the place-names are forgotten or becoming incomprehensible'. Often in the Outer Hebrides I have been told that younger generations are losing a literacy of the land. Cox remarks that the previously 'important role' of place-names and 'natural' language in the Carloway culture has 'recently' been sharply diminished. In 2006 Finlay observed that as people's 'working relationship with the moorland [of Lewis] has changed, [so] the keen sense of conservation that went with it has atrophied, as has the language which accompanied that sense'.

What is occurring in Gaelic is, broadly, occurring in English too – and in scores of other languages and dialects. The nuances observed by specialized vocabularies are evaporating from common usage, burnt off by capital, apathy and urbanization. The terrain beyond the city fringe has become progressively more understood in terms of large generic units ('field', 'hill', 'valley', 'wood'). It has become a blandscape. We are *blasé* about place, in the sense that Georg Simmel used that word in his 1903 essay 'The Metropolis and Mental Life' – meaning indifferent to the distinction between things.

It is not, on the whole, that natural phenomena and entities themselves are disappearing; rather that there are fewer people able to name them, and that once they go unnamed they go to some degree unseen. Language deficit leads to attention deficit. As we further deplete our ability to name, describe and figure particular aspects of our places, our competence for understanding and imagining possible relationships with non-human nature is correspondingly depleted. The ethno-linguist K. David Harrison bleakly declares that language death means the loss of 'long-cultivated knowledge that has guided human–environment interaction for millennia . . . accumulated wisdom and observations of generations of people about the natural world, plants, animals, weather, soil. The loss [is] incalculable, the knowledge mostly unrecoverable.' Or as Tim Dee neatly puts it, 'Without a name made in our mouths, an animal or a place struggles to find purchase in our minds or our hearts.'

IV

In Which Enchantment Is Practised

In 1917 the sociologist and philosopher Max Weber named 'disenchantment' (*Entzauberung*) as the distinctive injury of modernity. He defined disenchantment as 'the knowledge or belief that . . . there are no mysterious incalculable forces that come into play, but rather that one can, in principle, master all things by calculation'. For Weber, disenchantment was a function of the rise of rationalism, which demanded the extirpation of dissenting knowledge-kinds in favour of a single master-principle. It found its expressions not just in human behaviour and policy – including the general impulse to control nature – but also in emotional response. Weber noted the

widespread reduction of 'wonder' (for him the hallmark of enchantment, and in which state we are comfortable with not-knowing) and
the corresponding expansion of 'will' (for him the hallmark of disenchantment, and in which state we are avid for authority). In
modernity, mastery usurped mystery.

Our language for nature is now such that the things around us do
not talk back to us in ways that they might. As we have enhanced
our power to determine nature, so we have rendered it less able to
converse with us. We find it hard to imagine nature outside a
use-value framework. We have become experts in analysing what
nature can do *for* us, but lack a language to evoke what it can do *to*
us. The former is important; the latter is vital. Martin Heidegger
identified a version of this trend in 1954, observing that the rise of
technology and the technological imagination had converted what
he called 'the whole universe of beings' into an undifferentiated
'standing reserve' (*Bestand*) of energy, available for any use to which
humans choose to put it. The rise of 'standing reserve' as a concept
has bequeathed to us an inadequate and unsatisfying relationship with the natural world, and with ourselves too, because we
have to encounter ourselves and our thoughts as mysteries before
we encounter them as service providers. We require things to
have their own lives if they are to enrich ours. But allegory as a mode
has settled inside us, and thrived: fungibility has replaced
particularity.

This is not to suggest that we need adopt either a literal animism
or a systematic superstition; only that by instrumentalizing nature,
linguistically and operationally, we have largely stunned the earth
out of wonder. Language is fundamental to the possibility of
re-wonderment, for language does not just register experience, it
produces it. The contours and colours of words are inseparable from

the feelings we create in relation to situations, to others and to places. Language carries a formative as well as an informative impulse – the power known to theorists as 'illocutionary' or 'illative'. Certain kinds of language can restore a measure of wonder to our relations with nature. Others might offer modest tools for modest place-making. Others still might free objects at least momentarily from their role as standing reserve. As Barry Lopez urges: 'One must wait for the moment when the thing – the hill, the tarn, the *lunette*, the kiss tank, the *caliche* flat, the *bajada* – ceases to be a thing and becomes something that knows we are there.'

Between 2002 and 2006 a group of researchers compiled a place-dictionary called *Home Ground: Language for an American Landscape*. Their ambition was to retrieve, define and organize nearly 1,000 terms and words for specific aspects of US topography. Its ethical presumption was that having such a language to hand is vital for two reasons: because it allows us to speak clearly about such places, and because it encourages the kinds of allegiance and intimacy with one's places that might also go by the name of love, and out of which might arise care and good sense. Inspired by Lopez, the research team located their terms, defined them, and illustrated them with usages from American literature, science and art. The result – as with Finlay's glossary – is a kind of sustained prose-poem, exquisite in its precision and its metaphors.

For *Home Ground* does not so much define as evoke; or rather it defines through evocation. 'That rivers and streams seldom flow naturally in straight lines is a gift of beauty; otherwise we would not have canyons that bear the shape of moving water,' begins the entry for *gooseneck*, meaning those 'deeply entrenched river meanders . . . so tight in succession that their bows nearly meet one another'. *Shinnery* is 'a type of low brush thicket . . . difficult or impossible to cross on foot or horseback . . . taking its name from the shin oak (*Quercus havardii*)'. *Cowbelly* describes super-soft river mud:

> [I]t is along the banks of slow-moving creeks, where the current slackens completely, that the very finest particles of sediment settle out of the water . . . at the boundary where water becomes silt, the bottom is so plush that the sinking foot of the barefoot wader barely registers the new medium, only a second change of temperature.

What a finely particular definition for a finely particular phenomenon! Thus this dictionary proceeds, lyrically renewing a language of place. The aim of *Home Ground*, wrote Lopez in his Introduction, was 'to recall and to explore [such] language . . . because we believed in an acquaintance with it, that using it to say more clearly and precisely what we mean, would bring us a certain kind of relief [and] would draw us closer to . . . landscapes'. This is the language, he concluded, that 'keeps us from slipping off into abstract space'.

It is true that once a landscape goes undescribed and therefore unregarded, it becomes more vulnerable to unwise use or improper action. This is what happened to the Lewisian moor in 2004.

V

In Which Songlines Are Sung

In November of that year the engineering company AMEC, in conjunction with British Energy, filed an application to build a vast wind farm on the Brindled Moor. The proposed farm – which would have been Europe's largest – consisted of 234 wind turbines, each of them

140 metres high (more than twice the height of Nelson's Column) and with a blade-span of more than 80 metres (longer than a Boeing 747 measured nose-to-tail). Each turbine would be sunk into a foundation of 700 cubic metres of concrete. The generated energy was to be ducted off the island and down to the centres of need by 210 pylons, each 26 metres high, joined by overhead lines. To service the turbines and pylons, 104 miles of roads would be built, as well as nine electrical substations. Five new rock quarries would be opened, and four concrete-batching plants established. In total, around 5 million cubic metres of rock and 2.5 million cubic metres of peat would be excavated and displaced. By AMEC's own account in their initial application, 'the effect on the landscape resource, character and perception [of Lewis would be] major and long-term'. AMEC's application began a three-and-a-half-year battle over the nature and the future of the moor. It was fought between the majority of Lewisians (around 80 per cent of the island's inhabitants expressed opposition to the plans), and AMEC together with its local supporters – for whom the wind farm meant jobs and money on an island long troubled by emigration and low employment.

The crux of the debate concerned the perceived nature and worth of the moor itself, and the language that was used – and available – to describe it. It was in the interests of AMEC to characterize the moor as a wasteland, a *terra nullius*. The metaphors used to describe the moor by those in favour of the plans repeatedly implied barrenness. One pro-farm local councillor dismissed the island's interior as 'a wilderness', suggesting a space both empty of life and hostile in its asperities (wilderness in the old American-Puritan sense of the word, then, or that implied by the desert 'wilderness of Zin' through which the Israelites wander in Exodus). If the pro-farm lobby charged the moor with an affective power, it was the capacity to depress and oppress the mind. The journalist Ian Jack, arguing in support of AMEC's application in 2006, described it as 'a vast, dead place: dark brown moors and black lochs under a grey sky, all swept by a chill wet wind'. Jack's comment, like those of the two people I overheard on the plane, has precedents in earlier modern encounters with moors: Daniel Defoe, for instance, who in 1725 rode over the ling moors above Chatsworth in Derbyshire, and found them 'abominable', 'a waste and a howling wilderness'. It recalls the many nineteenth-century white settler accounts of the Australian desert interior as a 'hideous blank': 'everywhere the same dreadful, dreary, dismal desert', lamented the *Argus* newspaper of Melbourne in an 1858 editorial against the 'interior'. And it anticipated James Carnegy-Arbuthnott, the estate owner in Angus who notoriously argued in 2013 that it is right that few people own most of the land in Scotland because 'so much [of it] is unproductive wilderness'.

The American geographer Yi Fu Tuan proposes that 'it is precisely what is invisible in the land that makes what is merely empty space to one person, a place to another'. The task that faced the Lewisians, when the conflict with AMEC began, was to find ways of expressing the moor's 'invisible' content: the use-histories, imaginative shapes, natural forms and cultural visions it had inspired, and the ways it had been written into language and memory. They needed to create an account of the moor as 'home ground' – and for that they needed to renew its place-language. 'Those who wish to explain to politicians and others why landscape should be nurtured and made safe for all living things face a daunting task where the necessary concepts and vocabulary are not to hand,' wrote Finlay in a public essay; 'it is therefore difficult to make a case for conservation without sounding either wet or extreme.'

Beginning in early 2005, the islanders began to devise ways of making that case by re-enchanting the moor. They started both to salvage and to create accounts – narrative, lexical, poetic, painterly, photographic, historical, cartographical – which, taken in sum or interleaved, might restore both particularity and mystery to the moor, and thus counter the vision of it as a 'vast, dead place'. Among the most memorable moor-works to emerge out of this period of resistance was one made by Anne Campbell and her collaborator, Jon MacLeod. It was a booklet entitled *A-mach an Gleann*, which translates as 'A Known Wilderness'. Anne's family had lived in the township of Bragar for generations, and she and MacLeod wanted to evoke a sense of the moor as a wild place, but also to demonstrate its long-term enmeshment with human culture. They became interested in the criss-crossing paths and tracks – both human and animal – that existed on the moor, each of which they saw as a story-line of a kind.

So they began to map their own moor-walks, recording paths taken and events that occurred or were observed along the way. On 27 June 2005, for instance, they walked between '*An Talamh Briste, Na Feadanan Gorma, Gleann Shuainagadail*, and *Loch an Òis*' and saw in these places 'drifts of sparkling bog-cotton', 'scarlet damselflies', 'a long wind, carrying bird-calls'. They 'crossed a greenshank territory' and 'disturbed a hind in long grass', before 'stopping at a shieling where an eagle had preened'. MacLeod delved further back, making speculative reconstructions of the memory maps of 'the people who traversed this landscape before and after the peat grew, naming features to navigate their way around, or to commemorate stories' and events. In these ways, Campbell and MacLeod began to create their own repertoire of songlines – ancient and new – for the moor.

Another group of islanders gathered poems and folk songs concerning the moor, mostly from the nineteenth and early twentieth centuries, including Padraig Campbell's 'The Skylark' and Derick Thomson's 'The Side of the Hill' and 'The Moor'. These were texts written on the moor in both senses, and they testified to its subtlety. Meanwhile, Finlay and Anne began to compile their Peat Glossary. In their wish to record the particularities of the moor, they shared an ethic if not a tone with Hugh MacDiarmid's angry poem rebuking a 'fool' who has dismissed Scotland as 'small'. 'Scotland small? Our multiform, our infinite Scotland *small*?' cries MacDiarmid furiously. 'Only as a patch of hillside may be a cliché corner / To a fool who cries "Nothing but heather!"' Taking that patch of hillside as his metonym for Scotland, MacDiarmid's poem 'gazes' hard at it, singling out this and that for our attention. He finds in moorland 'not only heather' but also blueberries (green, scarlet, blue), bog myrtle (sage green), tormentil (golden), milkworts ('blue as summer skies') flourishing on the patches that sheep have grazed bare, down in the unworked peat hags, sphagnum mosses (yellow, green and pink), sundew and butterwort, nodding harebells that 'vie in their colour' with the butterflies that alight on them, and stunted rowan saplings with their 'harsh dry leaves'. ' "Nothing but heather!" ' the poem mocks sharply at its close; 'How marvellously descriptive! And incomplete!'

'What is required,' wrote Finlay in a public appeal to save the Brindled Moor, 'is a new nomenclature of landscape and how we relate to it, so that conservation becomes a natural form of human awareness, and so that it ceases to be under-written and under-appreciated and thus readily vulnerable to desecration.' 'What is needed,' he concluded superbly, 'is a Counter-Desecration Phrasebook.' He and his fellow islanders worked to produce some version of that phrasebook for Lewis.

After three and a half years the Scottish Executive ruled on

AMEC's proposal. Taking into consideration the protective designations that the moor possessed (including a UN Ramsar designation) and the protests against the development (including 10,924 letters of objection) it decided to reject the wind-farm application.

The moor was saved.

VI

In Which a Baroque Fantasia Is Imagined

We need now, urgently, a Counter-Desecration Phrasebook that would comprehend the world – a glossary of enchantment for the whole earth, which would allow nature to talk back and would help us to listen. A work of words that would encourage responsible place-making, that would keep us from slipping off into abstract space, and keep us from all that would follow such a slip. The glossaries contained here in *Landmarks* do not constitute this unwriteable phrasebook – but perhaps they might offer a sight of the edge of the shadow of its impossible existence.

Such a phrasebook, as I imagine it – as thought-experiment, as baroque fantasia – would stand not as a competitor to scientific knowledge and ecological analysis, but as their supplement and ally. We need to know how nature proceeds, of course, but we need also to keep wonder alive in our descriptions of it: to provide celebrations of not-quite-knowing, of mystification, of excess. Barry Lopez again: 'something emotive abides in the land, and . . . it can be recognized and evoked even if it cannot be thoroughly plumbed'. This 'something' is 'inaccessible to the analytic researcher, and invisible to the ironist'.

Like Lopez, I am drawn to this idea of a valuable superfluity in nature: a content to landscape that exceeds the propositional and that fails to show up on the usual radar sweeps – but which may be expressible, or at least gesturable towards, in certain kinds of language. I relish the etymology of our word *thing* – that sturdy term of designation, that robust everyday indicator of the empirical – whereby in Old English *thynge* does not only designate a material object, but can also denote 'a narrative not fully known', or indicate 'the unknowability of larger chains of events'.

As I imagine it, futilely, this phrasebook would be rich with language that is, as the poet Marianne Moore put it in an exceptional essay of 1944 entitled 'Feeling and Precision', 'galvanized against inertia', where that 'galvanized' carries its sense of flowing current, of energy received by contact, of circuitry completed. For Moore, precision of language was crucial to this galvanism. 'Precision,' she wrote – in a phrase with which I could not be in more agreement – 'is a thing of the imagination' and produces 'writing of maximum force'. 'Precision' here should not be taken as cognate with scientific language. No, precision for Moore is a form of testimony different in kind to rational understanding. It involves not probing for answers, but watching and waiting. And precision, for Moore, is best enabled by metaphor: another reminder that metaphor is not merely something that adorns thought but is, substantively, thought itself. Writers must be, Moore concludes finely, 'as clear as our natural reticence allows us to be', where 'reticence' mutely reminds us of its etymology from the Latin *tacere*, 'to be silent, to keep silent'. I recall Charles Simic: 'For knowledge, add; for wisdom, take away.'

This phrasebook would help us to understand that there are places and things which make our thinking possible, and leave our thinking changed. In this respect it would inhabit what linguistics calls the 'middle voice': that grammatical diathesis which – by hovering between the active and the passive – can infuse inanimate objects with sentience and so evoke a sense of reciprocal perception between human and non-human. It would possess the unfeasible alertness of Jorge Luis Borges's character Ireneo Funes, who develops perfect recall after a riding accident. 'John Locke, in the seventeenth century, postulated (and rejected) an impossible language in which each individual thing, each stone, each bird and each branch, would have its own name,' wrote Borges there; 'Funes once projected an analogous language, but discarded it because it seemed too general to him, too ambiguous. In fact, Funes remembered not only every leaf of every tree of every wood, but also every one of the times he had perceived or imagined it . . .'

This phrasebook would find ways of outflanking the cost-benefit framework within which we do so much of our thinking about nature. Again and again when we are brought short by natural events – the helix of a raptor's ascent on a thermal; a flock of knots shoaling over an east-coast estuary; the shadows of cumulus clouds moving across Lewisian moorland on a sunny day – the astonishment we feel concerns a gift freely given, a natural potlatch. During such encounters, we briefly return to a pre-economical state in which things can be 'tendered', as Adam Potkay puts it, 'that is, treated with tenderness – because of the generosity of their self-giving, as if alterity were itself pure gift'.

Above all, then, this phrasebook would speak the language of tact and of tenderness. The Canadian poet Jan Zwicky writes of the importance of 'having language to hand' in our dealings with the natural world. There is a quiet reminder in her phrase of the relationship between tactfulness and tactility, between touch and ethics. As the *Oxford English Dictionary* defines it:

> *Tact*: 1*(a)*. The sense of touch, the act of touching or handling. 1*(b)* A keen faculty of perception or discrimination likened to the sense of touch. 2*(b)* Musicologically, a stroke in beating time which 'directs the equalitie of the measure' (John Downland, writing in 1609, translating Andreas Ornithoparcus).

Tact as due attention, as tenderness of encounter, as rightful tactility. Tactful language, then, would be language which sings (is lyric), which touches (is born of contact with the lived and felt world), which touches us (affects) and which keeps time – recommending thereby an equality of measure and a keen faculty of perception.

GLOSSARY I

Flatlands

Flowing Water

bugha green bow-shaped area of moor grass or moss, formed by the winding of a stream **Gaelic**

caochan slender moor-stream obscured by vegetation such that it is virtually hidden (possibly from Old Irish *caeich*, meaning 'blind', i.e. the stream is so overgrown that it cannot see out of its own bed) **Gaelic**

èit practice of placing quartz stones in moorland streams so that they would sparkle in moonlight and thereby attract salmon to them in the late summer and autumn **Gaelic (Isle of Lewis)**

feadan small stream running from a moorland loch **Gaelic**

fèith watercourse running through peat, often dry in summer, the form of which resembles veins or sinews **Gaelic**

lòn small stream with soft, marshy banks **Gaelic**

rife small river flowing across the coastal plain **Sussex**

sike small stream, often flowing through marshy ground **Yorkshire**

Mists, Fogs, Shadows

ammil 'The icy casings of leaves and grasses and blades and sprigs were glowing and hid in a mist of sun-fire. Moor-folk call this morning glory the ammil' Henry Williamson, *Tarka the Otter* (1927) **Exmoor**

burnt-arse fire will-o'-the-wisp, ignis fatuus **Fenland**

daal'mist mist which gathers in valleys overnight and is exhaled when the sun rises **Shetland**

dag dew or heavy-lying mist on the marsh **Suffolk**

grumma mirage caused by mist or haze rising from the ground **Shetland**

haze-fire luminous morning mist through which the dawn sun is shining **poetic**

muggy dull, misty weather; cf. Welsh *mwg*, meaning 'smoke, fume' **Northamptonshire**

na luin fast-moving heat-haze on the moor **Gaelic**

rafty of weather: misty, damply cold **Essex**

rionnach maoim shadows cast on the moorland by clouds moving across the sky on a bright and windy day **Gaelic**

roke fog that rises in the evenings off marshes and water meadows **East Anglia**

summer geese steam that rises from the moor when rain is followed by hot sunshine **North Yorkshire**

thick wet dense mist **Exmoor**

Pasture, Transhumance and Grazing

a' chailleach — stone coping topped with dry turf, forming a seat at the end of the bed in the shieling **Gaelic**

àirigh — shieling: i.e. summer pasture, or shelter established near the pasture **Gaelic**

astar, innis — area of moor where sheep spend their first summer and to which they tend to return **Gaelic**

botann — hole in the moor, often wet, where an animal might get stuck **Gaelic**

both — 'beehive' shieling with a corbelled stone roof, usually covered in turf such that it resembles a drumlin from a distance **Gaelic**

clach-tachais — upright stone standing outside a shieling, intended for cows to scratch against **Gaelic**

cotan — place made of turf where calves are kept on the shieling **Gaelic**

doras-iadht — door in the shieling which faces the wind and is therefore closed with turfs (the sheltered door being left open) **Gaelic**

geàrraidh — group of shielings **Gaelic**

làrach àirigh — mark where a shieling has been, its vestigial remains **Gaelic**

leabaidh liatha — mossy bed where the cattle lie at a distance from the shieling **Gaelic**

mow, mowfen — name formerly given to a fen which in the summertime yielded fodder for cattle **Northamptonshire**

rathad nam banachagan	path to the shieling (literally 'the road of the dairymaids') **Gaelic**
sgombair	old grass found around the edges of lochs after storms and used as bedding for cattle **Gaelic**
sgrath	thin turf used to roof the shieling **Gaelic**
teine leathan	fire made from heather and moor-grass bedding on the morning before returning home from the shieling at the end of summer. This fire was the signal to the cattle to set off home **Gaelic**
tulach na h-àirigh	site of the shieling **Gaelic**
uinneagan	alcoves set into shieling walls for holding basins of milk **Gaelic**

Peat, Turf and Earth

an caoran	lowest layer of a peat bank **Gaelic**
baitíneach	fibrous turf **Irish**
bàrr-fhàd	topmost layer of peat cut **Gaelic**
beat	rough sod of moorland (along with the heather growing on it) which is sliced or pared off, and burnt when the land is about to be ploughed **Devon**
blàr mònach	field of peat banks **Gaelic**
bruach	natural peat bank **Gaelic**

brug   stump of earth standing with the sward intact where the ground has been broken by the continued action of the weather **Shetland**

bull-pated   applied to a tuft of grass driven by the wind into a quiff, i.e. standing up like the tuft on a bull's forehead **Northamptonshire**

bungel   clod of turf used as a missile, for pelting with **Shetland**

caorán   peat embers, used to light or relight a fire **Irish**

carcair   turfed surface of a peat bank **Gaelic**

ceap murain   turf that is difficult to cut because of the tough grassy growth through it, and which is therefore often used as a seat in the shieling **Gaelic**

coirceog mhóna   small heap or 'beehive' (*coirceog*) of turf left for drying **Irish**

cruach mhònach   peat stack **Gaelic**

delf   sod or cut turf **Scots**

densher, devonshire   paring off the top layer of turf in a field and burning it in order to enrich the soil with ash **Dorset, Somerset**

flaa   hunk of turf, matted with roots of heather and grass, torn up by hand without a spade and used in thatching **Shetland**

flag   turf **Suffolk**

fòid depth of a peat bank measured in the number of peats that can be cut from the top of bank; thus *poll aon fòid, poll dà fhòid, poll thrì fòid* – a bank one, two, three peats deep **Gaelic**

gàrradh peats placed on top of each other in such a way as to let the air circulate through them, on the bank **Gaelic**

hassock, hussock tuft of coarse grass growing on boggy land **Northamptonshire**

kast to cut peats out of the ground and cast them onto the bank to dry **Shetland**

maoim place on the moor where there has been peat movement in the past **Gaelic**

mawn peat **Herefordshire**

mòine peat, once it is cut and dried **Gaelic**

mòine dhubh heavier and darker peats which lie deeper and older into the moor **Gaelic**

mump block of peat dug out by hand **Exmoor**

rathad an isein narrow gap left on top of the peat bank (literally 'the bird's road') **Gaelic**

rind edge of a peat bed **Scots**

rùdhan set of four peat blocks leaned up against one another such that wind and sun hasten their drying **Gaelic**

rùsg turf covering a peat bank **Gaelic**

skumpi clumsy, lumpish peat; outermost peat in each row as the peats are cut out of the bank **Shetland**

stèidheadh peat stack constructed in such a way as to shed rain. Various patterns are used in the side wall of the stack, e.g. sloping wall, flat wall, herringbone **Gaelic**

teine biorach flame or will-o'-the-wisp that runs on top of heather when the moor is burnt during the summer **Gaelic**

teine mònach peat fire **Gaelic**

tott clump or tuft of grass **Kent**

tubins grass sods **Cornwall**

turbary the right to cut turf or peat for fuel on a common or on another person's land **legal**

tusk tuft of grass or reeds **Northamptonshire**

veggs peat **Devon**

watter-sick of peats: saturated with water; of land: needing to be drained **Cumbria**

yarpha peat full of fibres and roots **Orkney**

Raised Ground, Flat Ground

bivan puv clover field **Anglo-Romani**

breck breach, blemish or failing; thus 'Brecklands', the name given to the broken sandy heathlands of south Norfolk **Middle English**

bruerie heath, common **Suffolk**

bukkalo tan heath, common **Anglo-Romani**

cnoc low-lying hill, often with surrounding flat or low ground **Gaelic**

druim wide ridge of high ground **Gaelic**

eig raised area of land or lifted turf mark used to designate a boundary **Gaelic**

eiscir ridge of ground separating two plains or lower land-levels **Irish**

ffridd moorland; mountain pasture **Welsh**

gallitrop fairy ring **Devon, Gloucestershire, Somerset**

gwaun moor; meadow; downland, usually walkable **Welsh**

hoath heath **Kent**

knowe field head; hillock; fairy mound **Scots**

ling sandy heathland **Norfolk, Suffolk**

má plain; region of level and even country **Irish**

machair rich grasslands and flower meadows that overlie shell-sand on the west coasts of Scotland, especially the Atlantic coast of Outer Hebridean islands **Gaelic**

machaireach inhabitant of low-lying landscapes **Gaelic**

maghannan open moorland, sometimes with low hills **Gaelic**

mall of land: bad, quaggy **Welsh**

mign   bog, mire **Welsh**

reeast   moorland **Manx**

rhos   moor, heath; extent of level land **Welsh**

roddam   raised silt bank left behind by a drained river, as the surrounding peat dries and lowers following the drainage. Land with an undulating surface is known as *roddamy* land or rolling land **Fenland**

saltings   salt marshes, usually on the seaward side of sea walls **Essex, Kent**

sìthean   derived from *sìth* (fairy hill or mound), by association with features within which fairies were thought to dwell: applied to small knolls, in most cases crowned by green grass **Gaelic**

skradge   small bank raised on an old one to prevent flooding **Fenland**

smeeth   level space **East Anglia**

tafolog   abounding in dock leaves (now found only as place-name element) **Welsh**

tòl   moor-mound **Gaelic**

tom   round hillock, small raised area **Gaelic**

wong   portion of unenclosed land under the open-field system **agricultural**

wonty-tump   molehill **Herefordshire**

Rushes, Mosses, Grasses, Heathers

canach white cotton grass, bog cotton: a sedge that typically grows on wet moor and produces tufts of long white silky hairs **Gaelic**

falaisgeir burning of heather to encourage fresh growth **Gaelic**

fianach deergrass, usually purple **Gaelic**

fizmer rustling noise produced in grass by petty agitations of the wind **East Anglia**

foggagey of grass: rank, tufted, matted **Scots**

foggit covered in moss or lichen **Scots**

fraoch heather **Gaelic**

fub long withered grass on old pastures or meadows **Galloway**

gads rushes and sedges that grow on wet, marshy ground **Kent**

gersick reed swamp **Cornish**

grugog heath-covered, abounding in heather **Welsh**

hover floating island, bed of reeds **Norfolk**

juncary land overgrown with rushes **southern English**

kite-log coarse grass on marshland, used for making doormats **Suffolk**

lìananach type of filamentous green algae that grows in moorland rivers and streams **Gaelic** *may-blobs*   kingcups, marsh marigolds **Herefordshire**

mycelia   network of fine filaments constituting the tissue of a fungus **botanical**

quealed   of vegetation: curled up, withered **Exmoor**

quicks   roots of stubbornly vivacious grasses harrowed out of long-neglected soil **East Anglia**

quill   to dry up or wither; to part with its sap: applied to grass or any green vegetable matter **Exmoor**

roshin   large lump of weeds **Galloway**

scraunching   withering with heat (vegetation) **Exmoor**

stàrr   sedge that grows in moorland lochs **Gaelic**

swailing, swaling,   burning heather, bracken and gorse on
zwealing   moorland **Cornwall, Devon**

zwer   whizzing noise made by a covey of partridges as they break suddenly from cover **Exmoor**

Watery Ground

aller-grove   marshy place where alders grow **Exmoor**

báisín   natural well or spring in a bog, which carries cleaner water (literally 'basin') **Irish**

blàr   very flat area of moor, often boggy **Gaelic**

boglach   general term for boggy area **Gaelic**

boglet little bog (coined by R. D. Blackmore in *Lorna Doone* (1869)) **poetic**

botach reedy bog **Gaelic**

bottoms marshy ground **Irish English**

breunloch dangerous sinking bog that may be bright green and grassy **Gaelic**

brochan miry soft ground (literally 'porridge') **Gaelic**

carr boggy or fenny copse **northern English**

clachan sìnteag stepping stones across boggy areas of moor **Gaelic**

corrach bog, marsh **Irish**

curhagh-craaee quagmire **Manx**

dams drained marshes **East Anglia**

didder of a bog: to quiver as a walker approaches **East Anglia**

donk, donkey of land: wet, moist or damp **Northamptonshire**

dub very deep bog or mire **Shetland**

each-uisge waterhorse, kelpie: a supernatural creature associated often with moorland lochs **Gaelic**

eanach marsh; narrow path or passage through a marsh **Irish**

ēg-land low-lying land, marshland, land liable to flooding **Old English**

fideach green stretch of a salt marsh which is flooded at high tide **Gaelic** *flow*   springy, mossy ground **Scots**

gotty, gouty   wet and boggy; a gouty field is a piece of land intersected with many small streams **Northamptonshire**

grasy-land   rich pastureland; marshland **Suffolk**

gwern   alder; alder marsh **Welsh**

haggy   boggy and full of holes **Scotland**

halophilous   salt-loving: growing in salt marshes **ecological**

headbolt   road over bog or morass, liable to flooding **Scottish Borders**

heugh   damp dip in a field **Doric**

inchland   marshland, low land near water **Northern Ireland**

ing   wet meadow, especially one by the side of a river **northern England**

lé stchez   place at the edge of a marsh which dries up in summer (toponym) **Jèrriais (Jersey Norman)**

leacon   wet, swampy common **Kent**

lèig-chruthaich   quivering bog with water trapped beneath it, and an intact surface **Gaelic**

lode   fen drain **Fenland**

mòinteach   moorland **Gaelic**

morbhach   grassy plain so near to the sea that it is often flooded by the tide **Gaelic**

moss   bog **Scots**

muireasc low-lying marshy land **Irish**

pee-wit-land cold, wet land which the lapwing haunts
North Sea coast

plim to swell with moisture **Cotswolds**

poise-staff jumping pole: a long staff with a small block of
wood at the lower end, used for jumping dykes
Fenland

polder area of marshy or boggy land **Kent**

pull-over way for carriages over the fen banks **Fenland**

pyllau pools, puddles **Welsh**

quacky of ground: springy, mossy **Galloway**

quick-fresh spring that rises in mossy ground **Scots**

quob quicksand; shaking bog **Herefordshire**

raon wide flat area of moorland **Gaelic**

ross morass **Herefordshire**

slack soft or boggy hollow **northern England, Scotland**

slamp boggy strip of land bordering fen riverbanks
Fenland

sliabh wide sloping area of moorland **Gaelic**

slunk muddy or marshy place, a miry hollow **Scots**

snape, sneap boggy place in a field, often containing small
springs and requiring to be drained **West
Country**

soke patch of marshy land **Northamptonshire**

spew   wet, marshy piece of ground **southern England**

spootie-place   area of land where water is rising from below **Galloway**

stoach   to churn up waterlogged land, as cattle do in winter **Kent, Sussex**

stugged   of a person or animal: enmired in a bog **Devon**

sùil-chruthaich   bog with water trapped under an intact surface layer of turf, which trembles on approach **Gaelic**

swang   low-lying piece of ground liable to be flooded **northern England**

turlach   land-lake: an area of ground, usually in limestone landscapes, that floods from beneath via a sinkhole or swallow, during periods of heavy rain or in winter **Irish**

walee   mossy ground **Galloway**

warp   mixture of fine sand and mud left on meadowland after the receding of floods **Northamptonshire**

weepy   of land: rife with springs **Exmoor**

wham   swamp **Cumbria**

yarf   swamp **Shetland**

zam-zody   soft, damp, wet **Exmoor**

zugs   bogs, soft wet ground; little bog islands, about the size of a bucket, of grass and rushes **Exmoor**

3

The Living Mountain

The Cairngorm Mountains of north-east Scotland are Britain's Arctic. In winter, storm winds of up to 170 miles per hour rasp the upper shires of the range, and avalanches scour its slopes. Even in high summer, snow still lies in the deepest corries, sintering slowly into ice. The Northern Lights flare green and red above its summits. The wind is so strong that on the plateau there are bonsai pines, fully grown at six inches, and juniper bushes which flatten themselves across the rocks to form densely woven dwarf forests. Two of Scotland's great rivers – the Dee and the Avon – have their sources there: falling as rain, filtered by rock, pooling as the clearest water into which I have ever looked, and then running seawards with gathering strength. The range itself is the eroded stump of a mass of magma that rose up through the earth's crust in the Devonian, cooled into granite, then emerged out of the surrounding schists and gneiss. The Cairngorms were once higher than today's Alps, but over billennia they have been eroded into a low-slung wilderness of whale-backed hills and shattered cliffs. Born of fire, carved by ice, finessed with wind, water and snow, the massif is a terrain shaped by what Nan Shepherd – in her slender masterpiece about the region, *The Living Mountain* – calls 'the elementals'.

Anna 'Nan' Shepherd was born near Aberdeen in 1893 and died there in 1981, and during her long life she spent hundreds of days and thousands of miles exploring the Cairngorms on foot. For decades her reputation rested on her three fine modernist novels, *The Quarry Wood* (1928), *The Weatherhouse* (1930) and *A Pass in the Grampians* (1933), all set in small communities in north-east Scotland, and all concerned with strong young women making their way against the current of convention. But to my mind her most important book was a work of non-fiction, *The Living Mountain*, written in the 1940s but not published until 1977.

Shepherd was a localist of the best kind: she came to know her chosen place closely, but that closeness served to deepen rather than to limit her vision. She had a modest middle-class upbringing and what looked like a modestly regional life: she attended Aberdeen High School for Girls, graduated from Aberdeen University in 1915 and was appointed to the staff of the Aberdeen Training Centre for Teachers, where she became a full-time lecturer in 1919 and from which she retired in 1956 (she wryly characterized her role there as the 'heaven-appointed task of trying to prevent a few of the students who pass through our Institution from conforming altogether to the approved pattern'). She travelled widely – including to Norway, France, Italy, Greece and South Africa – but lived for eighty-eight years in the same house in the Deeside village of Cults, now a suburb of Aberdeen. 'I have had the same bedroom all my life!' she once said, gladly. The house was called Dunvegan, and it was a two-storey granite Victorian villa sunk in its own steeply sloping grounds, with a pine-treed garden backing onto the railway line. Inside, it was a maze of curtained alcoves, frosted glass, oak-lined corridors, worn flagstones, and stairs that led upwards into shadow. The house served as Shepherd's retreat and also – in time – as a defence against those who were curious about her own refusal to conform 'altogether to the approved pattern'. For she never married, was never known to be in a relationship, and devoted the second half of her life to the care first of her mother, and then of her housekeeper and friend, Mary 'Mamie' Lawson.

Dunvegan was Nan's demesne; the Cairngorms, which rose to the west of her home, were her heartland. Into and out of those mountains she went in all seasons, by dawn, day, dusk and night, walking sometimes alone, and sometimes with friends, students or fellow hikers from the Deeside Field Club. She had use of a howff above Braemar on the side of Morrone, which served as a base for exploring the southern reaches of the range, and access to a shepherd's bothy north of the Lairig Ghru which was equipped with camp beds and sleeping bags. Like all true mountain-lovers, she got altitude sickness if she spent too long at sea level.

From a young age, Nan was hungry for life. She seems to have lived with a great but quiet gusto. Writing to a friend about a photograph of her as a toddler, she describes herself as 'all movement, legs and arms flailing as though I were demanding to get at life – I swear those limbs move as you look at them'. Intellectually, she was what Coleridge once called a 'library-cormorant' – omnivorous and voracious in her reading. On 7 May 1907, aged fourteen, she started the first of what she called her 'medleys' – commonplace books into which she copied literary, religious and philosophical citations, and which reveal the breadth of her reading as a young woman.

An extraordinary studio portrait exists of Shepherd as a university student. Her chin is tilted up, and she stares out of the top right of the frame, as if at a far-off prospect of hills. She is wearing a brocaded blouse and a broad headband with a jewel set into its centre. Her hair is parted down the middle, and thick glossy plaits tumble either side of her brow. The overall appearance is faintly Native American, without any implication of parody or foolish fancy-dress.

She is a charismatic presence: strong, bold-eyed and strikingly beautiful. This is the Shepherd who was remembered by a fellow undergraduate as 'a tall slim figure with a halo of chestnut plaits, a Blessed Damozel expression and an awe-inspiring dispatch case'. That 'dispatch case' was evidence of her commitment to study. She was shaped by the teaching of Herbert Grierson, the first Professor of English Literature at the University of Aberdeen, a 'long lean man' who 'spoke like a torrent'. It was Grierson who led her, she later recalled, 'to understand how minute, precise and particularised knowledge had to be, and then [to see] to our delight that it need not cease to exhilarate'. An allegiance to 'precise' and 'particularised' knowledge would become an insignia of Shepherd's own 'exhilarating' work. Throughout her life she carried with her an air of what her friend Erlend Clouston calls 'dark wisdom, almost sorcery'. 'Close up there were these tingling hazel eyes set between copper cheeks and a froth of wiry hair – Nan never went to a hairdresser,' he remembers, 'and seen from further off – striding over the moors, say – she was a swirling ziggurat of tawny cardigans, scarves and skirts. Never trousers. When the wind blew against her slender frame, she resembled a giant ruffled eagle's feather.'

Shepherd published her three novels in an extraordinary five-year burst of creativity. Shortly afterwards came a collection of poetry entitled *In the Cairngorms* (1934), published in a handsome green-and-sable hardback by the Moray Press of Edinburgh. The print run was tiny and the copies of this original edition are now almost impossible to find. It was the book of which she seems to have been most proud. Shepherd had a clear genre hierarchy in her mind, and poetry was at its pinnacle. 'Poetry', she wrote to the novelist Neil Gunn – with whom she had a flirty and intellectually ardent correspondence – holds 'in intensest being the very heart of all experience' and offers glimpses of 'that burning heart of life'. She felt that she could produce poetry only when she was 'possess[ed]', when her 'whole nature . . . suddenly leaped into life'. This happened rarely: it took her a quarter of a century to gather the forty-six poems of *In the Cairngorms*, and it was to be her only collection of poetry. Despite taking such patient care over the book's creation, she was dissatisfied with it, worrying aloud to Gunn that her poetry – 'about stars and mountains and light' – was too 'cold', too 'inhuman'. Still, she admitted, 'When I'm possessed that's the only kind of thing that comes out of me.'

It is true that her poems are often 'cold', for they excel in a spare boreal grammar (the 'snow driving dim on the blast', or a winter sky that is 'green as ice'). But they are not chilly and they are certainly not inhuman. Shepherd's great subject as a writer across all forms was the inter-animating relationship of mind and matter. She was thrilled by evidence of the earth's vast indifference to human consciousness: the granites and schists of the corries, and the upwelling stream water of the plateau that 'does nothing, absolutely nothing, but be itself'. But she also believed, like Wordsworth in *The Prelude*, that sustained contemplation of outer landscapes led – at last, after 'toil' – to a subtler understanding of the 'spirit'. In the Cairngorms, therefore, she came to feel 'not out of myself, but in myself', and this doubled motion – the exploratory movement out into wild landscape simultaneous with the confirming movement back into the self – lends her poems their uncanny atmosphere, whereby the hills are both hostile and habitual, unsettling and enfolding. This is keenest in the four short lyrics written in Doric, the north-east dialect of Scots, which stud the book like garnets in granite. Keen, also, in the first two lines of the opening poem of the collection, which catch much of her poetry's strange magic: 'Oh burnie with the glass-white shiver, / Singing over stone . . .' What a start it is – at once homely and eerie, pitched somewhere between lullaby and cantrip. Out of the water's stone-song springs Nan's own quick lyric. I have read those lines a dozen times or more, and they send a glass-white shiver down my spine on each new occasion. The tiny poem of which they are part still haunts my ear; I hear it when I am in the hills.

Shepherd produced four books in six years and then, for almost half a century – nothing. It is hard now to tell if her literary silence was down to discretion or to block. In 1931 – even at the apex of her output – she was smitten by something close to depression at her inability to write. 'I've gone dumb,' she wrote blackly to Gunn that year:

> One reaches (or I do) these dumb places in life. I suppose there's nothing for it but to go on living. Speech may come. Or it may not. And if it doesn't I suppose one has just to be content to be dumb. At least not shout for the mere sake of making a noise.

'Speech' did come back to her after 1934, but only intermittently. She wrote little save for *The Living Mountain* – itself only about 30,000 words long – and the articles she contributed occasionally to the journal of the Deeside Field Club.

The Living Mountain was written mostly during the closing years of the Second World War, though it draws on Shepherd's earlier decades of mountain experiences. War exists as distant thunder in the book: there are the aeroplanes that crash into the plateau, killing their crew; the blackout nights through which she walks to hear news of the campaigns on the one radio in the area; the felling of Scots pines on the Rothiemurchus estate for the war effort. We know that

Shepherd had completed a draft of her book by the late summer of 1945, because she sent a version to Gunn then for his scrutiny and opinion.

'Dear Nan, You don't need me to tell you how I enjoyed your book,' begins his astute reply:

> This is beautifully done. With restraint, the fine precision of the art-
> ist or scientist or scholar; with an exactitude that is never pedantic
> but always tribute. So love comes through, & wisdom . . . you deal
> with facts. And you build with proposition, methodically and calmly,
> for light and a state of being are facts in your world.

Gunn instantly identifies the book's distinctive manners: precision as a form of lyricism, attention as devotion, exactitude as tribute, description structured by proposition, and facts freed of their ballast such that they levitate and otherwise behave curiously. But then his letter turns a little patronizing. He thinks that it will be 'difficult, perhaps' to get it published. He suggests that she add photographs, and a map to help readers for whom the 'proper nouns' of the Cairngorms will mean nothing. He warns her away from Faber, who are in a 'mess', and suggests considering serial publication in *Scots Magazine*. He congratulates her – his 'water sprite!' – on having written something that might interest 'hill & country lovers'.

Unable or unwilling to secure publication at the time, Shepherd placed the manuscript in a drawer for more than forty years, until Aberdeen University Press finally and quietly published it in 1977, in an unlovely edition with a purple hillscape on its dust jacket. The same year Bruce Chatwin's *In Patagonia*, Patrick Leigh Fermor's *A Time of Gifts* and John McPhee's *Coming into the Country* appeared; a year later came Peter Matthiessen's mountain epic, *The*

Snow Leopard. To my mind, *The Living Mountain* stands easily equal to these four better-known classics of place and travel.

~

Shepherd was a word-hoarder. As Finlay and Anne gathered the Gaelic of the Hebridean moors, so Nan collected the Scots of the Cairngorms. *The Living Mountain* carries a glossary that is longer than its last chapter, and that is vivid with walking words (*spangin'*, meaning 'walking vigorously') and weather words (*smored*, meaning 'smothered in snow', and *roarie-bummlers*, meaning 'fast-moving storm clouds'). She also treasured the Gaelic place-names of the range: Loch an Uaine, 'the green loch', or Stac Iolaire, 'the eagle's crag'. To Shepherd, such terms were means to convey both 'exactitude' and 'tribute', as Gunn had put it. She described her book as 'a traffic of love', with 'traffic' implying 'exchange' and 'mutuality' rather than 'congestion' or 'blockage', and with a shudder of eroticism to that word 'love'. It is both exhilaratingly materialist, and almost animist in its account of how mind and mountain interact; both a geo-poetic quest into place, and a philosophical enquiry into the nature of knowledge.

The Living Mountain needs to be understood as a parochial work in the most expansive sense. Over the past century, *parochial* has soured as a word. The adjectival form of *parish*, it has come to connote sectarianism, insularity, boundedness: a mind or a community turned inward upon itself, a pejorative finitude. It hasn't always been this way, though. Patrick Kavanagh (1904–67), the great poet of the Irish mundane, was sure of the parish's importance. For Kavanagh, the parish was not a perimeter but an aperture: a space through which the world could be seen. 'Parochialism is universal,' he wrote.

'It deals with the fundamentals.' Kavanagh, like Aristotle, was careful not to smudge the 'universal' into the 'general'. The 'general', for Aristotle, was the broad, the vague and the undiscerned. The 'universal', by contrast, consisted of fine-tuned principles, induced from an intense concentration on the particular. Kavanagh often returned to this connection between the universal and the parochial, and to the idea that we learn by scrutiny of the close-at-hand. 'All great civilisations are based on parochialism,' he wrote:

> To know fully even one field or one land is a lifetime's experience.
> In the world of poetic experience it is depth that counts, not width.
> A gap in a hedge, a smooth rock surfacing a narrow lane, a view of
> a woody meadow, the stream at the junction of four small fields –
> these are as much as a man can fully experience.

Shepherd came to know the Cairngorms 'deeply' rather than 'widely', and they are to her what Selborne was to Gilbert White, the Sierra Nevada were to John Muir, and the Aran Islands are to Tim Robinson. They were her inland-island, her personal parish, the area of territory that she loved, walked and studied over time such that concentration within its perimeters led to knowledge cubed rather than knowledge curbed. What, Shepherd once wondered to Gunn, if one could find a way to 'irradiate the common'. That, she concluded, 'should make something universal'. This irradiation of the 'common' into the 'universal' is what she achieved in *The Living Mountain*.

Most works of mountaineering literature have been written by men, and most male mountaineers are focused on the summit: a mountain expedition being qualified by the success or failure of ascent. But to aim for the highest point is not the only way to climb a mountain, nor is a narrative of siege and assault the only way to write about one. Shepherd's book is best thought of not as a work of mountaineering literature but of mountain literature. Early on, she confesses that as a young woman she had been prone to a 'lust' for 'the tang of height', and had approached the Cairngorms egocentrically, appraising them for their 'effect upon me'. *The Living Mountain* relates how, over time, she learnt to go into the hills aimlessly, 'merely to be with the mountain as one visits a friend, with no intention but to be with him'. 'I am on the plateau again, having gone round it like a dog in circles to see if it is a good place,' she begins one section, chattily; 'I think it is, and I am to stay up here for a while.' Circumambulation has replaced summit-fever; plateau has substituted for peak. She no longer has any interest in discovering a pinnacle point from which she might become the looker-down who sees all with a god-like eye. Thus the brilliant image of the book's opening page (which has for ever changed the way I perceive the Cairngorms), where she proposes regarding the massif not as a series of distinct zeniths, but instead as an entity: 'The plateau is the true summit of these mountains; they must be seen as a single mountain, and the individual tops . . . no more than eddies on the plateau surface.'

As a walker, then, Shepherd practises a kind of unpious pilgrimage. She tramps around, over, across and into the mountain, rather than charging up it. There is an implicit humility to her repeated acts of traverse, which stands as a corrective to the self-exaltation of the mountaineer's hunger for an utmost point.

~

The Cairngorms were my first mountain range, and they are still the hills I know best. My grandparents lived in a converted forestry cottage on a rare limestone upsurge on the north-eastern slopes of the massif, and the field of rough pasture which they owned ran down to the banks of the River Avon. From a young age, I visited them with my family, usually in the summers. On a wall of the house hung a framed Ordnance Survey map of the whole massif, on which we would finger-trace walks done and walks planned. My grandfather was a diplomat and mountaineer who had spent his life climbing around the world, and it was he and his Cairngorm world which cast the spell of height upon me as a child. His yard-long wooden-hafted ice-axe and his old iron crampons seemed to my young imagination like the props of wizardry. I was shown black-and-white photographs of the peaks he had climbed in the Alps and the Himalayas, and it was miraculous to me that such structures could be ascended by humans. Mountaineering seemed to me then, as Shepherd puts it, 'a legendary task, which heroes, not men, accomplished'.

For me, as for Shepherd, childhood exposure to the Cairngorms 'thirled me for life to the mountain'. I have since crossed the massif on foot and ski many times, and my maps of the region are spidery with the marks of tracks followed and routes attempted. I have seen dozens of blue-white snow hares, big as dogs, popping up from behind peat hags over the back of Glas Maol, I have followed flocks of snow buntings as they gust over the Braeriach plateau, and I once spent hours sheltering in a snow-hole above the Northern Corries while a blizzard blew itself furiously out.

So I knew the Cairngorms long before I knew *The Living Mountain*. I first read it in 2003, and was changed. I had thought I knew the Cairngorms well, but Shepherd showed me my complacency. Her writing taught me to *see* these familiar hills, rather than just to look at them.

The Living Mountain is thick with the kinds of acute perception that come only from staying up 'for a while'. 'Birch needs rain to release its odour,' Shepherd notes. 'It is a scent with body to it, fruity like old brandy, and on a wet warm day one can be as good as drunk with it.' I had never before noticed the 'odour' of birches, but now cannot be in a stand of birch trees on a rainy summer's day without smelling its Courvoisier whiff. Elsewhere Shepherd remarks and records 'the coil over coil' of a golden eagle's ascent on a thermal, 'the minute scarlet cups of lichen', a white hare crossing sunlit snow with its accompanying 'odd ludicrous leggy shadow-skeleton'. She has a sharp eye for the inadvertent acts of land art authored by nature: 'Beech bud-sheaths, blown in tide-mark lines along the edge of the roads, give a glow of brightness to the dusty roads of May.' She spends an October night in air that is 'bland as silk', and while half asleep on the plutonic granite of the plateau feels herself become stone-like, 'rooted far down in their immobility', metamorphosed by the igneous rocks into a newly mineral self.

Shepherd is a fierce see-er, then, and like many fierce see-ers, she is also a part-time mystic, for whom intense empiricism is the first step to immanence. 'I knew when I had looked for a long time,' she writes, 'that I had hardly begun to see.' Her descriptions often move beyond the material. Up on the mountain, after hours of walking and watching:

> the eye sees what it didn't see before, or sees in a new way what it
> had already seen. So the ear, the other senses. These moments come
> unpredictably, yet governed, it would seem, by a law whose working
> is dimly understood.

Shepherd – like Neil Gunn, and like the Scottish explorer-essayist W. H. Murray – was influenced by her reading in Buddhism and the Tao. Shards of Eastern philosophy glitter in the prose of all three writers, like mica flecks in granite. Reading their work now, with its fusion of Highland landscape and Buddhist metaphysics, remains astonishing: like encountering a Noh play performed in a kailyard, or chrysanthemums flourishing in a corrie.

~

Late one March I left my home in Cambridge and travelled north to the Cairngorms. In the south of England, blackthorn was foaming in the hedges, tulips and hyacinths were popping in suburban flower-beds, and spring was reaching full riot. Arriving in the Cairngorms, I found I had travelled back into high winter. Avalanches were still rumbling the lee slopes, Loch Avon was frozen over, and blizzards were cruising the plateau. Over three days, with four friends, I crossed the massif from Glenshee in the south-east to Loch Morlich in the north-west. Up on the wide summit plateau of Ben a' Bhuird, I found myself in the purest white-out conditions I have ever experienced. Those who have travelled in high mountains or to the poles are likely to be familiar with the white-out: the point at which snow, cloud and blizzard combine such that the world dissolves into a single pallor. Scale and distance become impossible to discern. There are no shadows or waymarks. Space is depthless. Even gravity's hold feels loosened: slope and fall-lines can only be inferred by the tilt of blood in the skull. It felt, for that astonishing hour up on Ben a' Bhuird, as if we were all flying in white space.

The mountain world, like the desert world, is filled with mirages: tricks of light and perspective, parhelia, fogbows, Brocken spectres, white-outs – illusions brought on by snow, mist, cloud or distance. These optical special effects fascinated Shepherd. In winter, she sees a 'snow skeleton, attached to nothing', which turns out to be the black rocks of a cliff high above, whose apparent levitation is due to the imperceptibility of the snow banks below it. At midsummer, she looks through lucid air for hundreds of miles and spies an imaginary peak, a Hy Brasil of the high tops: 'I could have sworn I saw a shape, distinct and blue, very clear and small, further off than any hill the chart recorded. The chart was against me, my companions were against me, I never saw it again.'

One winter morning in the Cairngorms, following the cloud base up from Loch Etchachan to the top of Ben Macdui, I looked upwards and – through a break in the clouds – saw the white summit ridge of an impossibly high mountain, Himalayan in altitude, rising many thousands of feet above me, though I was within an hour of the top of Macdui. My friend David saw it too, and we regarded it together in wonderment and faint fear. 'We seem to be lost in the foothills of another range entirely,' David said. I still cannot account for the sight of that unreal peak. I remember that vision of impossible distance also because, a few hours later, after we had reached the summit of Macdui and begun the descent to the north, we passed into mobile-phone reception and I learnt that someone very close to me had very suddenly died.

Shepherd punningly calls such mountain illusions 'mis-spellings': visual 'errors' that possess an accidental magic and offer unlooked-for revelation. She delights in these moments, rather than holding them in suspicion or correcting for them:

> Such illusions, depending on how the eye is placed and used, drive home the truth that our habitual vision of things is not necessarily right: it is only one of an infinite number, and to glimpse an unfamiliar one, even for a moment, unmakes us, but steadies us again.

This is brilliantly seen and said. Our vision is never correct but only ever provisional. 'Illusions' are themselves means of knowing (a reminder of James Joyce's aside about errors being the portals of discovery). Importantly, these illusions cannot be summoned into being or ordered on request. They are unpredictable conspiracies of the material and the sensory; like the mountain as a whole, they are 'impossible to coerce'. Shepherd doesn't systematically traverse the Cairngorms, or seek by some psychogeographic ruse to prise them open. The massif is graceful in the Augustinian sense; its gifts cannot be actively sought (mind you, there's more than a hint of good Dee-side Presbyterianism in Shepherd's preoccupation with 'toil': 'On one toils, into the hill' . . . one enjoys 'a tough bit of going' . . . one 'toil[s] upwards').

In an amazing passage about illusions, Shepherd describes looking from a distance at a stone barn on a humid day. The moist air acts as a lens, multiplying and redistributing her sightlines, so that she seems to view all sides of the barn simultaneously. Her own style possesses a similar dispersive quality. While reading *The Living Mountain* your sight feels scattered – as though you have suddenly gained the compound eye of a dragonfly, seeing through a hundred different lenses at once. This multiplex effect is created by Shepherd's refusal to privilege a single perspective. Her own consciousness is only one among an infinite number of focal points on and in the mountain. Her prose watches now from the point of view of the eagle, now from that of the walker, now from that of the creeping juniper. By means of this accumulation of exact attentions we are brought – in her memorable phrase – to see the earth 'as the earth must see itself'.

The first law of ecology is that everything is connected to everything else, and *The Living Mountain* is filled – woven – with images of weaving and interconnection. There are pine roots that are 'twisted and intertwined like a cage of snakes'; the tiny Scots pines high on the hill that are 'splayed to the mountain and almost roseate in structure'; the duck and drake that, rising together, appear to form a single bird with 'two enormous wings'; the loch currents which knit thousands of floating pine needles into complex spheres, similar to wren's nests: structures so intricately bound that 'they can be lifted out of the water and kept for years, a botanical puzzle to those who have not been told the secret of their formation' (these pine-needle balls are also, of course, surreptitious emblems of Shepherd's own tightly knit and tiny work, itself kept for years). Reading through the book, you realize that its twelve sections are bound laterally to each other by rhymes of colour, thought and image, so that they offer not a dozen different facets of the mountain but rather a transverse descriptive weave – the prose equivalent of a dwarf juniper forest.

In one scene Shepherd describes a long winter dusk spent watching two rutting stags, whose antlers have become 'interlaced' during a joust, such that they cannot separate. She watches as they 'drag . . . each other backwards and forwards across the ringing frozen floor of a hollow', and waits for answers: who will win, how will they disentangle? But darkness falls, Shepherd is forced to return indoors, and even a return to the site of the battle the next morning yields neither corpses nor clues. The episode is yet another image of the mountain's refusal to answer to questions which are explicitly asked of it. That which 'interlocks' is rarely opened here, even by the 'keyed' senses of the walker. Deer run in a way that resembles flight, and yet their motion is 'fixed to the earth and cannot be detached from it'. A fawn lies in a 'hidden hollow', so camouflaged that its presence is given away only by the flick of its eyelid. Knowledge is never figured in *The Living Mountain* as finite: a goal to be reached or a state to be attained. The massif is not a crossword to be cracked, full of encrypted ups and downs. Man 'patiently adds fact to fact', but such epistemological bean-counting will take you only so far. Greater understanding of the mountain's interrelations serves to finesse the real into a further marvellousness – and reveal other realms of incomprehension.

What Shepherd learns – and what her book taught me – is that the true mark of long acquaintance with a single place is a readiness to accept uncertainty: a contentment with the knowledge that you must not seek complete knowledge. 'Slowly I have found my way in,' she says: slowly, but not fully, for '[i]f I had other senses, there are other things I should know'. This is not a book that relishes its own discoveries; it prefers to relish its own ignorances – the water that is 'too much' for her, or the dark line of geese that melts 'into the darkness of the cloud, and I could not tell where or when they resumed formation and direction'. Shepherd is compelled by the massif's excesses, its unmappable surplus: 'The mind cannot carry away all that it has to give, nor does it always believe possible what it has carried away.'

~

I worry that I am making *The Living Mountain* sound abstruse, cold, over-intellectual. It isn't. It is deeply wise and it is propositionally structured, but not abstruse. It is also avidly sensual. What physical joy Shepherd records! Up in the mountains she lives off wild food, foraging for cranberries, cloudberries and blueberries, drinking from the 'strong white' water of rivers. 'I am like a dog – smells excite me. The earthy smell of moss . . . is best savoured by grubbing.' She swims in lochs, and sleeps on hillsides to be woken by the sharp click of a robin's foot upon her bare arm, or the snuffle of a grazing deer. She observes with brilliant exactness how frost 'stiffens the muscles of the chin' (a part of the body we don't usually associate with muscularity, let alone thermometric sensitivity), or the pleasure of 'running my hand after rain through juniper . . . for the joy of the wet drops trickling over the palm'. Heather pollen which feels 'silky to the touch' rises from the moor. The body is made 'limber' by the rhythm of walking. There is, unmistakably, an eroticism tingling through this book, clandestine and surreptitious – especially thrilling because Shepherd was a woman writing at a time and in a culture where candour about physical pleasure was widely regarded with suspicion.

'That's the way to see the world: in our own bodies,' says the poet, Buddhist and forester Gary Snyder, and his phrase could stand as an epigraph to *The Living Mountain*. True, Shepherd knows well how rough mountains can be on the human body – sometimes fatally so. She admits to the 'roaring scourge' of the plateau in summer, when the midges are out in their millions and the heat rises in jellied waves from the granite; and she deplores the 'monstrous place' the mountain becomes when rain pours for hours on end. She describes getting burnt by snow-glare until her eyes are weeping, she feels sick and her face for days afterwards is left scorched 'as purple as a boozer's'. She demonstrates – like many mountain-goers, myself included – a macabre fascination with the dead of the hills: the five killed in falls; the crew of Czech airmen whose plane crashes into Ben a' Bhuird in low cloud; the four 'boys' who are caught and killed by storms, including two who leave a 'high-spirited and happy report' in the waterproof logbook beneath the Shelter Stone at the west end of Loch Avon, but whose frozen bodies are later discovered on the hill, their knees and knuckles raw with abrasions from the granite boulders over which they had crawled, trying desperately to make their way in the blizzard wind.

Yet if the body is at risk in the mountains, it is also, for Shepherd, the site of reward, a fabulous sensorium – and the intellect's auxiliary. In the mountains, she writes, a life of the senses is lived so purely that 'the body may be said to think'. This is her book's most radical proposition. Radical because, as a philosophical position, it was cutting-edge. In the same years that Shepherd was writing *The Living Mountain*, the French philosopher Maurice Merleau-Ponty was developing his influential theories of the body-subject, as laid out in his *Phenomenology of Perception* (1945). Merleau-Ponty was at the time working as a professional philosopher in Paris with all the institutional support and vocational confidence that such a position brings. He had been trained as one of the French philosophical elite, studying alongside Sartre, De Beauvoir and Simone Weil at the École Normale Supérieure, where he passed the *aggrégation* in philosophy in 1930. Shepherd was a teacher in an Aberdeen tertiary college, but her philosophical conclusions concerning colour-perception, touch and embodied knowledge are arrestingly similar to those of Merleau-Ponty.

For Merleau-Ponty, post-Cartesian philosophy had cleaved a false divide between the body and the mind. Throughout his career he argued for the foundational role that sensory perception plays in our understanding of the world as well as in our reception of it. He argued that knowledge is 'felt': that our bodies think and know in ways that precede cognition. Consciousness, the human body and the phenomenal world are therefore inextricably intertwined. The body 'incarnates' our subjectivity and we are thus, Merleau-Ponty proposed, 'embedded' in the 'flesh' of the world. He described this embodied experience as 'knowledge in the hands'; our body 'grips' the world for us and is 'our general medium for having a world'. And the material world itself is therefore not the unchanging object presented by the natural sciences, but instead endlessly relational. We are co-natural with the world and it with us – but we only ever see it partially.

You will already be able to hear the affinities between Merleau-Ponty's thought and Shepherd's, as well as between their dictions. On the mountain, she writes, moments occur at which 'something moves between me and it. Place and mind may interpenetrate until the nature of both are altered. I cannot tell what this movement is except by recounting it.' 'The body is not . . . negligible, but paramount,' she elsewhere declares, in a passage that could have come straight from *Phenomenology of Perception*. 'Flesh is not annihilated but fulfilled. One is not bodiless, but essential body':

> The hands have an infinity of pleasure in them. The feel of things, textures, surfaces, rough things like cones and bark, smooth things like stalks and feathers and pebbles rounded by water, the teasing of gossamers . . . the scratchiness of lichen, the warmth of the sun, the sting of hail, the blunt blow of tumbling water, the flow of wind – nothing that I can touch or that touches me but has its own identity for the hand as much as for the eye.

Shepherd's belief in bodily thinking gives *The Living Mountain* a contemporary relevance. We are increasingly separated from contact with nature. We have come to forget that our minds are shaped by the bodily experience of being in the world – its spaces, textures, sounds, smells and habits – as well as by genetic traits we inherit and ideologies we absorb. We are literally 'losing touch', becoming dis-embodied, more than in any historical period before ours. Shepherd saw this process starting over sixty years ago, and her book is both a mourning and a warning. 'This is the innocence we have lost,' she says, 'living in one sense at a time to live all the way through.' Her book is a hymn to 'living all the way through': to touching, tasting, smelling and hearing the world. If you manage this, then you might walk 'out of the body and into the mountain', such that you become, briefly, 'a stone . . . the soil of the earth'. And at that point then, well, then 'one has been in'. 'That is all,' writes Shepherd, and that 'all' should be heard not diminutively, apologetically, but expansively, vastly.

Like Martha Ironside, the heroine of her first novel, *The Quarry Wood*, Shepherd 'coveted knowledge and willingly suffered priva-tions in the pursuit of learning', and among those privations were the hardships of hill-walking (the toil, the cold, the rain), for to Shepherd walking was inextricable from 'learning'. Her relationship with the massif was lifelong. She kept walking 'into' the Cairngorms until infirmity made it impossible.

In her final months, harrowed by old age, she was confined to a nursing home near Banchory. She began to suffer illusions, confu-sions, 'mis-spellings'. She hallucinated that the whole ward had been moved out to a wood in Drumoak: 'I can see the wood – I played in it as a child.' She began to see Grampian place-names blazoned in 'large capital letters' in a glowing arc across the 'dark and silent' room in which she slept. Even in this troubled state, Shepherd was still thinking hard about the nature of perception and about how to represent perception in language. 'It took old age to show me that time is a mode of experiencing,' she wrote then to her friend, the

Scottish artist Barbara Balmer, 'but how to convey such inwardness?' Reading true literature, she reflected, 'it's as though you are standing <u>experiencing</u> and suddenly the work is there, bursting out of its own ripeness . . . life has exploded, sticky and rich and smelling oh so good. And . . . that makes the ordinary world magical – that rever-berates/illuminates.' This 'illumination' of the ordinary world was, of course, what Shepherd's own work achieved, though it would never have occurred to her to acknowledge her immense talent as a writer.

Shepherd was, the novelist Jessie Kesson recalled, 'reticent about herself'. She possessed a 'grace of the soul' that expressed itself in part as discretion. But she was also a person of passions. She lived with zeal, right to the end. Speaking of the poet Charles Murray – the man to whom Shepherd is thought to have become closest – Shepherd attributed the 'striking power' of his poetry to the fact that 'he said yes to life'. So did she, and the huge 'power' of her writing is also born of this affirmative ardour. Kesson, at one time a student of Shepherd's, asked her if she believed in an afterlife. 'I hope it is true for those who have had a lean life,' she replied. 'For myself – *this* has been so good, so fulfilling.'

~

The more I read *The Living Mountain*, the more it gives to me. I have read it perhaps a dozen times now, and each time I re-approach it as Shepherd re-approaches the mountain: not expecting to exhaust it of its meaning, rather to be surprised by its fresh yields. New ways of seeing emerge, or at least I find myself shown how to look again from different angles. This book is tutelary, but it is not the expression of any system or programme, spiritual or religious. It advances no manifesto, offers no message or take-home moral. As on the mountain, so in the book: the knowledge it offers arrives from unexpected directions and quarters, and seemingly without end. It is a book that grows with the knowing.

In the last days of September, ten years after first reading Shepherd, I returned to the Cairngorms. I wanted to spend days and nights in the hills without fixed destinations. Too often I had been hurried across them by weather and logistics, unable to linger and pry. Shepherd called herself 'a peerer into corners', and I took this as my mandate to wander and be distracted.

With two friends I walked in from the north, through the dwarf pines of the Rothiemurchus Forest, under a blue sky and a daytime moon, and into the Lairig Ghru. It was hot work for autumn. The sun was slant but bright. Mare's-tail clouds furled 30,000 feet above us. A mile into the Ghru, I saw a golden eagle catch a thermal near Lurcher's Crag, rising coil over coil in slow symmetry. It was only the second eagle I had ever seen in the Cairngorms, and it set my heart hammering. Up the long shoulder of Sròn na Lairige we toiled, over the tops of Braeriach and at last onto the plateau proper: a huge upland of tundra and boulder at an altitude of around 4,000 feet. I heard a barking and saw to my north-east a flight of a hundred or so geese arrowing through the Lairig Ghru in a ragged V. Because I had height, I looked down onto their flexing backs rather than up at their steady bellies as they passed.

We made camp far across the plateau, near to the source of the Dee – the highest origin of any British river. I pitched my tent by a stream, looking south-east over the Lairig Ghru towards the battleship flanks of Carn a'Mhaim. Butterflies danced. There were no midges. I had some real coffee with me for the morning brew. I was very happy indeed.

Later that afternoon we dropped 600 feet north off the plateau in search of Loch Coire an Lochain, the 'loch of the corrie of the loch', which Shepherd prized as one of the range's 'recesses', or hidden places. She had also visited it on a late-September day, and marvelled at the chilly clarity of its water, and its secrecy as a site. 'It cannot be seen until one stands almost on its lip,' she wrote. At the hour we reached it, a curved shadow had fallen across the corrie which, when doubled by the surface of the water, perfectly mimicked the form of a raven's beak. We swam in the loch, which was steel-blue and speckled on its surface with millions of golden grains of dust or pollen. The water was gin-clear and bitingly cold.

Sunset was close as we climbed back up to the plateau, so we waited for it on a westerly slope. As the sun lowered and reddened, cloud wisps blew up from the valley and refracted its light to form a dazzling parhelion: concentric halos of orange, green and pink that circled the sun. Once the sun had gone a pale mist sprang up from the plateau, and we waded knee-deep in its milk back to camp, from where we watched a yellow moon rise above the Braeriach tors. After dark had fallen I walked to the edge of the plateau, where the young Dee crashed down 1,000 feet into the great inward fissure of the Garbh Coire.

The air that night was so mild there was no need for a tent. I woke soaked in dew and shrouded in cloud that had rolled up out of the Lairig Ghru. We were in a white world. Visibility was twenty yards at most. Blinded of sight, for a full hour, in a way I have never done before, I sat and simply listened to the mountain. Ptarmigans zithered and churred to one another, dotterels kewed, and water moved: chuckled, burred, glugged, shattered. 'The sound of all this moving water is as integral to the mountain as pollen to the flower,' Shepherd reflected beautifully:

> One hears it without listening as one breathes without thinking. But to a listening ear the sound disintegrates into many different notes — the slow slap of a loch, the high clear trill of a rivulet, the roar of spate. On one short stretch of burn the ear may distinguish a dozen different notes at once.

That morning we searched in the mist for the Wells of Dee, the springs that mark the river's true birthplace. We began at the plateau rim, and from there we followed it back uphill, always taking the larger branch where the stream forked. At last we reached a point where the water rose from within the rock itself. Shepherd had also made this 'journey to the source', and confronted matter in its purest form:

> Water, that strong white stuff, one of the four elemental mysteries, can here be seen at its origins. Like all profound mysteries, it is so simple that it frightens me. It wells from the rock, and flows away. For unnumbered years it has welled from the rock, and flowed away.

This proof of the mountain's mindlessness was to Shepherd both thrilling and terrifying. The Cairngorms exceeded human comprehension: what she called the 'total mountain' could never totally be known. Yet if approached without expectation, the massif offered remarkable glimpses into its 'being'.

Walking under Shepherd's influence, led by her language, I had enjoyed an astonishing time of gifts. The eagle, the geese, the blue-gold loch, the parhelion, the mists, the springs, those few days in the hills had compressed into them a year's worth of marvels – and each had its precedent in *The Living Mountain*. The fortuity of it all was acute, approaching the eerie. It was as if we had walked *into* the pages of Nan's book, though of course her book had emerged out of the Cairngorms themselves, so we were merely completing that circuit of word and world.

GLOSSARY II

Uplands

Hills, Fells and Peaks

abri   shelter used by mountaineers, typically an overhanging rock **mountaineering**

alpenglow   light of the setting or rising sun seen illuminating high mountains or the underside of clouds **mountaineering**

amar   hill with precipices **Gaelic**

arête   sharp ascending ridge of a mountain **mountaineering**

banc   hill; bank or breast of a hill **Welsh**

bans, vans   high place **Cornish**

barr   summit **Irish**

batch   hillock **West Country**

beacon   conspicuous hill with long sightlines from its summit (suitable for a beacon-fire) **southern England, Wales**

beinn   usually the highest peak in an area; visually dominant summit **Gaelic**

biod   pinnacle; pointed knoll **Gaelic**

bioran   peak of medium height, usually sharp and rugged **Gaelic**

bothy   hut or shelter maintained in remote country **Scots**

brent brow of a hill **Northamptonshire**

bron hillside, slope **Welsh**

byurg rocky hill **Shetland**

cadair mound or hill shaped like a seat (as place-name element); fort, defensive settlement **Welsh**

caisteal peak of medium height, usually without corries (literally 'castle', 'fort') **Gaelic**

càirn, càrn substantial, complex peak, with corries, shoulders and ridges **Gaelic**

chockstone stone wedged in a vertical cleft or chimney of rock, impeding progress **mountaineering**

choss rock that is unsuitable for climbing due to its instability or friability **mountaineering**

cleit peak usually with a rounded base and a craggy summit **Gaelic**

cnap small but very rugged peak, often an outlying summit of a *beinn* or *càirn* **Gaelic**

cnoc hill, usually though not always smaller than a *sliabh* **Irish**

cnwc hillock, knoll **Welsh**

coire high, hanging, glacier-scooped hollow on a mountainside, often cliff-girt (anglicized to *corrie*) **Gaelic**

cragfast unable to advance or retreat on a steep climb; stuck, usually requiring rescue **mountaineering**

creachann grassless, stony hilltop **Gaelic**

creagan knoll **Gaelic**

croit humpbacked hill or group of hills **Gaelic**

cruach rugged peak with pinnacled tops, sometimes resembling a rick or stack ('*cruach*') in outline **Irish**

dod, dodd rounded summit, either a separate hill, or more frequently a lower summit or distinct shoulder of a higher hill **northern England, southern Scotland**

droim ridge or 'back' of hills **Irish**

drum small, rectangular hillock; a field sloping on all sides **Galloway**

dūn low hill with a fairly level and extensive summit, providing a good settlement site in open country **Old English**

gala, olva lookout point **Cornish**

gob beak or projecting point of mountain **Gaelic**

grianan knoll or hillock that is often sunny **Gaelic**

gualainn shoulder of a hill **Gaelic**

hōh projecting or heel-like ridge **Old English**

hope hill **Cotswolds**

kame comb or ridge of hills **Shetland**

knob round-topped hill **Kent**

landraising waste disposal site which is above the height of the surrounding land **official** *maol* bare and rugged peak, usually of middling height **Gaelic**

meall high and rounded summit, often heathery **Gaelic**

mena hill, high point **Cornish**

moel of a hilltop or mountain summit: treeless, rounded (literally 'bald') **Welsh**

mynydd mountain, hill **Welsh**

nab summit of a hill **Sussex**

pap mountain or hill whose shape is thought to resemble that of a woman's breast **Irish English, Scots**

pinch short, steep hill **Kent**

rajel scree **Cornish**

rake steep path or track up a fell- or crag-side, often leading to the summit **Cumbria**

ruighe grassy place on a hillside **Gaelic**

saidse sound of a falling body **Gaelic**

sgòr, sgùrr sharp and steep-sloped summit, often rising to a craggy top **Gaelic**

skord deep indentation in the top of a hill at right angles to its ridge **Shetland**

slaag low part of the skyline of a hill **Shetland**

sliabh single mountain; range of mountains **Irish**

soo's back sharp long ridge (literally 'sow's back') **Scots**

spidean sharp summit or top, often rising above a corrie **Gaelic**

sròn shoulder of land rising from a valley towards the higher reaches of a peak **Gaelic**

stob high, rugged peak, often with numerous corries **Gaelic**

strone hill that terminates a range; the end of a ridge **Scots**

stùc sharp subsidiary peak, often conical in form **Gaelic**

tap, top summit **Scots, especially Aberdeenshire**

tom hill or hillock, normally free of rocks and of relatively gentle elevation **Gaelic**

toot isolated hill suitable for observation, lookout hill **western England**

tòrr craggy-topped hillock **Gaelic**

tulach green place on a hillside **Gaelic**

Ice and Snow

aquabob icicle **Kent**

billow snowdrift **East Anglia**

bleb bubble of air in ice **north-east Ireland, northern England**

blee high, exposed **Northamptonshire**

blenk light snow, resembling the 'blinks' or ashes that fly out of a chimney **Exmoor**

blin' drift drifting snow **Scots**

blunt heavy fall of snow **East Anglia**

clinkerbell, cockerbell, conkerbell icicle **Dorset**

clock-ice ice cracked and crazed by fissures, usually brought about by the pressure of walkers or skaters **Northamptonshire**

dagger, daggler, dagglet icicle **Hampshire**

feetings footprints of creatures as they appear in the snow **Suffolk**

feevl snow falling in large flakes **Shetland**

fievel thin layer of snow **Shetland**

firn old, consolidated snow, often left over from the previous season **mountaineering**

flaucht snowflake **Scots**

fleeches large snowflakes **Exmoor**

flukra snow falling in large, scale-like flakes **Shetland**

frazil loose, needle-like ice crystals that form into a churning slush in turbulent super-cooled water, for example in a river on a very cold night **hydrological**

glocken   to start to thaw (compare the Icelandic *glöggur*, 'to make or become clear') **Yorkshire**

graupel   hail **meteorological**

hailropes   hail falling so thickly it appears to come in cords or lines (Gerard Manley Hopkins) **poetic**

heavengravel   hailstones (Gerard Manley Hopkins) **poetic**

ickle   icicle **Yorkshire**

iset   colour of ice: *isetgrey, isetblue* **Shetland**

moorie caavie   blinding snowstorm **Shetland**

névé   consolidated granular snow formed by repeated freeze-and-thaw cycles, hard and skittery underfoot **mountaineering**

penitent   spike or pinnacle of compact snow or ice left standing after differential melting of a snowfield **geographical**

pipkrakes   needle-like crystals of ice **geographical**

rone   patch or strip of ice **north-east Scotland**

sheebone   snowdrift, heavy fall of snow **Northern Ireland**

shockle   lump of ice; icicle **northern England, Scotland**

shuckle   icicle **Cumbria**

skalva   clinging snow falling in large damp flakes **Shetlands**

skith   thin layer of snow **Herefordshire**

smored   smothered in snow **Scots**

snaw grimet   colour of the ground when lying snow is partly melted **Shetland**

snipe   hanging icicle (so named for its resemblance to the bill of a snipe) **Northamptonshire**

snitter   to snow **Sheffield**

snow-bones   patches of snow seen stretching along ridges, in ruts or in furrows after a partial thaw **Yorkshire**

snow-devil, snow-djinn   mini-cyclone or whirling dervish made of spindrift (loose particles of snow) wind-whipped into a vortex, which roams the slopes of winter hills **mountaineering**

snyauvie   snowy **Scots**

stivven   become filled with blown or drifted snow **East Anglia**

tankle   icicle **Durham**

ungive   to thaw **Northamptonshire**

unheeve   to thaw or to show condensation **Exmoor**

up'lowsen, up'slaag   to thaw **Shetland**

verglas   thin blue water-ice that forms on rock **mountaineering**

windle   snowdrift **Fenland**

wolfsnow   dangerously heavy and wind-driven snow; a sea blizzard (Gerard Manley Hopkins) **poetic**

Slopes and Inclines

allt   slope, usually wooded **Welsh**

ard   rising ground; height **Irish**

banky-piece   field on a steep slope **Herefordshire**

brae   brow of a hill; high ground sloping down to a riverbank **Scots**

buaim, maidhm   steep or steepish slopes, though metaphorically used to suggest 'rush' or 'onset' **Gaelic**

carrach   rocky, boulder-strewn **Irish**

chossy   of a slope or cliff: loose, unreliable underfoot or under hand **mountaineering**

clegr   crag; rugged place **Welsh**

cliath   slope **Gaelic**

côti   hill field that slopes down to the sea **Jèrriais (Jersey Norman)**

downy   meadow on a hillside **Essex**

gnùig   pejorative for slope with a 'scowl' or 'surly expression' **Gaelic**

headwall   steep rock slope at the head of a valley; cliff at the back of a corrie **geographical**

hook   piece of land situated on a slope **Northamptonshire**

hylde   slope of a hill **Old English**

jig   steep slope **Staffordshire**

kaim, kame elongated mound of post-glacial gravel
geological

kleef field on the steep side of a hill
Northamptonshire

leathad slope **Gaelic**

leitir slope, gradient **Gaelic**

li sloping hillside, often adjacent to a sea inlet
Shetland

linch small precipice, usually grassy **Cotswolds**

lynchet slope or terrace along the face of a chalk down
southern England

pant small declivity on the side of a hill, generally
without water **Herefordshire**

pent slope, inclination **Kent**

rinn projecting part of a slope or hill **Gaelic**

scarp steep face of a hill **English**

scree mass of small stones and pebbles that forms on
a steep mountain slope **geological**

skruid steep, slippery place where the loose earth has
run down or been washed away by the action
of the weather **Shetland**

tarren knoll; rocky hillside **Welsh**

Valleys and Passes

bealach pass between two hills **Gaelic**

bearna ghaoithe wind gap in the mountains **Irish**

bellibucht hollow in a hill **Galloway**

bwlch pass **Welsh**

caigeann rough mountain pass **Gaelic**

ciste pass **Gaelic**

clinks, clints steep glens **Galloway**

combe, coombe valley: in the chalk-lands of southern England, a hollow or valley on the flank of a hill, or a steep short valley running up from the sea coast; in Cumbria or Scotland, a crescent-shaped scoop or valley in the side of a hill **English**

cumhang narrow ravine, defile **Gaelic**

cwm valley **Welsh**

dale valley **northern England**

glaab opening between hills or between isles through which a distant object may be seen **Shetland**

gleann, glen valley **Gaelic, Scots**

hass sheltered place on or near a hill **Galloway**

hope small enclosed valley, especially one branching out from a main valley, or a blind valley **north-east England, southern Scotland**

kynance   gorge **Cornish**

làirig   gap or pass between hills **Gaelic**

mám   mountain pass **Irish**

nick   gap in the hills through which weather comes **Yorkshire**

peithir   crooked valley or ravine (literally 'lightning bolt') **Gaelic**

pingo   circular depression, often water-filled, thought to be the remains of a collapsed mound formed under permafrost conditions during an earlier periglacial period **geological**

porth   pass **Cornish**

sgrìodan   stony ravine on a mountainside **Gaelic**

slack   small shallow dell or valley **northern England, Scotland**

slidder   trench or hollow running down a hill; a steep slope **northern England, Scotland**

swire   hollow near the summit of a mountain or hill; gentle depression between two hills **northern England, Scotland**

taca   very steep slope, close to precipice **Gaelic**

yett   low pass in hills (literally 'gate') **Shetland**

4

The Woods and the Water

Roger Deakin was a water-man. He lived for most of his life in a timber-framed Suffolk farmhouse with its own spring-fed moat, the arms of which extended around the house such that it was, in Roger's phrase, 'part-islanded'. The moat was connected to a cattle pond that jutted out into the largest grazing common in Suffolk, and that pond was one of twenty-four set around the common, each linked to each by an ancient labyrinth of tunnels and drains. We think of an archipelago as a scatter of land existing within water, but Roger lived on an inverse archipelago – a scatter of water existing within land. Mellis Common itself, when the wind blew in summer, appeared to him like 'a great inland sea of rippling grasses', so that 'although the sea itself is twenty-five miles due east at Walberswick', he could 'still enjoy some of the pleasures of living beside it'.

Roger was a film-maker, environmentalist and writer who is best known for his trilogy of books about nature and adventure: *Waterlog* (1999), *Wildwood* (2007) and *Notes from Walnut Tree Farm* (2008). His work can be located at the convergence point of three English traditions of rural writing: that of dissent tending to civil disobedience (William Cobbett, Colin Ward); that of labour on the land (Thomas Bewick, John Stewart Collis, Clare Leighton); and that of the gentle countryman or the country gentleman, of writer as scrupulous watcher and phenologist (Gilbert White, Richard Mabey,

Ronald Blythe). Roger travelled widely, but always returned to his farmhouse and the twelve acres of meadow and hedgerow that surrounded it. This was his fixed point, where one foot of his compass was planted, while the other roved and circled.

Walnut Tree Farm was first raised in the Elizabethan era, ruined when Roger found it in 1969, and then rebuilt by him according to an East Anglian method of timber-framing whereby the frame 'sit[s] lightly on the sea of shifting Suffolk clay like an upturned boat'. At the back of the house was an old claw-footed iron bathtub he had salvaged from a skip or auction yard (he foraged avidly; he cherished used objects that wore their histories as patina; he disliked waste). On hot summer days, Roger would snake out twenty metres of water-filled hosepipe onto the ground near the bath, leave the pipe to lounge for hours in the sun like a lazy python, then run that solar-heated water into the outdoor bath for an al fresco wallow. The bath was his tepidarium; a cooling plunge into the moat usually followed. Out of the bath, across the grass, between the two apple trees, round the big willow to where he had staked a ladder to the moat's bank, three steps into the water, and then softly down among the weed and the ducks and the ramshorn snails for a few lengths of breaststroke or crawl.

'It's extraordinary what you see in an English moat,' said Roger once. Water was to him a visionary substance. It was homoeopathic, it was cheering, it was beautiful in its flex and flow – and it was lensatic. Prepositions matter again here: we might say that Roger Deakin thought not just *about* water, he thought *in* water or *with* water. His imagination was watery not in the sense of dilute, but in the senses of ductile, mobile, lucid, reflective. Open water offered a glass into which one peered to see local miracle and revelation (and not – for Roger was no Narcissus – oneself). 'All water,' he wrote in a notebook, 'river, sea, pond, lake, holds memory and the space to think.'

It was while doing lengths in his moat during a rainstorm that the idea came to Roger for a swimmer's journey around Britain – no, not *around* Britain, *through* Britain, via its lakes and rivers – the account of which was subsequently published as *Waterlog*. For a year Roger swam in some of the iconic waters of the country (Dancing Ledge on the Dorset coast; the tidal rips off the Isle of Jura; the clear-running trout streams of Hampshire), as well as less predictable places (the estuary of the Fowey in Cornwall; the mud-channels that wriggle through the East Anglian salt marshes). That journey gave Roger, and in turn its hundreds of thousands of readers, a magically defamiliarizing 'frog's-eye view' of the country: a world seen freshly from water level. It is a witty, lyrical, wise travelogue that sketches a people's history of open-water swimming in Britain and offers a defence of the open water that remains, and an elegy for that which has gone (culverted, privatized, polluted).

Waterlog quickly became an exceptionally influential book. *Influence* is itself a watery word: the *Oxford English Dictionary* gives us as its first definition: '1. The action or fact of flowing in; inflowing, inflow, influx, said of the action of water and other fluids, and of immaterial things conceived of as flowing in.' The affective sense of influence, the notion of being influenced by another person or property, is also aquatic in its connotations: '3. The inflowing, immission, or infusion (*into* a person or thing) of any kind of . . . secret power or principle; that which thus flows in or is infused.'

I know of few other writers whose influence has been as strong as Roger's, in the sense of 'infusing' itself into people, of possessing a 'secret power' to 'flow' into and change them. You finish reading *Waterlog* invigorated, and with a profoundly altered relationship to water. It is a book which leaves you, as Heathcote Williams nicely punned, with 'a spring in your step'. Despite its deep Englishness, it has won admirers internationally, and been translated into languages as various as Italian, Korean and Japanese. In the two years after its first publication, Roger would typically receive three or four letters or telephone calls each day from readers seeking to make contact and tell him their own swimming stories, or share their swimming spots. The book prompted a revival of the lido culture in Britain, as well as of outdoor swimming more widely. It led to the founding of a wild-swimming company, and the emergence of 'wild swimming' as a cliché, appearing in the title of numerous books and the straplines of countless newspaper articles (a trend Roger held in suspicion during its early stages as the corporatization of a dissident and self-willed act).

Certainly, Roger influenced my behaviour. After reading *Waterlog*, and coming to be friends with Roger, I ceased to see open water as something chiefly to be driven around, flown over or stopped at the brink of. It became, rather, a realm to be entered and explored. Britain seemed newly permeable and excitingly deepened: every lake or loch or lough or llyn a bathing pool, each river a journey, each tide a free ride. Swimming came to involve not chlorine, turnstiles and verrucas, but passing through great geological portals (Durdle Door in Dorset), floating over drowned towns (Dunwich) or spelunking into long sea caves that drilled way back into sea cliffs, as I did off the Llyn Peninsula in north Wales, swimming alone down a tidal tunnel-cave and discovering at the back of that long chamber of mudstone a vast white boulder, a ton or more in weight, shaped roughly like a throne, the presence of which I cannot explain and whose existence I have not since returned to verify.

In May 2004 I was in Sutherland, in the far north-west of

Scotland, on a cold and rainy late-spring day. I was travelling alone at that time, pursuing my own journeys into the landscapes of Britain for other reasons, but under the influence of *Waterlog*. A few days earlier I had climbed the camel-humped mountain of Suilven, and from its summit had looked south-east to a sprawling loch called Sionascaig. Its water was speckled with micro-islands, and shone silver-blue in the sun. From an altitude of nearly 2,400 feet and a distance of several miles, it looked fabulously inviting and full of adventure.

In actuality, it was less accommodating. I parked near the loch and battled down through wet moor grass and tick-thick birch trees to the shore, and then swam out in bitingly cold water to the nearest island, a humpback of gneiss with a rock-garden of heathers. I explored the island briefly, found it to be uninteresting, and swam back to shore. The midges came up in clouds as I tried to change into warm clothes on the sharp-pebbled beach, so I gathered my trousers and jumper and retreated in my trunks, shivering and bitten, back to the road. I was approaching my car, where a flask of hot tea was waiting on the front seat, when another vehicle came into view over the hill. Its driver stopped beside me, wound down her window and turned off her radio.

'You've been swimming, haven't you?' she said.

Dripping wet, dressed only in my trunks, clutching my clothes, I could not deny it.

'A bit early in the year, isn't it?'

Goose-bumped, flinching in the wind, I could not deny that either.

'Midges are bad today, aren't they?'

At this point my patience for rhetorical questions expired, so I briefly explained that a friend of mine had written a book about wild swimming and as a result I couldn't keep out of the water, and so if she would excuse me? She gave a surprised smile, reached down and picked up the audiotape of *Waterlog*, to which she had been listening as she drove that lonely road on that grey day past that remote loch. It was a memorable meeting of influences – a point at which water came together with other water.

~

Roger and I first encountered one another in late 2002, and were friends until his death in the summer of 2006. In that short time a friendship grew up between us that was in part paternal–filial in its nature, but more significantly comprising shared passions (land-scape, literature, nature, exploration) with regard to which the thirty years between us in age seemed irrelevant. We visited each other often, corresponded by letter and email, travelled together in Ireland and the south-west of England, and Roger became unofficial god-parent to my daughter Lily, for whose first visit to Walnut Tree Farm he raked into being a circular maze made of yellow mulberry leaves. Roger once wrote that he wanted his friendships to grow 'like weeds . . . spontaneous and unstoppable', and for me at least it was a weedy friendship in that sense.

Roger once came to Cambridge, where I teach, to give an invited seminar to the assembled modern literature experts and graduate students of my faculty, in a high room at King's College on whose walls Virginia Woolf had once doodled murals and graffiti. Roger's chosen theme was water in literature – and the subject ran through his fingers. He sat at the polished table, ruffled his papers, hesitated, murmured, then moved too quickly from John Keats to Wallace Stevens to Woolf to Ted Hughes. I stared dedicatedly at my shoes, embarrassed that my friend was failing to perform in front of my academic peers.

It was only later that I realized it wasn't a failure to perform, but a refusal to conform. Cambridge seminars expect rigour and logic from their speakers: a braced subtlety of exposition and explanation, tested proofs of cause and consequence. But water doesn't do rigour in that sense, and neither did Roger, though his writing was often magnificently precise in its poetry (precision being, to my mind, preferable to rigour – the former being exhilaratingly exact and the latter grimly exacting). For Roger, water flowed fast and wildly through culture: it was protean, it was 'slip-shape' – to borrow Alice Oswald's portmanteau from her river poem, *Dart* – and so that was how he followed it, *slipshod* and *shipshape* at once, moving from a word here to an idea there, pursuing water's influences, too fast for his notes or audience to keep up with, joining his archipelago of watery subjects by means of an invisible network of tunnels and drains.

Waterlog also possesses this covertly connected quality, this slip-shapeness. It feels spontaneous, written as if spoken – but as the dozens of closely annotated drafts of the book reveal, it was in fact densely contrived in its pattern-makings and metaphors. In one chapter, Roger explored the Rhinogs, a small and wild mountain-group in north Wales:

Searching the map, I had seen some promising upland streams, a waterfall, and a tarn, so I hiked off uphill through the bracken. There is so much of it in the Rhinogs that the sheep all carry it around on their coats like camouflaged soldiers. I watched a ewe standing between two rocks the shape of goats' cheeses. They were just far enough apart to allow the animal in, and I began to understand the relationship Henry Moore perceived between sheep and stones. He saw sheep as animate stones, the makers of their own landscape. By grazing the moors and mountains they keep the contours – the light and shade – clear, sharp and well-defined, like balding picture-restorers constantly at work on every detail. The black oblongs of their pupils set deep in eyes the colour and texture of frog skin are like the enormous slate coffin-baths you see in the farmyards here; seven-foot slabs of slate hollowed into baths.

Sheep like soldiers, sheep like picture-restorers, sheep like stones, stones like cheeses, sheep's eyes like frog skin, sheep's pupils like slate baths – this joyful promiscuity of comparison, this sprawl of simile, is characteristic of Roger's prose. The finding of 'likeness' was a function of his generosity and his immense curiosity; it was also a literary expression of the idea that, as John Muir put it, 'when we try to pick out anything by itself, we find it hitched to the whole world'. Roger loved language for its capacity to connect and relate, and as he swam through Britain he collected some of the wondrous words that ran through its waterways:

dook (noun, Scots) – a swim in open water

gull (verb, East Anglian) – to sweep away by force of running water

tarn (noun, Cumbrian/northern English) – an upland pool or small lake

winterburna (noun, Old English) – an intermittent or ephemeral stream, dry in the summer and running in the winter

bumbel (verb, Shetlandic) – to flounder around in water

Waterlog, unlike much that gets labelled as nature writing, is very funny. There is plenty of bumbelling in it. Roger's gently subversive sense of humour recalls that of Kenneth Grahame, Jerome K. Jerome and A. A. Milne: all of them, in their ways, water-men and river-rats. In one chapter, Roger decides to swim up the estuary of the River Erne in Cornwall. He discovers that by catching the incoming tide in the estuary mouth, he will be carried rapidly upstream:

> I threw myself in and . . . felt the incoming tide lock onto my legs, and thrust me in towards the distant woods along the shore. Each time a frond of sea-lettuce lightly brushed me, or glued itself around my arms, I thought it was a jellyfish, and flinched. But I soon grew used to it; seaweed all around me, sliding down each new wave to drape itself about me. I kept on swimming until I practically dissolved, jostled from behind by the swell. Then, as the tide rose higher, the sandy estuary beach came into focus. The woods reached right over the water, and began accelerating past me. I found I was moving at exhilarating speed, in big striding strokes, like a fell-runner on the downhill lap. It was like dream swimming, going so effortlessly fast, and feeling locked in by the current, with no obvious means of escape. I was borne along faster and faster as the rising tide approached the funnel of the river's mouth until it shot me into a muddy, steep-sided mooring channel by some old stone limekilns on the beach. I had to strike out with all my strength to escape the flood and reach the eddy in the shallows. I swam back up to the limekilns and crawled out onto the beach like a turtle.

Much of the magic of *Waterlog* is apparent here: the adventure, the unostentatious bravery, the sense of life as a game with joy as its gain, a pleasure at moving with the world and being swept along by its rhythms rather than sweeping it along with ours – and the soft bathos of that final image. He crawls out onto the beach 'like a turtle', which is at once comic and true, for he has been transformed by the water, much as Wart – the hero of T. H. White's *The Sword in the Stone* – magicked by Merlyn, dives into a river and becomes a trout as soon as he breaks the surface. Roger felt himself at various times in the course of his swimming journeys to have become part otter, part fish, part turtle: a compound being, a merman, some of his humanity 'dissolved' away and replaced with the creaturely. Metempsychosis, metamorphosis: these were ideas to which Roger and I found ourselves returning in conversation – talking about Hughes and Hopkins and J. A. Baker, or the frontiers we perceived to exist within even familiar landscapes (hill-passes, watersheds, snow-lines; the move from chalk onto greenstone, or from boulder-clay onto breckland), and the transformations that might occur as you crossed them.

To enter water is, of course, to cross a border. You pass the lake's edge, the sea's shore, the river's brink – and in so doing you arrive at a different realm, in which you are differently minded because differently bodied. To Roger, treelines and forest fringes also offered such frontiers. 'To enter a wood is to pass into a different world in which we ourselves are transformed,' he wrote; 'it is where you travel to find yourself, often, paradoxically, by getting lost.'

For Roger was a woodsman as well as a wordsman and a water-man. 'The woods and the water as two poles in nature,' he scribbled in one of the dozens of Moleskine notebooks he filled and kept over the years: 'The one ancient, cryptic, full of wisdom. The other the vitality of water. The wood and the wet . . . would be good for us to understand more thoroughly.' Roger dedicated his writing life to improving our understanding of the woods and the water – the volatilities of the latter, and the patient engrainings of the former. After the demands that followed the success of *Waterlog* had ebbed, he began work on what was to become a life-absorbing and eventually unfinishable book about trees and wood. It was the natural next subject for him – an investigation of what Edward Thomas elected as the 'fifth element'.

Trees grew through Roger's life. His mother's maiden name was Wood, the third of his father's three Christian names was Green-wood, and his great-grandfather ran a timber yard in Walsall. Roger worked for Friends of the Earth on campaigns to protect rainforests, and he co-founded the charity Common Ground, which among its many good offices championed old orchards and the pomological diversity of British apple culture. The house in which he lived was named for the big walnut that flourished alongside it, and that in autumn thunked its green fruit down onto the orange pantiles of the farm, and rattled the wrinkly tin of the barn roof. Walnut Tree Farm was surrounded by water and by trees: in hedges and copses, and as splendid singletons – walnut, mulberry, ash, willow. Roger planted wood, coppiced it, worked it, and he burnt it by the cord in the inglenook fireplace at the heart of the farm, which was itself timber-framed, its vast skeleton made of 323 beams of oak and sweet chestnut, some of them more than four centuries old, held and jointed together with pegs of ash. In total, around 300 trees were felled to make the house, and the result was a structure that was organic to the point of animate. Truly, it was a tree-house, and in big winds it would creak and shift, riding the gusts so that being inside it felt like being in the belly of a whale, or in a forest in a gale. 'I am a woodlander,' Roger wrote, 'I have sap in my veins' – and as such he was a waterlander too, for 'a tree is itself a river of sap'.

Roger once sent me a list of the apple varieties in the orchards of Girton College in Cambridge. He read them out when we next met, dozens of them, each a story in miniature, making together a poem of pomes: King of the Pippins, Laxton's Exquisite, American Mother, Dr Harvey, Peasgood's Nonsuch, Scarlet Pimpernel, Northern Greening, Patricia and (my favourite) Norfolk Beefing. It was a celebration of diversity and language, and it represented, Roger said, only a fraction of the pomology recorded in the *Herefordshire Pomona*, the great chronicle of English apple varieties.

In the years he spent researching *Wildwood*, Roger travelled to Kyrgyzstan, Kazakhstan, the Pyrenees, Greece, Ukraine, Australia, North America and all over Britain and Ireland. He gathered a vast library of tree books, the pages of which he leaved with jotted-on Post-it notes. As it took root, the project also branched, digressing into studies of the hula-hoop craze, Roger's anarchist great-uncle, the architecture of pine cones, the history of cricket bats and Jaguar dashboards, hippy communes, road protestors, the uses of driftwood . . . but returning always to individual trees and tree species.

This specifying impulse distinguished Roger's approach. In September 1990 he gave a World Wildlife Fund lecture on education, literature and children at the Royal Festival Hall, in which he spoke passionately about the virtues of precision. 'The central value of English in education has always been in its poetic approach,' he said, 'through the particular, the personal, the microscopic observation of all that surrounds us.' It was attention to such particularity, he argued, that best permitted a Keatsian 'taking part in the existence of things', and 'the development of this ability to take part in the existence of things' was in turn 'the common ground of English teaching and environmental education'. Roger ended the lecture with an attack on generalism as an enemy of wonder because it suppressed uniqueness. He quoted a passage from his beloved D. H. Lawrence in support of his argument:

> The dandelion in full flower, a little sun bristling with sun-rays on the green earth, is a non-pareil, a nonsuch. Foolish, foolish, foolish to compare it to anything else on earth. It is itself incomparable and unique.

Foolish, foolish, foolish Lawrence, though, for even as he celebrates the 'non-pareil' and berates the comparative impulse, he cannot prevent himself figuring the dandelion as a 'little sun', so that it is itself and not-itself at once. But Lawrence, like Roger, would have defended the metaphor as an intensifier rather than a comparator – a means of evoking the dandelion-ness of that dandelion, instead of diffusing its singularity. Some of Roger's most precise observations of natural events used figurative language to sharpen, rather than to blunt, their accuracy. When he writes that '[r]edstarts flew from tree to tree, taking the line a slack rope would take slung between them; economy in flight is what makes it graceful', it is the aptness of the 'slack rope' that makes the observation itself graceful. Like Baker, he was unafraid of elaborate comparisons: the 'park-bench green' of a pheasant's neck; a hornet 'tubby, like a weekend footballer in a striped vest'.

~

In the spring of 2006 I drove over to Walnut Tree Farm with my friend Leo and my son Tom, then only a few months old. Leo and I swam in the moat, and we noticed that Roger did not join us. The water still had the chill of winter to it, and though the weed growth was low it twined around my neck and shoulders as I swam. Two lengths were as much as we could manage, and we came out buzzed. We hung our towels on the rails of the Aga, and Roger pressed our swimming trunks into waffle grills and dried them out over the hot plates, before returning them to us crispy, with the bow and mock flourish of a waiter serving valued customers. He cooked us a real meal of peppers and garlic. Roger wasn't hungry himself, so he held Tom while Leo and I ate, sitting at the scarred and dinted wooden table in the kitchen. We talked, I remember, about Andy Goldsworthy and his sculptural work with drystone walls, that looped across hillsides and fields with such cursive elegance that they appeared a natural landform – as spontaneous in their rhythms as rivers. We talked, too, about Annie Dillard, and the years she had spent watching and walking the landscape of the Blue Mountains in Virginia, filling thousands of notebook pages, from which she had then distilled *Pilgrim at Tinker Creek* (1974), a book that both Roger and I held in awed esteem. Roger fetched his copy of *Pilgrim*, and read out Dillard's vision of a cedar tree struck by sunlight so strong that each cell seemed to hum with the charge of its illumination. And from there, of course we talked about *Wildwood*, and how vigorously it had branched out as a subject, an organism.

After lunch, as usual, we tramped the fields. Roger pointed out where he had recently seen a tawny owl, a barn owl, a muntjac deer. The blackthorn was just starting to flower: the first flakes of the avalanche. We wandered to the little triangle of trees in the far corner of the outermost meadow, bordered on one side by the railway line, where Roger had planted a sapling wood of hornbeam and beech, the trees of which were now twenty-five feet tall, and understoried by blackthorn. 'Look at them now!', Roger said. 'High enough for you to climb!'

Throughout the visit Roger seemed more distracted than usual, though, and more distant. The jokes did not flow from him as they usually did, the great smile came more rarely, and he was oddly less ready to connect subject to subject, word to word. Privately, I worried that I had somehow upset him. I talked it over with Leo on the drive home, trying to work out where I'd mis-stepped, what I might have mishandled. I wrote to Roger that night, apologizing for phantom faults.

A few weeks later, Roger was diagnosed with an aggressive and incurable brain tumour. Its progress was bitterly swift. In early June, he called to ask if I would act as his literary executor. I said I would. It was a difficult conversation. His illness was seriously advanced. He was having trouble forming speech. I was having trouble not crying. He died soon afterwards. The coffin he lay in had a wreath of oak leaves on its lid. Just before it glided through the velvet curtains and into the cremating flames, Loudon Wainwright's 'The Swimming Song' was played, full of hope and loss. It brought me to shuddering tears that day, and whenever it pops up now and then out of the thousand songs on my phone, it still stops me short like a punch to the chest.

~

Roger rarely threw anything away. He was an admirer of old age, and he lived in the same place for nearly forty years – so whenever he ran out of space to store things, he just built another shed, raised another barn, or hauled an old railway wagon or shepherd's hut into a patch of field and began to fill that up with stuff too. In the strange months after his funeral, it became clear that the main question facing me as his executor was what to do with all the language he had left behind: the hundreds of notebooks, letters, manuscripts, folders, box-files, cassettes, videotapes and journals in which he had so memorably recorded his life.

Six months after Roger's death, Walnut Tree Farm passed into the ownership of two remarkable people, Titus and Jasmin Rowlandson, friends of Roger and now friends of mine. They moved into the farm with their two young daughters and began – slowly, respectfully – to make it their home. As they moved from room to room and barn to barn, so they found more of Roger's papers, stashed in trunks and boxes, pushed under beds or shoved into sheds where the mice had made nests of his notes. They kept everything, storing it all in the attic room of a steep-eaved barn that Roger had raised in the early 1970s.

Four years after Roger's death, I could no longer put off confronting his archive. I drove across to the farm on a warm early-summer day. Jasmin led me up one ladder to the first floor of the barn, then pointed up another that led through a flip-back trapdoor and into the narrow attic.

'Up you go! Good luck. It's going to take you a while . . .'

Dusty light fell from a gable window. The air was hot and musty. There was a single bed under the window, a clear aisle down the centre of the room leading to it, and otherwise the attic room was full, floor to slanted ceiling, of boxes and crates. Eighty? A hundred? I felt overwhelmed. How could this volume of documents ever be brought under control? I sat down on a box, took a notebook from the top of a crate and leafed through it. 'Angels are the people we care for and who care for us,' read the sentence at the top of one page, in Roger's spidery black handwriting. There followed a jotted thought-stream on angels, which moved out to the double

hammer-beam roof of the church in the fenland village of March –
where the wings of the 200 wooden angels in the roof are feathered
like those of marsh harriers – and then back again to further reflection on the nature of friendship.

With Titus and Jasmin's generous help, I began the process of
working out what Roger had left behind. Digging through boxes;
brushing away mouse droppings and spiders' webs; scanning letters
from friends and collaborators; putting letters from lovers and family to one side unread. Each box I opened held treasure or puzzles:
early poems; first drafts of *Waterlog*; a copy of the screenplay for *My
Beautiful Laundrette* sent to Roger by Hanif Kureishi; word-lists of
place-language (*tufa*, *bole*, *burr*, *ghyll*); a folder entitled 'Drowning
(Coroners)', which turned out not to be a record of coroners that
Roger had drowned, but an account of his research into East Anglian
deaths-by-water. It was hard not to get distracted, especially by his
notebooks. Each was a small landscape through which it was possible
to wander, and within which it was possible to get lost. One had a
paragraph in which Roger imagined a possible structure for *Wildwood*: he compared it to a cabinet of wonders, a chest in which each
drawer was made of a different timber and contained different
remarkable objects and stories. The notebooks, taken together, represented an accidental epic poem of Roger's life, or perhaps a
dendrological cross-section of his mind. In their range and random-
ness, they reminded me that he was, as Les Murray once wrote, 'only
interested in everything'.

~

The last three boxes of Roger's archive were found in 2013, in the
dusty corner of a dusty shed. Jasmin called to let me know that more

material had turned up; would I like to come and collect it? I drove over, had lunch, walked the fields with Titus and Jasmin and took the boxes home. That evening, kneeling on the floor of my study, I began to sort through the contents. There were files and notebooks from Roger's schooldays, A4 notepads with scribbles and jottings, a new clutch of letters and pamphlets from the early years of Common Ground, and then, with a jolt of shock, I found a blue foolscap folder with a white label on the front, on which Roger had written 'ROBERT MACFARLANE'.

I paused. I thought about throwing it away unopened. What if it held hurt for me? I opened it. It contained five letters. The letters weren't about me – they were *from* me, to Roger, all written in 2002–3, when I was first coming to know him. Two were handwritten, two were typed, and one was the printout of an email. I had no memory of any of them, and for that reason I encountered my own voice almost as a stranger's:

Tuesday 11 February 2003

It was great to get your letter, Roger, and to be transported out of my bunker-office in Cambridge, to the walnut woods of Kyrgyzstan. The word that really leaped out at me, oddly, from your description, was 'holloway' for the sunken lanes you saw. My wonderful editor is called Sara Holloway, and reading your letter, her name – which I have said often but never thought of as possessing an origin in the landscape – suddenly became rich with association and image. I could infer a meaning for it from your description, but wanted to know more, so went to my Shorter Oxford Dictionary. *It wasn't there, so I hauled out the complete OED, and discovered, buried in the small print of the 'variants' of meaning No. 7, the following: 'hollow-way, a way,*

*road or path, through a defile or cutting, also extended, as quot. in
1882)'. That was all, but it was enough. I wonder where you picked
the term up from? What a word it is! It made me think of the description
of a holloway – though he does not call it such – in Gilbert White's*
Natural History of Selborne. *A friend and I are fascinated by ways,
paths, ancient roads, ley-lines, dumbles, cuttings and – I now know –
by holloways. So: thank you for the gift of the word.*

Roger's gift of that word would set further ripples of influence
ringing outwards. Two years later he and I would travel together to
the 'holloways' of south Dorset, in search of the hideout of the hero
of Geoffrey Household's cult 1939 novel, *Rogue Male*, who goes to
ground in a sandstone-sided sunken lane in the Chideock Valley.
Seven years after that I would return to Chideock with the artist Stanley Donwood and the writer Dan Richards, with whom I subsequently
co-wrote a small book called *Holloway* – though by then I had fully
forgotten the work's true origin in that letter from Roger to me about
the walnut woods of Kyrgyzstan and their deep-trodden lanes.

The other gift I received from Roger's trip to Central Asia was
an apple pip. He had travelled to the Talgar Valley in the mountains
of Kazakhstan in search of the ur-apple – the wild apple, *Malus
sieversus*, that was thought to have evolved into the domestic apple,
Malus domesticus, and in that form found its way to Britain thanks to
the Romans. On the northern slopes of the Tien Shan massif, Roger
had filled three film canisters with wild-apple pips and damp cotton
wool, and carried them home to Suffolk. He planted the pips in pots
on his kitchen windowsill and there they had grown to seedlings. But
then Roger died and the seedlings almost died with him, as the
creepers on the outside of the farm grew untended over the kitchen
window and shut out the sun. Potbound and light-hungry, each

seedling developed an obvious kink in its trunk from the months around Roger's death, where they had leaned desperately sunwards.

Then Titus and Jasmin rescued them, re-potted them and gave them light. The seedlings flourished into saplings. When spring came, Titus planted out ten of the ur-apples in a field just behind the barn where Roger's archive was kept, making an apple avenue. And Jasmin gave one of the saplings to me. I planted it in the chalky clay of my suburban garden, and to my surprise it flourished there.

It takes about twelve years for an apple tree to grow from pip to first fruiting. I write this in the spring of 2014, eleven years after Roger returned from Central Asia. My ur-apple flowers with white blossom, its leaves are a keen green, and it still has the sharp crook near the base of its trunk that remembers Roger's death. Next year, all being well, it will fruit for the first time.

~

A life lived as variously as Roger's, and evoked in writing as powerful as his, means that even after death his influence continues to flow outwards. Green Man-like, he appears in unexpected places, speaking in leaves. There is, of course, a tendency to hero-worship those who lived well and died too young, as Roger did. Laundry lists and emails become holy writ; hallowed places become sites of pilgrimage; admiration is expressed through ritual re-performance; and idealism threatens to occlude the actual. I know that Roger was no pure Poseidon or Herne: that he flew often and without apparent pangs to his conscience, that he could at times talk too much and at times too little, and that he was unrepeatably rude to any Jehovah's Witnesses who made the long trudge down the track from Mellis

Common to the front door of Walnut Tree Farm. But his writing did show people how to live both eccentrically and responsibly, and by both dwelling well and travelling wisely, he resolved in some measure the tension between what Edward Thomas called the desire to 'go on and on over the earth' and the desire 'to settle for ever in one place'. Above all he embodied a spirit of childishness, in the best sense of the word: innocent of eye and at ease with wonder.

Though Roger is gone, many of his readers still feel a need to express their admiration for him, and the connection they felt with his work and world view, and so they still write letters, as if he might somehow read them. As I am Roger's literary executor, and as our writings have become intertwined, many of these letters find their way to me. They come from all over the world, and from various kinds of people: a professional surfer from Australia, a Canadian academic, a woman from Exeter confined to her house due to mobility problems, a young man re-swimming the route of *Waterlog*, lake by lake and river by river, in an attempt to recover from depression. Titus and Jasmin have to cope with the scores of Deakinites who come on pilgrimage to Mellis each year, wanting to see the farm and its fields. Most are polite. Some expect it all to have been kept as a shrine or museum, and are offended by the changes they perceive. Some, inspired by Roger's insouciant attitude towards trespass, wander the fields uninvited, or take unannounced dips in the moat.

But all of the pilgrims, and all the letter writers, are under Roger's influence, and as I know that feeling well I do not begrudge them it. Among the letters I have received, one of the most heartfelt came from a Dutch-English reader, and this is how it began:

I am Hansje, born and bred in the north Netherlands where I bathed from age one in lakes, rivers and cold-water outdoor pools. Here in

Landmarks

Warwickshire, where I have lived for some thirty-three years, I am among other things a swimmer, and if you ever wish to swim in the beautiful Avon, then do tell me and I will show you to the best and secret places. I have never experienced the profound sense of loss of someone I have never met as when I learnt that Roger had died. Many sentences in each of his books are as if engraved in me, find a resting place, a recognition, they are magnifying glass, lens and microscope to the natural world, a watery surface through which I look to see the earth clarified.

GLOSSARY III

Waterlands

Moving Water

aber   mouth of a river (into the sea), estuary; confluence of a lesser with a larger river **Welsh**

abhainn   substantial river, often running to the sea, with numerous tributaries **Gaelic**

ǣwell   source of a stream **Old English**

aghlish   crook or sharp curve of a river (literally 'armpit') **Manx**

aker   turbulent current **East Anglia**

allt   strong stream or burn, usually running into an *abhainn* **Gaelic**

bala   outflow of a river from a lake **Welsh**

bathshruth   calm stream, smoothly flowing stream **Irish**

bay   slow water above a weir **Cumbria**

beck   stream **northern England**

berw   of water: boiling, foaming **Welsh**

beuc-shruth   roaring stream; cataract **Gaelic**

beum-slèibhe   sudden torrent caused by the bursting of a thundercloud **Gaelic**

blaen   of a river: source, headwater **Welsh**

borbhan   purling or murmur of a stream **Gaelic**

brook   small stream **English**

burn, burnie   small stream **northern England, Scots**

burraghlas torrent of brutal rage **Gaelic**

caa'l mill dam; place in a stream where salmon jump **North Sea coast**

calbh gushing of water or blood **Gaelic**

caol stream flowing through a marsh **Irish**

cartage violent stream of water that runs through a town and carries away the off-scourings **Manx**

catchment area from which precipitation and groundwater will collect and contribute to the flow of a specific river **ecological**

cenllif torrent, swift-flowing stream **Welsh**

comb feature of a stream where water pours over a rock such that it stands upwards in glossy ridges, separated by grooves (Gerard Manley Hopkins) **poetic**

cora weir or ford that might be used as a crossing place; also a rocky ridge extending into a sea or lake **Irish**

còs-shruth stream running partly underground or forming hollows in its course **Gaelic**

crìon-allt small stream often dried up by the sun's heat in summer **Gaelic**

currel small stream **East Anglia**

cymer confluence of two or more rivers or streams **Welsh**

drindle diminutive run of water, smaller than a *currel* **East Anglia** *eagmin mall* slow meander or winding of a river **Gaelic**

easaraich boiling of a pool where a cascade falls **Gaelic**

faoi noisy stream **Gaelic**

ffrwd swift-flowing stream, gushing rill **Welsh**

force powerful waterfall **northern England**

gairneag noisy little stream **Gaelic**

ghyll, gill deep rocky cleft or ravine, usually wooded and forming the course of a stream **northern England**

glaise rivulet, stream **Irish**

gore muddy obstruction in a watercourse **Essex**

grain point where a stream branches **Yorkshire**

gull to sweep away by force of running water **East Anglia**

gulsh to tear up with violence, as a stream when swollen with floods **Northamptonshire**

iomashruth eddying current **Gaelic**

keld deep, still, smooth part of a river **northern England**

lade watercourse to or from a mill **Galloway**

land-shut flood **Herefordshire**

lane slow stream **Galloway**

latch occasional watercourse **Cumbria**

lum	slack water at the bend of, or a pool in, a stream **Cumbria**
marbh-shruth	that part of a river or stream the current of which is scarcely perceptible **Gaelic**
mill-race, mill-tail	stream of water as it runs out from under the waterwheel **English**
nailbourne	intermittent stream **Kent**
nant	stream; stream-cut gorge, usually rocky **Welsh**
òs	inlet or outlet of a loch **Gaelic**
pill	creek capable of holding small barges **Herefordshire**
pistyll, rhaeadr	waterfall, water-spout **Welsh**
potamic	of or relating to rivers; riverine **ecological**
pow	naturally sluggish, slow-moving stream, generally with a muddy bottom **Cumbria**
reach	level, uninterrupted stretch of water on a river **English**
riag-allt	fast-flowing, noisy stream **Gaelic**
rin	stream **Shetland**
ruadh-bhuinne	torrent embrowned by peat **Gaelic**
seabhainn	very small river **Gaelic**
sgoinn	small pool in the rocky bed of a stream in which salmon get imprisoned and caught when the tide is low **Gaelic**
sgòr-shruth	rocky stream **Gaelic**

sill of a weir: the glassy curve where the water tips over the level **English**

speat sudden flood (spate) in a river following rain, snow or thaw **Cumbria**

spout waterfall, smaller than a *force* **northern England**

stripe small stream, *burn* **Shetland**

taghairm noise; echo; type of divination by listening to the noise of waterfalls **Gaelic**

threeple, tripple gentle sound made by a quick-flowing stream (incessant chattering, monotony and repetition being implied) **Cumbria**

tolg to sputter, vomit, as a mountain torrent **Gaelic**

turn-whol deep, seething pool where two streams meet **Cumbria**

twire movement of slow and shallow river water **Exmoor**

ùidh stream with a slow but strong current running between two freshwater lochs **Gaelic**

vaedik channel, small stream **Shetland**

whelm half a hollow tree, placed with its hollow side downwards, to form a small watercourse **East Anglia**

winterbourne intermittent or ephemeral stream, dry in the summer and running in winter, usually found in chalk and limestone regions **Berkshire, Dorset, Wiltshire**

wirli place where a dyke crosses a burn **Shetland**

ystum of a river: a bend, curve, meander **Welsh**

Pools, Ponds and Lakes

blatter puddle **Yorkshire**

botunn deep pool **Gaelic**

cesspools water that gathers on the 'cess', or land between a river and its bank, when the river is low **Fenland**

flosh stagnant pool overgrown with reeds **Lancashire**

fuarán spring, pool or fountain **Irish**

glumag deep pool in a river **Gaelic**

grimmer large, shallow, weed-infested pond **East Anglia**

hassock large pond **Kent**

lacustrine of or pertaining to a lake or lakes; lake-like **geographical**

leech pond or pool of water lying in the hollow of a road **Lancashire**

lidden pond **west Cornwall**

linne pool in a river, deeper than a _glumag_ **Gaelic**

llyn lake **Welsh**

loch lake **Gaelic**

lochan small lake **Gaelic**

lodan little pool; water in one's shoe **Gaelic**

loom slow and silent movement of water in a deep pool **Cumbria**

lough lake **Irish**

mardle small pond convenient for watering cattle; also to gossip, to waste time gossiping **Suffolk**

mere marsh; pool (used of Grendel's abode in *Beowulf*) **Old English**

pell hole of water, generally very deep, beneath an abrupt waterfall **Sussex**

plash small pool **Cotswolds**

pudge little puddle **Northamptonshire**

puil pool or small marsh **Scots**

pulk small dirty pool **Essex**

stank pool caused by a dam or a stream; also the dam itself **Cotswolds**

staran causeway of stones built out into a loch in order to fetch water **Gaelic**

swidge puddle **Suffolk**

tarn mountain pool or small upland lake **northern England**

wake piece of open water in the midst of a frozen river or broad **East Anglia**

Rain and Storm

after-drop raindrop which falls after a cloud has passed (first cited in Sir Philip Sidney's *Arcadia*, c. 1580) **poetic**

bachram very heavy rain (literally 'boisterous behaviour') **Irish**

bange light rain **East Anglia**

bashy of a day: wet **Northamptonshire**

basking drenching in a heavy shower **East Anglia**

blashy of a day: wet **north-east England**

blatter to rain heavily, noisily; also to beat, thrash **Galloway**

bleach of rain and snow: to lash, blow in your face **North Sea coast**

bleeterie showery **Scots**

blirt short dash of rain coming with a gust of wind **Scots**

boinneartaich isolated drops of rain **Gaelic**

brais sudden heavy shower of rain **Irish**

braon heavy shower at the beginning of summer, favourable to the growth of plants and crops **Gaelic**

brenner sudden sharp gust of wind and rain on the water **Suffolk**

brishum, briskeno rain **Anglo-Romani**

chucking, henting, raining hard **English, Scots, with countless**
hooning, hossing, **regional variants**
hoying, kelching,
lashing, pissing,
wazzing it down

cith, cith-uisge shower of warm, drizzling rain **Gaelic**

ciùran drizzling rain **Gaelic**

clagarnach clatter; noise of heavy rain on an iron roof **Irish**

dabbledy of a day: showery **Herefordshire**

dag to spit with rain **North Sea coast**

dibble to rain slowly in drops **Shropshire**

dimpsey low cloud with fine drizzle **Cornwall, Devon**

dinge drizzle or rain mistily **East Anglia**

down-come, fall of rain **Yorkshire**
down-faw

dravely of a day: showery **Suffolk**

dreich dull, overcast, misty, cold **Scots**

dribs rain which falls in drops from the eaves of
thatched houses **Leicestershire, Northamptonshire**

dringey light rain that still manages to get you soaking
wet **Lincolnshire**

drizzle fine precipitation with droplets less than 0.5mm
in diameter **meteorological**

drochy   warm, moist, misty **Galloway**

drookit   soaked, drowned **Doric**

dropple   to rain in large drops **Northamptonshire**

flist   sudden squall with heavy rain **Scots**

frisk   gentle rain **Exmoor**

gagey   showery weather, unsettled and changeable **south-east England**

garbh-fhras   boisterous shower **Gaelic**

gleamy   showers and fitful sunshine **Essex**

glìbheid   mixture of rain, sleet and hail **Gaelic**

glut   long stretch of wet weather **Northamptonshire**

gulching   downpour of rain **Essex**

haitch   slight passing shower **Sussex**

heavy rain   rainfall with a precipitation rate of between 4 and 16mm per hour **meteorological**

humidity   very gentle rain **Northern Ireland**

hurly-burly   thunder and lightning **England**

juggin   raining steadily, not as bad as *kelching* **Lincolnshire**

land-lash   high winds and heavy rain **English**

lattin, letty   enough rain to make outdoor work difficult (as in 'let and hindrance') **Shropshire and Somerset respectively**

leasty   of weather: dull, wet **Suffolk**

light rain   rainfall with a precipitation rate of between 0.25 and 1mm per hour **meteorological**

lummin   raining heavily **Galloway**

mì-chàilear   even more *dreich* than *dreich* **Gaelic**

misla, misla-in   rain, raining **Shelta (Irish traveller dialect)**

mizzling   raining lightly and finely **north-west England**

moderate rain   rainfall with a precipitation rate of between 1 and 4mm per hour **meteorological**

owdrey   overcast, cloudy **Exmoor**

pash   heavy fall of rain or snow **northern England**

payling   wind-driven shower **Northamptonshire**

perry   wet squall **Lincolnshire**

planets   extremely localized rain, falling on one field but not another, is said to fall in *planets* **Northamptonshire**

plothering   raining heavily **Leicestershire**

plype   heavy sudden shower **Scots**

posh   strong shower **Shropshire**

rain   precipitation with droplets of 0.5mm or more **meteorological**

scoor shower of rain **Scotland**

scud light, quickly passing shower **Herefordshire**

serein fine rain falling from an apparently cloudless sky **meteorological**

shatter scattering or sprinkling of rain **Kent**

shuggi drizzly **Shetland**

skat brief shower **Northamptonshire**

skew driving but short-lived rain **Cornwall**

skiff light shower **Northern Ireland**

slappy rainy **West Yorkshire**

slottery of weather: foul, rainy **Exmoor**

smirr extremely fine, misty rain, close to smoke in appearance when seen from a distance **Scots**

smither light rain **East Anglia**

soft of weather: overcast, lightly misty or drizzly **Hiberno-English**

teem to rain **Northumberland**

thunder-lump rain-cloud hanging over a place **Shetland**

thunner-pash heavy shower, with thunder **Durham**

upcasting uprising of clouds above the horizon, threatening rain **North Sea coast**

very heavy rain rainfall with a precipitation rate of between 16 and 50mm per hour **meteorological**

very light rain rainfall with a precipitation rate of less than 0.25mm per hour **meteorological**

virga observable streak or shaft of precipitation that falls from a cloud but evaporates before reaching the ground **meteorological**

water-dogs, messengers small floating clouds separated from larger masses, which signal rain **Norfolk, Northamptonshire**

watery-headed anxious about rain **Essex**

weet to rain slightly **Cheshire**

wetchered wet through after being caught out in the rain **Lincolnshire**

williwaw sudden violent squall **nautical**

Riverbed, Riverbank

aa ford, shallow place in a river **Manx**

æ-stán stone taken from a river **Old English**

alluvial fan fan-shaped deposit of sediment left by a fast-flowing river or stream that has lost velocity due to a change in gradient or profile **geographical**

áth ford **Irish**

beul-àtha ford, shallow part of a river **Gaelic**

bior-shruth old bed of a river's former course **Gaelic** *bodha*   bank jutting out below the water level, good for fishing from **Gaelic**

brink-ware   small bundles of wood, generally whitethorn, used to repair the banks of a river **East Anglia**

bun   of a river: bottom or bed **Irish**

carse   level land by river **Galloway**

ceulan   riverbank, river brink, especially one that has been hollowed by the current **Welsh**

draw-ground   stretch of riverbank on which a draw-net was pulled and the fish removed **Suffolk**

dubhagan   deep part of a pool; also the pupil of the eye **Gaelic**

faodhail   narrow channel fordable at low water **Gaelic**

fleiter   prop or pile used to support the bank of a brook or bridge damaged by flood **Northamptonshire**

foolen   space between the usual high-water mark in a river and the foot of the wall thrown up on its banks to prevent occasional overflowing **Suffolk**

gaffle   of ducks: to feed together in the mud **Northamptonshire**

laid   of a river or stream: frozen to the bottom **East Anglia**

plumb   deep hole in the bed of a river **Scots**

redd, rud   hollow or nest made in the gravel of the riverbed by fish prior to spawning **English** *soss* navigable sluice or lock **Fenland**

srath level ground beside a river **Gaelic**

stickle river rapid **south-west England**

thalweg deepest part of the bed or channel of a river or lake **geographical**

trabhach rubbish of any kind cast ashore by the flood on the bank of a river, or on the seashore **Gaelic**

watering road or path liable to flooding **Essex**

wath ford in a river, place through which one can wade **Cumbria**

Springs and Wells

eylebourne intermittent spring that overflows, usually at the end of the winter rains **Kent**

fenten well **Cornish**

gofer overflow of a well **Welsh**

peath sunken well **Cornish**

pulk-hole small open ditch or well **Suffolk**

rock-spring perennial spring, the channels of which are in the fissures of rocks **Northamptonshire**

shute well **Cornwall**

stone-water petrifying spring (found in limestone landscapes) **Northamptonshire**

<dl>

upboil water springing in the bottom of a well or drain, and powerful enough to cause the appearance of boiling on the surface **Cumbria**

willis rill from a spring **Exmoor**

wilm of water: a fount or stream that surges **Old English**

</dl>

Swimming and Splashing

bumbel to flounder around in water **Shetland**

dook to swim in open water **Scots**

endolphins swimmers' slang for the natural opiates ('endorphins') released by the body on contact with cold water (Roger Deakin) **poetic**

glumadh big mouthful of liquid **Gaelic**

jabblin, jappin, jiddlin, jirblin, jirglin playing around with water as children do **Galloway**

plab soft noise, as of a body falling into the water **Gaelic**

plumadaich making a noise in the water **Gaelic**

puddle to play messily with or in water **Galloway**

skiddle to throw flat stones so that they skim on the surface of water **Galloway**

skite to splash, usually with muddy water **Northern Ireland**

squashle to squelch, make a splashing noise **Kent**

wæter-egesa water-terror **Old English**

Water's Surface

acker ripple on the surface of the water **North Sea coast**

beggar's-balm froth collected by running streams in ditches, or in puddles by the roadside **Northamptonshire**

caitein first slight ruffling of the water after a calm **Gaelic**

cockle ripple on the water caused by the wind **Exmoor**

cuairt-shruth stream abounding in whirlpools or eddies **Gaelic**

cuilbhean cup-shaped whirl in a stream or eddy **Gaelic**

eynd water-smoke **East Anglia**

giel ripple on the surface of the water **Shetland**

jabble agitated movement of water; a splashing or dashing in small waves or ripples; where currents meet, the surface of the water may be *jabbly* **Scots**

lhingey-cassee whirlpool **Manx**

luddan-mea oily slick on water **Manx**

raith weeds, sticks, straw and other rubbish in a pool or in running water **Herefordshire**

sgùm patch of white foam on an eddying river **Gaelic**

shirr ruffle or ripple on water; also a gather in the texture of a fabric **Cumbria**

skim-ice wafer-thin ice that forms especially on the surface of puddles and pools **meteorological**

smother foam on the edge of a river when it is in flood **Cumbria**

swelk whirlpool, especially the eddies and swirls of the Pentland Firth **Scots**

twindle of stream-foam: to divide into two rows or braids (Gerard Manley Hopkins) **poetic**

Wetlands

allan piece of land nearly surrounded by water **Cumbria**

amod green plain almost encircled by the bend of a river **Gaelic**

crannóg prehistoric lake dwelling **Irish**

dòirling islet to which one can wade at low water **Gaelic**

eyot small island, especially in a river **English**

feorainn grassy area of riverside or shore **Irish**

haft island in a pool **Midlands**

halh nook; spur of land between two rivers (place-name element) **Old English**

holm river island; land formerly covered with water **Fenland**

peninsula piece of land that is almost, but not wholly, surrounded by water **geographical**

wæter-fæsten place protected by water **Old English**

warth flat meadow close to a stream **Gloucestershire, Herefordshire**

ynys island; raised area in wet ground **Welsh**

5
Hunting Life

What did I see that morning? Hot winter sun on the face's brink, felt as red but seen as gold. Air, still, blue. Tremors at the edge of vision: quick dark curve and slow straight line over green, old in the eye. Intersection, shrapnel of down, grey drop to crop, flail and clatter, four chops and the black star away with quick wing flicks.

Let me tell that again, clearer now, if clearer is right. What did I see that morning? A green field dropping citywards. The narrow track at the bronze wood's border. The sun low but strong in the cold. Then odd forms glimpsed in the eye's selvedge. The straight line (grey) the flight-path of a wood pigeon passing over the field. The fast curve (dark) the kill-path of a peregrine cutting south from the height of the beech tops. The pigeon is half struck but not clutched, chest-feathers blossom, it falls to the low cover of the crop and flails for safety to a hedge. The falcon rises to strike down again, misses, rises, misses again, two more rises and two more misses, the pigeon makes the hedge and as I rush the wood-edge to close the gap the falcon, tired, lifts and turns and flies off east and fast over the summits of the hilltop trees, with quick sculling wing flicks.

And let me tell it one last time, clearer still perhaps. What did I see that morning? It was windless and late autumn. The sky was milky blue, and rich leaves drifted in the path verges, thrown from the trees by a night frost and a gale not long since dropped away. That afternoon I was due to drive to Essex to see the archive of a man called John Alec Baker, author of *The Peregrine*, and among the contents of the archive were Baker's binoculars and telescopes, with which he had spent a decade (1955–65) watching and tracking the falcons that wintered each year in the fields and coastal margins of Essex. Before leaving, I decided to go for a run up to the beech woods that stand on a low hill of chalk, a mile or so from my home in south Cambridge. A thin path leads to the woods; a path that I have walked or run every few days for the last ten years, and thereby come to know its usual creatures, colours and weathers. I reached the fringe of the beech wood, where the trees meet a big sloping field of rapeseed, when my eye was caught by strange shapes and vectors: the low slow flight of a pigeon over the dangerous open of the field, and the quick striking curve of a sparrowhawk – no, a peregrine, somehow a peregrine, unmistakably a peregrine – closing to it from height. The falcon slashed at the pigeon, half hit it, sent up a puff of down; the bird dropped into the rape and panicked towards the cover of the hawthorn hedge. The falcon rose and fell upon it as it showed above the surface of the crop, striking four more times but missing each time. I ran to get closer, along the fringe of the wood, but the falcon saw me coming, had known I was an agent in the drama since before it had first struck, and so it lifted and flew off east over the beech tops, black against the blue sky, its crossbow profile – what Baker calls its 'cloud-biting anchor shape' – unmistakable in silhouette, as my blood thudded.

I had followed the path to the beech woods a thousand times, and I had seen kestrels, sparrowhawks, buzzards, once a tawny owl, twice a red kite – but never a peregrine. That one had appeared there on that morning seemed so unlikely a coincidence as to resemble contrivance or magical thinking. But no, it had happened, and though it felt like blessing or fabrication it was nothing other than chance, and a few hours later, still high from the luck of it, I left for Essex to look through Baker's eyes.

~

J. A. Baker made an unlikely birdwatcher. He was so short-sighted that he wore thick glasses from an early age, and he was excused National Service during the Second World War on grounds of his vision. But this myopic man would write one of the greatest bird books ever, the fierce stylistic clarity of which must be understood in part as a compensation for the curtailed optics of its author's eyes. As an elegy-in-waiting for a landscape, *The Peregrine* is comparable with Barry Lopez's *Arctic Dreams* (1986). In its dredging of melancholy, guilt and beauty from the English countryside, it anticipates W. G. Sebald's *The Rings of Saturn* (1995). Along with *The Living Mountain* – with which it shares a compressive intensity, a generic disobedience, a flaring prose-poetry and an obsession (ocular, oracular) with the eyeball – it is one of the two most remarkable twentieth-century accounts of a landscape that I know.

If Baker's book can be said to possess anything so conventional as a plot, it is that one autumn, two pairs of peregrines come to hunt over a broad area of unspecified English coastline and hinterland – a mixed terrain of marshland, woods, fields, river valleys, mudflats, estuaries and sea. Baker becomes increasingly obsessed with the birds. From October to April he tracks them almost daily, and watches as they bathe, fly, kill, eat and roost. 'Autumn,' he writes, 'begins my season of hawk-hunting, spring ends it, and winter glitters between like the arch of Orion.' The book records these months of chase in all their agitated repetitiveness. Everything that occurs in *The Peregrine* takes place within the borders of the falcons' hunting grounds, and with respect to them. No cause is specified for the quest itself, no triggering detail. No other human character of significance besides Baker is admitted. His own presence in the book is discreet, tending to paranoid. We are told nothing of his life outside the hunt: we do not know where he sleeps at night, or to what family – if any – he returns. The falcons are his focus.

~

I reached the University of Essex soon after noon. I was shown into a room with a large table, in the centre of which had been placed two big clear plastic packing crates with snap-lock lids: a life reduced to 100 litres. The table was otherwise empty, so I unpacked the boxes and laid out their contents.

There were several maps: half-inch Ordnance Surveys of the Essex coast near Maldon, a road atlas, a large-scale map of northern Europe. There were rubber-banded bundles of letters by Baker, and other bundles of letters to him from readers and friends. There was a folder containing yellowed newspaper clippings of review coverage of *The Peregrine*. There was a curious collection of glossy cut-out images of peregrines and other raptors, scissored from magazines, bird-guides, calendars and cards. There was a list of the contents of his library. There were drafts – in manuscript and typescript – of *The Peregrine* and his second book, *The Hill of Summer*. There were proof copies in red covers of both books, every paragraph of which, I saw as I flicked through them, had been arcanely annotated by Baker using a system of ticks, numbers and symbols. There were the field journals he had kept during his years of 'hawk-hunting'. There was a sheaf of early poems. And there were his optics. A pair of Miranda 10x50 binoculars in a black case with a red velvet interior. A brass telescope, heavy in the hand, which collapsed to ten inches, extended to a foot and a half, and was carried in a double-capped brown leather tube. A featherweight spotter-scope, light and quick to lift, from J. H. Steward's in London. And a pair of stubby Mirakel 8x40s, German-made, in a carry-case of stiff brown leather lined with purple velvet, the base of which had at some point come loose, and which had been carefully repaired with pink strips of sticking plaster that still held it together.

There were also dozens of photographs, some of them still in the branded envelopes of their developers ('Instamatic – Magnify Your Memories!'). Among them I found a black-and-white shot of Baker taken in 1967, the year *The Peregrine* was published. He was forty-one at the time. I had not seen it before, though it was the photograph he chose as his author image on the jacket flap of the first edition. He is seated in an armchair and dressed in a collared white shirt and a dark woollen tank-top. He has wavy brown hair and an owlish gaze. He is resting his chin upon his hand, and looking away from the camera, over the left shoulder of the viewer, towards a sun-lit six-paned window – we know this because there is a curved reflection of the window visible in each of the thick lenses of the spectacles he is wearing.

There was something unusual about the image, though, and it took me time to realize what it was. Baker's right hand, the hand on which his chin rests, is distorted. The knuckles of the first and second finger appear to have fused together, and the back of his hand has swollen and stiffened into a pale spatulate shape, so all that can be seen is the plain white paddle of the hand's back. His fingers are invisible to the viewer, curled tightly into his palm like talons.

~

Baker was born on 6 August 1926 in Chelmsford, Essex, the only child of an unhappy marriage. His parents were Congregationalists: his father, who worked as an electrical designer, suffered prolonged mental ill health due to a bony growth that pressed onto his brain (his treatment was, brutally, a lobotomy).

At the age of eight, Baker contracted rheumatic fever, the after-effects of which would be lifelong. It induced arthritis that spread and worsened as Baker aged, and at seventeen he was diagnosed with ankylosing spondylitis, an inflammatory form of acute arthritis that fuses muscle, bone and ligament in the spine. Codeine managed but did not eliminate the chronic pain, and Baker underwent agonizing long-needle 'gold' injections into his joints, hoping to slow the progression of his disease. But his body nevertheless succumbed: his knees and hips first, and then his hands, which were thoroughly stricken by the 1960s. Thus the fused knuckles, the curled fingers, the stiffened shield of his right hand – so bravely on show in his author photograph.

Despite the pain, photographs from Baker's youth show him as a cheerful and sociable young man. Golden hair, hands in pockets, always the thick spectacles. Arms round his friends, drunken embraces in wartime pubs, walks along the sea wall. He was six feet tall, deep-voiced and strongly built, though the spondylitis diminished his stature. He was an eager reader and a prolific correspondent: his letters from the war years speak of an intellectually adventurous teenager – passionate above all about landscapes and literature. He would often spend weeks writing single letters, and because of this tended to double-date his letters 'Comm:' and 'Conc:'. A letter to his friend Don Samuel was 'Comm: Sept 19th 1945' and 'Conc: Oct 4th 1945', and ran to sixty-four pages of blue notepaper. 'Dear Sam,' it opened. 'Here beginneth what promises to be indeed a "weird" if not a "wonderful" letter. Many subjects will drift leisurely across the pages – vague substances phantasmal, trailing clouds of unwieldy imagery . . .' It ended with loving descriptions of the 'delicately balanced' Essex landscape: 'green undulating fields, rugged, furrowed earth, luscious orchards, pine clumps, rows of stately elms'. 'In things beautiful there is an eternity of peace, and an infinity of sight,' concluded the myopic Baker, longingly.

In the early 1950s, while working for the Automobile Association in Chelmsford, he met his wife, Doreen, a wages clerk at the company. They married in October 1956: the marriage would be durable, childless and loving, although – one suspects – difficult at times for Doreen. Also in the early 1950s Baker was introduced to birdwatching by a friend from work, Sid Harman. What began as a distraction became first a passion and then an obsession for Baker. Soon he was birding alone. Whenever possible, he would cycle – on his Raleigh bike, with khaki canvas saddle-bags – in search of birds, out into the 200 square miles of coastal Essex that comprised his hunting ground. He would pass London's overspill factories and car dumps, heading for the inland fields and woods, or to the lonely sea wall and saltings of the shore. He would wear his standard birdwatching clobber: grey flannel trousers, an open-necked shirt, a jumper knitted by his mother, a Harris tweed jacket, a flat cloth cap, and a gaberdine mac to keep the weather off. He would take a packet of sandwiches (made by Doreen), and a flask (filled with tea by Doreen). He would also carry a pair of binoculars or a telescope. He took a map on which he marked the locations of his sightings, and a Boots spiral-bound notebook in which he kept his field records. At the end of each bird-day he would return to a big meal (cooked by Doreen) and then retreat up to his den, the spare bedroom, to transpose and refine his notes. He was, Doreen remembered after his death, 'a prickly customer', who became a 'loner' as an adult. Limited in sight and mobility, and suffering near-constant pain, he was prone to bursts of anger.

Birdwatching helped Baker thwart his short sight, and offered him a form of relation. 'Binoculars and a hawk-like vigilance,' he wrote, 'reduce the disadvantage of myopic human vision.' Aided by optics and instincts, a new world became visible to him: the beyond-world of wildness that proceeds around and within the human domain. He recorded his discoveries in his notebooks and journals, in total more than 1,600 pages of field notes taken over the course of ten years, made in black and blue ink and his looping handwriting, the legibility of which deteriorated as his illness advanced.

~

The journals are coal to *The Peregrine*'s diamond. Crushed, they became his book. The first journal entry is dated 21 March 1954: it is functional and unadorned: a partridge is seen in the meadows opposite a church on 'Patching Hall Lane', in 'long', 'rich' grass. Thirteen species are seen in the day; a wren is heard 'singing lustily'. Habits of annotation that will last are established: each date is underlined; each bird name is double-underlined and capitalized (lending a Germanic feel to the prose); weather and wind direction are recorded.

Within weeks of that first entry, Baker had begun to experiment with his language, sensing that the field note might be a miniature literary form of its own. He soon employed metaphor and simile to evoke details and aspects that conventional field notes would have eschewed as irrelevant. Such comparative tropes, often elaborate, served to sharpen rather than blur observation:

> <u>Sunday May 9th</u>. Wood Hall Wood – <u>Nightingale</u> singing well, and perched amongst brambles and white may. Throat working convulsively as it sang, like an Adam's Apple, or bobbing, like a pea in a whistle, tremendous sound to come from such a narrow place as a bird's throat.

As I read the journals that afternoon, Baker's well-hidden personality became more visible to me: a private and pained man, in flight himself, who discovered a dignity and purpose in the work of watching – and whose encounters with birds supplied him with kinds of happiness that were otherwise unavailable. On 16 June 1954, five days before midsummer, he went out with Sid late in the evening in search of nightjars, undeterred by the heavy rain. Suddenly, unexpectedly, they heard the song of a wood lark and, inspired, they impetuously 'plunged into the wet wood' to find its source:

> I had a handkerchief over my head, like a puddingcloth, and followed the sound – at first along the footpath, then through the bracken, the ditches, and the bushes, until . . . we stood under that wonderful sound, coming down to us in the thick darkness and the pouring rain. And a feeling of great exhilaration possessed me, like a sudden lungful of purer air. The great pointlessness of it, the non-sense of nature, was beautiful, and no one else would know it again, exactly as we knew it at that moment. Only a bird would circle high in the darkness, endlessly singing for pure, untainted,

instinctive joy, and only a bird-watcher would stand and gorp up at something he could never hope to see, sharing that joy.

A feeling of exhilaration possessed me as I read that entry, smiling at the detail of the handkerchief, sharing something of Baker's joy. But I was aware of the reflexivity, too: that I had become a watcher myself, a second-order spotter, trying to see Baker through the darkness of six decades – 'gorping' after something I could never really hope to perceive.

Half a year or so into his journal-keeping, Baker started to produce more intense entries: brief prose-poem paragraphs, modernist and spiky, that anticipate the dense energies of *The Peregrine*:

Saturday November 20th 1954 Great SE/SW gales each night, Rooks were swept from home to roost on immense waves of wind, thrown like burnt paper, very high, revellers in the wind.

Tuesday November 1st 1955 50 degrees. Edney Wood was quiet, but frighteningly beautiful. The sodden glow of the millions of leaves burnt my eyes. But after sunset it was just a desolate, deserted autumn slum of trees.

Light fascinated him, as he worked at how to represent its volatilities in language. He tried out phrase after phrase, remaining hostile to cliché: 'clear varnish of yellow, fading sunlight'; 'that quality of sunlight, which is like the dusty golden varnish on some old Rembrandt oil-painting'. Occasionally he relinquished simile in favour of common adjectives, uncommonly combined: 'Wednesday April 23rd 1958. Light was tricky and strange.'

The early years of Baker's journals reveal him to be a good writer but a rather bad birdwatcher. Partly because of his myopia, he did not develop what birders call 'the jizz': the gestalt of body shape, flight-style, song or call, context, behaviour and location within a landscape that allows an experienced birder to make an instantaneous identification. The jizz is the knowledge-without-reflection that the bird glimpsed at the edge of vision is a *kestrel*, a *firecrest*, a *curlew*. Baker, though, was often uncertain as to what he had seen. Early one January he watched a bird in 'glorious light':

> moving very fast, with wing's [*sic*] beating quickly, rolling slightly from side to side. Its tail looked longish and tapering. The instant I saw it I thought it was a <u>Hawk</u>, a <u>Kestrel</u> or a <u>Sparrowhawk</u>, or even a <u>Peregrine</u> [. . .] or a <u>Wood Pigeon</u> or <u>Stock Dove</u>. . . . No markings could be seen in the glasses, so it wasn't a <u>Wood Pigeon</u>. Either a <u>Stock Dove</u>, or a falcon, presumably.

Another day he spots what he supposes to be a wood pigeon but 'the possibility of it's [*sic*] being an immature male Peregrine flashed across my mind'. 'Presumably', 'possibility': wish fulfilment is at work here: the beginnings of a longing for the peregrine so keen that it caused – in the blurry distance of Baker's far-sight – dove to morph into falcon, pigeon to pass into peregrine. From the start, the predatory nature of the falcons, their decisive speed, their awesome vision and their subtle killings all thrilled him. Baker was enraptored.

~

After two hours with the journals, I set them aside and turned to Baker's maps. The Essex maps, inch-to-a-mile Ordnance Surveys, had obviously been heavily used. At the corners where the panels met, the paper had worn through from folding, and threads of cloth were visible. The maps were also heavily annotated in ink and pencil. There were territories marked out with ruled biro-line perimeters, which presumably represented the area of a single day's exploration. Pocking the maps, too, were hundreds of inked circles, each containing a capital letter or pair of letters: LO, M, K.

It took me longer than it should have done to realize that each of the circles recorded a raptor sighting. P = peregrine. SH = sparrowhawk. M = merlin. LO = little owl. BO = barn owl. HH = hen harrier. K = kestrel. Only raptors – birds that hunt and feed on other animals – were recorded in this way by Baker. Our word *raptor* comes from the Latin *rapere*, meaning 'to seize or take by force'. I felt a sudden surge of unease at seeing Baker's obsession with raptors recorded in this way: as if I had stumbled into the room of someone fixated with serial-killers, note-boards and walls papered with yellowing news-clippings of past crimes . . .

The Peregrine is a book of bloodiness, strewn with corpses whose lacerations and dismemberments Baker records with the diligent attention of a crime-scene investigator. Indeed it is, in many ways, a detective story: there is the same procedural care, the gathering of clues as to the nature of the killer, the bagging of evidence, and the following of hunches when evidence falls short and deduction will not suffice. And as with so many crime dramas, the killer comes to fascinate the pursuer.

After he first saw (or believed himself to have seen) a peregrine, Baker quickly elected the bird – which he often, inaccurately, calls a 'hawk' rather than a 'falcon' – as his totem creature, rife with dark voodoo. In the late 1950s, peregrines become the chief object of his searchings, and his language from this period begins to invest the birds with disturbing powers and qualities: a northern purity, a shattering capacity for violence – and the ability to vanish.

~

The winter of 1962–3 was the fiercest since the mid eighteenth century. The sea froze for two miles out into the North Sea. Spear-length icicles hung from eaves and gutters, and snow drifted to twenty feet deep in places. The estuaries of Essex iced up, and the wading birds that depended upon access to the mudflats for their food supply died in their thousands. Not a day in England dawned above freezing from 26 December to 6 March.

Soon after the snow at last left the land, Baker resigned from his job at the Automobile Association in order to commit to his pursuit of the falcons and work on the book he was starting to compress out of the field journals. By day he watched, and by night he wrote. It was a frugal, focused life. He and Doreen lived off savings, a tiny pension and National Assistance. The house had no telephone, and Baker seems to have communicated little with friends. These were the circumstances he needed to convert the sprawling journals into a crystalline prose-poem.

Waiting for Godot was once described as a play in which nothing happens, twice. *The Peregrine* is a book in which little happens, hundreds of times. Dawn. Baker watches, the bird hunts, the bird kills, the bird feeds. Dusk. Thus again, over seven months. What Baker understood was that to dramatize such reiteration he had to forge a new style of description. The style he created, up in his Chelmsford spare room, was as sudden and swift as the bird to which it was devoted, and one that – like the peregrine – could startle even as it repeated itself.

Baker gained his effect by a curious combination of surplus (the proliferation of verb, adjective, metaphor and simile), deletion (the removal of articles, conjunctions, proper nouns) and compression (the decision to crush ten years of 'hawk-hunting' down to a single symbolic 'season', its year unspecified). This mixture of flaring out and paring away results in the book's shocking energies and its hyperkinetic prose. Neologisms and coinages abound. There are the adjectives Baker torques into verbs ('The north wind brittled icily in the pleached lattice of the hedges'), and the verbs he incites to misbehaviour ('Four short-eared owls soothed out of the gorse'). Adverbs act as bugle notes, conferring bright ritualism upon scenes ('Savagely he lashed himself free, and came superbly to the south, rising on the rim of the black cloud'). There are the audacious comparisons: the yellow-billed cock blackbird 'like a small mad puritan with a banana in his mouth', the wood pigeon on a winter field that 'glowed purple and grey like broccoli' – like broccoli! – or the 'five thousand dunlin' that 'rained away inland, like a horde of beetles gleamed with golden chitin'. Such flourishes have the appearance of surplus to them, but in fact they aspire to maximum efficiency. A baroque simile is offered because it seems to Baker the most precise way to evoke the thing to which it is being compared. These comparisons are 'far-fetched' in two senses: elaborate in their analogies, but also serving to fetch-from-far – to bring near the distant world of the birds.

I had known before coming to the archive that Baker had rewritten the book five times after its first draft. But until I opened the red-jacketed proof copy of *The Peregrine* I had no idea of the unique method of analysis he had devised for his own prose. Almost every page of the proof was rife with annotations. Ticks indicated phrases with which Baker was especially pleased. Here and there he had re-lineated his prose as verse. He had subjected his sentences to prosodic analysis, with stress and accent marks hovering above each syllable, as if scanning poetic meter (echoes of Gerard Manley Hopkins).

On every page, he had also tallied and totalled the number of verbs, adjectives, metaphors and similes. Above each metaphor was a tiny inked 'M', above each simile an 'S', above each adjective an 'A' and above each verb a 'V'. Written neatly in the bottom margin of each page was a running total for each category of word-type, and at the end of each chapter were final totals of usage. 'Beginnings', the first chapter of *The Peregrine*, though only six pages long, contained 136 metaphors and 23 similes, while the one-and-a-half-page entry for the month of March used 97 verbs and 56 adjectives.

There, laid bare, was the technical basis of Baker's style: an extreme density of verbs, qualifiers and images, resulting in a book in which – as the writer and ornithologist Kenneth Allsop put it in a fine early review – 'the pages dance with image after marvellous image, leaping forward direct to the retina from that marshland drama'. That quality of 'leaping forward' is distinctive of Baker's writing: distinctive, too, of course, of what the world does when binoculars are raised to it. Thus the stunning set-pieces of hunt and kill, close to imagist poems, describing chase and 'stoop' – that 'sabring fall from the sky' when the peregrine drops onto prey from a height of up to 3,000 feet, at a speed of up to 240 mph, slaying with the crash of impact as well as the slash of talons:

> A falcon peregrine, sable on a white shield of sky, circled over from the sea. She slowed, and drifted aimlessly, as though the air above the land was thick and heavy. She dropped. The beaches flared and roared with salvoes of white wings. The sky shredded up, was torn

by whirling birds. The falcon rose and fell, like a black billhook in splinters of white wood.

'What does a falcon see?' asked Anaximander in the sixth century BC. According to Baker, it sees like a Cubist painter gazing from the cockpit of a jet aircraft. It perceives in surface and plane, a tilt-vision of flow and slant. It remembers form and the interrelation of form:

> The peregrine lives in a pouring-away world of no attachment, a world of wakes and tilting, of sinking planes of land and water. The peregrine sees and remembers patterns we do not know exist; the neat squares of orchard and woodland, the endlessly varying quad-rilateral shapes of fields. He finds his way across the land by a succession of remembered symmetries . . . he sees maps of black and white.

One of the many exhilarations of reading *The Peregrine* is that we acquire some version of the vision of a peregrine. We look upon the southern English landscape from above and perceive it as almost pure form: partridge coveys are 'rings of small black stones' on the fields, an orchard shrinks 'into dark twiggy lines and green strips', the horizon is 'stained with distant towns', an estuary 'lift[s] up its blue and silver mouth'. These are things imperceptible at ground level. We become the *catascopos*, the 'looker-down': a role usually reserved for gods, pilots and mountaineers. This falcon-sight, this *catascopy*, makes Essex – a county that never rises higher than 140 metres above sea level, a county that one sees often across, but rarely down onto – new again. Baker gained this perspective for his prose by studying RAF and Luftwaffe aerial photographs of the south-east of England. To see like a peregrine, he had first to see like a helmeted airman. Short sight led to bomb-sight led to hawk-sight.

~

The Peregrine is not a book about watching a falcon but a book about becoming a falcon. In the opening pages, Baker sets out his manifesto of pursuit:

> Wherever he goes, this winter, I will follow him. I will share the fear, and the exaltation, and the boredom, of the hunting life. I will follow him till my predatory human shape no longer darkens in terror the shaken kaleidoscope of colour that stains the deep fovea of his brilliant eye. My pagan head shall sink into the winter land, and there be purified.

There, in four eldritch sentences, is the book's chill heart. Baker hopes that, through a prolonged and 'purified' concentration upon the peregrine, he might be able to escape his 'human shape' and abscond into the 'brilliant' wildness of the bird.

He begins his 'hunting life' by learning to track his predatory prey. Peregrines can often fly so fast, and at such altitude, that to the human eye – especially the myopic human eye – they are invisible from the ground. But Baker discovers that they can be located by the disturbance they create among other birds, almost as the position of an invisible plane can be told from its contrail: 'Evanescent as flame,' he writes on 7 October, 'peregrines sear across the cold sky and are gone, leaving no sign in the blue haze above. But in the lower air a wake of birds trails back, and rises upward through the white helix of the gulls.'

As he improves his tracking skills, so Baker draws closer to the bird, and he begins to seek contact with it, through ritual mimicry of its behaviour and habits (a method that has affinities with those of revolutionary mid-twentieth-century ethologists such as Frank Fraser Darling and Konrad Lorenz). One November day he rests his hand on the grass where a peregrine has recently come to ground, and experiences 'a strong feeling of proximity, identification'. By December he has gone fully feral. Crossing a field one afternoon, he sees feathers blowing in the wind:

> The body of a woodpigeon lay breast upward on a mass of soft white feathers. The head had been eaten . . . The bones were still dark red, the blood still wet.
>
> I found myself crouching over the kill, like a mantling hawk. My eyes turned quickly about, alert for the walking heads of men. Unconsciously I was imitating the movements of a hawk, as in some primitive ritual; the hunter becoming the thing he hunts . . . We live, in these days in the open, the same ecstatic fearful life. We shun men.

The pronouns tell the story – 'I' turns into 'we'; repetition becomes ritual; human dissolves into falcon. Allsop understood this drive for transformation to be the book's central psychodrama: 'The [book's] strange and awful grip,' he wrote, 'is in the author's wrestling to be rid of his humanness, to enter the hawk's feathers, skin and spirit.'

Why might a man want to become a bird? Baker's illness, and the pained discomfort of his daily life, bear upon this question. The peregrines – in their speed and freedom of manoeuvre, with their fabulous vision – idealized the physical abilities of which the earth-bound, joint-crabbed, eye-dimmed Baker had been deprived. One can hear a hint of envy when, one November, Baker notes seeing a peregrine moving with 'his usual loose-limbed panache'. The falcons embody all that is unavailable to him, and so they become first his prosthesis and then his totem: 'the hunter becoming the thing he hunts'.

Baker was also suffering from intense species shame. The peregrines of Europe and North America were, at the time he wrote, suffering severe population decline. In 1962 Rachel Carson had alerted the world to the calamitous effects of pesticides on bird populations in *Silent Spring*. A year later a British raptor specialist called Derek Ratcliffe had published a landmark paper revealing the terrible impact of agrichemicals upon peregrine numbers in Britain. Pesticide use, notably DDT, was leading to an aggregation of toxins in raptor prey species, which in turn was causing eggshell thinning and nesting failure in the falcons. Their breeding success rate plummeted, with chicks typically dying in the egg. In 1939, Ratcliffe noted, there were 700 pairs of peregrines in Britain. A 1962 survey showed a decline to under half of this number, with only 68 pairs appearing to have reared chicks successfully. Baker was aware of both Ratcliffe and Carson's work; as was J. G. Ballard, whose work Baker admired, and whose story 'Storm-bird, Storm-dreamer' (1966) imagines a future in which pesticide overuse has caused massive growth in the bird species of the country, who then begin coordinated attacks on the English crop-fields in an attempt to feed their vast hungers. The south-east English coastline becomes a militarized zone, with anti-aircraft guns mounted on barges, there to resist aerial attacks not by Heinkels but by hawks.

In the mid 1960s, as he laboured over his drafts of *The Peregrine*, it must have seemed likely to Baker that the peregrine would vanish from southern England, extinguished by what he called 'the filthy, insidious pollen of farm chemicals'. Over a decade he had watched the dwindling of peregrine numbers: 'Few winter in England now, fewer nest here . . . the ancient eyries are dying.' Thus the atmosphere of requiem that prevails in *The Peregrine*: a sadness that things should be this way, mixed with a disbelief that they might be changed. Occasionally, the elegiac tone flares into anger. Out walking on 24 December, a day of cusps and little light, Baker finds a near-dead heron lying in a stubble field. Its wings are frozen to the ground, but in a ghastly thwarted escape, it tries to fly off:

> As I approached I could see its whole body craving into flight. But it could not fly. I gave it peace, and saw the agonised sunlight of its eyes slowly heal with cloud.
>
> No pain, no death, is more terrible to a wild creature than its fear of man . . . A poisoned crow, gaping and helplessly floundering in the grass, bright yellow foam bubbling from its throat, will dash itself up again and again on to the descending wall of air, if you try to catch it. A rabbit, inflated and foul with myxomatosis . . . will feel the vibration of your footstep and will look for you with bulging, sightless eyes.
>
> We are the killers. We stink of death. We carry it with us. It sticks to us like frost. We cannot tear it away.

'We stink of death. We carry it with us.' By this point in *The Peregrine*, we understand these to be the words of a man who feels himself stricken with disease – and of a man appalled to belong to his own kind. He wants to resign his humanity, and to partake of both the far-sight and the guiltless murders of the falcon.

~

Towards the end of the afternoon in the archive, I took Baker's telescopes and binoculars one by one to the window. There was a view
of beech trees, concrete buildings, and a lecture hall with a curved
zinc roof. I tried out each instrument in turn. When I extended the
Steward scope, there was an ominous rattle from its interior. I held
it to my eye and stared into milk. The eyepiece was misty, glaucous.
I tried the other telescope, brass and heavy. But it was missing its
front lens, and there was only blackness to be seen, with a tiny circle
of light at its centre.

Both pairs of binoculars, though, were scratched but functioning.
Through the Mirakels I tracked wood pigeons on their *clap-clap-glide*
crossings of the campus sky, passing over the green-gold of
late-season oaks. Through the Mirandas I watched a wagtail
figure-eighting for flies above the zinc of the lecture hall.

Binocular vision is a peculiarly exclusive form of looking. It
draws a circle around the focused-on object and shuts out the world's
generous remainder. What binoculars grant you in focus and reach,
they deny you in periphery. To view an object through them is to
see it in crisp isolation, encircled by blackness – as though at the end
of a tunnel. They permit a lucidity of view but enforce a denial of
context, and as such they seemed to me then the perfect emblem of
Baker's own intense, and intensely limited, vision. I thought of him
out in the field towards the end of his decade of hedge-haunting and
hawk-hunting; how difficult it must have become to hold the binoculars, as his finger joints thickened and fused, and his tendons
tightened.

The Peregrine, a record of obsession, has itself in turn provoked
obsessions. It is a book which sets the mind aloft and holds it there.
In the archive I found scores of admiring letters written to Baker by
readers. Some wished to acquire his supernatural abilities as a

tracker: 'I hope to have the good fortune to see Peregrine somewhere in the [Blackwater] estuary on Thursday Feb 9th or Friday Feb 10th,' wrote one – as if Baker the magus might magic these wild birds up to order. A student of mine was so inspired by *The Peregrine*'s vision of human irresponsibility that she became an eco-activist, paddling kayaks up rivers to gain illegal access to coal-fired power stations. Several years ago I came to know a young musician living a marginal life in a south London squat and performing as the front man for a hardcore punk-rock band. He was a talented and troubled person, for whom 'nature' as conventionally experienced was irrelevant, tending to incomprehensible. But he had found his way to *The Peregrine*, and the book's dark fury spoke to him. He read it repeatedly, and began to mimic Baker's mimicry of the falcons: once, on a London street outside a club, he demonstrated the action of 'mantling' – when a peregrine spreads its wings, fans its tail and arches over its prey to hide it from other predators. He and I collaborated on a project one summer and made plans to work together again. Then that December he died of a heroin overdose, aged twenty-three. He was lowered into the cold hard earth of a Cornish field a few days before Christmas, with the cars of his friends pulled up around the grave, their stereos blasting out his music in tribute. Buried with him was a copy of the book he revered above all others.

I am another of those obsessives, differently stricken, unable to free myself from *The Peregrine*'s grip. As Nan changed the way I see mountains, so Baker changed the way I see coasts and skies. I have written often about the book, and followed Baker's own wanderings through Essex as best I have been able to reconstruct them: hunting the hunter's huntings. The opening sentences of a book of mine called *The Wild Places* knowingly invoke the opening sentences of

The Peregrine; Baker is present through the whole work, his style stooped into its prose.

When I have seen peregrines I have seen them, or I remember them, at least partly in Baker's language. A falcon up at the Mare's Tail waterfall in the Scottish Borders, *riding along the rim of the sky in a tremendous serration of rebounding dives and ascensions*, then dipping down in hooping dive to its nest on the cliffs of the cataract. A breeding pair high above a crag in misty sunlight on the side of long Loch Ericht in the Central Highlands, heard first, giving *high, husky muffled calls, keerk, keerk, keerk, keerk, keerk, sharp-edged and barbarous*, then appearing as *dark crossbow shapes*. And then the peregrine that morning, before leaving for the archive, first *a tremor at the edge of vision*, then at last *sculling away with quick wing flicks*.

The month I finished writing this chapter, eight months after I had been to the archive, a pair of peregrines took up residence on the great brown brick tower of the university library in Cambridge. They made their nest on a ledge high on the tower's south side, in front of one of the small windows that let light into the dim miles of book-stacks. A friend told me one afternoon that they had arrived, and gave me directions to the window: South Front Floor 6, Case Number 42. I went the next morning, rising up the tower in a cranky lift, and approaching the window cautiously. I could see feather fluff and guano; then, tucked in tight to the retaining tiles, a clutch of three eggs, brick-red and black-flecked. And suddenly I stepped back, because she was there also, *scything in and up* to the edge of the ledge and perching, the feathers of her piebald breast *rippled by the wind*, her yellow feet gripping the ledge, *the ridged knuckles tense, and big with muscle*, and her great *black eyes looking into mine*, or rather through me, *as though they see something beyond me from which they cannot look away*.

GLOSSARY IV

Coastlands

Bays, Channels and Inlets

barra channel cut in a rocky shore for boats to enter **Manx**

caol narrow channel between two islands, or between an island and the mainland **Gaelic**

caul embankment built across a river or an inlet of the sea to divert water **Galloway**

cilan small inlet, creek (place-name element) **Welsh**

crenulate of a shoreline: having many small irregular bays formed by the action of waves on softer rock **geographical**

firth arm of the sea; estuary **Scots**

gat gap in an offshore sandbank **East Anglia**

geo, gjo coastal cleft; narrow, rocky-sided bay **Gaelic, especially Orkney, Outer Hebrides, Shetland**

gunk-hole small narrow channel that is dangerous to navigate, owing to current and to numerous rocks and ledges **nautical**

hope inlet, small bay, haven **south-east England**

laimrig clear channel between rocks; marine landing place **Gaelic**

mijn mouth of a *voe* **Shetland**

oyce lagoon formed where a bar of shingle has been thrown up across the head of a bay **Orkney, Shetland** *pill*   tidal creek or stream **south-west England**

sump   muddy shallow near the mouth of a creek, offering anchorage **Kent**

swatch   passage or channel of water lying between sandbanks, or between a sandbank and the shore **East Anglia**

vaddel   gulf that fills and empties with the flowing and ebbing of the sea, commonly at the head of a *voe* **Shetland**

voe   inlet or arm of the sea **Shetland**

wik   little open bay **Shetland**

zawn   vertical fissure or cave cut by wave action into a coastal cliff **Cornwall**

Cliffs, Headlands and Defences

bill   promontory **southern England**

cadha   way up the ragged face of a cliff **Gaelic**

dragon's teeth   rows of concrete blocks or pyramidal shapes laid on beaches and tidal flats to prevent tanks from landing and becoming operational **military**

gabion   large wire or netting baskets containing earth or rubble to provide protection or reinforcing against military attack or coastal erosion **conservation, military**

heuch   cliff above water **Scots**

neap, noup lofty headland dropping steeply into the sea **Shetland**

ness promontory, cape or headland **North Sea coast**

revetment retaining wall, usually sloping: in military terms to defend a position or vulnerable site; in coastal management to protect the shoreline against erosion **conservation, military**

rhu, roo headland **Galloway**

rock armour large stones, boulders or concrete rubble used to defend a sea wall, usually in the form of a *revetment* **conservation**

score footway linking beach and cliff-top **Suffolk**

squilving-ground land which slants towards the sea at the edge of a cliff **Exmoor**

tairbeart isthmus between two sea lochs **Gaelic**

wannen-place 'one-end place', such as a projecting seaside resort only accessible from one direction **Suffolk**

Currents, Waves and Tides

adnasjur large wave or waves, coming after a succession of lesser ones **Shetland**

af'luva, af'rug reflex of a wave after it has struck the shore **Shetland**

ar'ris last weak movements of a tide before still water **Shetland**

bòc-thonnach covered with swelling waves **Gaelic**

bod jumping motion of waves **Shetland**

bore, eagre tide-wave of extraordinary height, usually caused by the rushing of the tide up a narrowing estuary **hydrological**

bretsh breaking of waves on a rocky shore **Shetland**

cockling of a sea: jerked up into short waves by contrary currents **Lancashire**

faks to swell up with a threatening motion without breaking, as a wave **Shetland**

ootrogue undercurrent from shore, taking sand out with it **North Sea coast**

pirr light breath of wind, such as will make a cat's paw on the water; a light breeze **Shetland**

roost turbulent tidal race formed by the meeting of conflicting currents **Orkney, Shetland**

saatbrak foam and spray of the surge **Shetland**

smooth calm sea, usually around the sixth or seventh wave in a sequence, used to launch and beach longshore boats **Suffolk**

sruthladh violent motion of waves advancing upon and receding from the shore **Gaelic**

Fishing and Boats

an'du to keep a boat in position by rowing gently against the tide **Shetland** *back fu'* wind on the wrong side of the sail **North Sea coast**

bak'flan sudden gust of wind which, by mischance, strikes a boat's sail on the back side (i.e. the lee side) and so endangers the boat **Shetland**

berth small area of beach on which a longshoreman kept his boats **Suffolk**

bichter stone used as an anchor to long lines **Shetland**

bill bubble-like ripple made by the stroke of an oar in water **Shetland**

blash, plash to hit the water with an oar (or similar) in order to disturb and drive fish when inshore, netting for salmon **North Sea coast**

blaze to take salmon by striking them at night, by torchlight, with a three-pronged spear **North Sea coast**

breast mark at sea, a landmark (church, lighthouse, coastguard buildings) sighted from abeam **Suffolk**

broached knocked sideways by the sea **North Sea coast**

cade measure of herrings or sprats **Suffolk**

caraidh fish-trap with low walls **Gaelic**

comharran twin markings on land used to give an offshore boat its location **Gaelic**

dabba stick with point on end used by children to catch flatfish on sand **North Sea coast**

dan flag on lobster pot **Cornwall**

dopper oilskin **North Sea coast**

eela fishing with a rod from a boat anchored in shallow water near the land **Shetland**

fendi capable of fending off the waves; having the qualities of a good sea boat **Shetland**

gansey fisherman's traditional woollen sweater, usually navy blue and patterned, with designs varying from family to family and area to area **North Sea coast, Scotland**

gear lobster pots **Cornwall**

girt to be caught by a powerful tide or surge of water while in a boat or craft **south-east England**

glister squall, squally weather **Manx**

griping groping at arm's length in the soft mud of the tidal streams for flounders and eels **Kent**

gyte fish-slime **North Sea coast**

herengro matcho crab **Anglo-Romani**

holly to leave lobsters in boxes in the sea for a period of time **North Sea coast**

jip to gut herrings **Suffolk**

kep-shite skua, so called because it chases other birds until they drop their food, thought by fishermen to be droppings **North Sea coast**

limmitter lobster with one claw missing **North Sea coast** *long-mark* landmark sighted from ahead **Suffolk**

luff to sail nearer to the wind **nautical**

matchkani gav Yarmouth (literally 'fish village', from the European Romani words *macho*, 'fish', and *gav*, 'village') **Anglo-Romani**

meith landmark used by sailors **Scots**

pallag lump on a hill as seen from the sea, used as a fishing mark in association with other objects **Manx**

plouncing beating the surface of the water of dykes in marshlands with leafy branches to drive fish along into nets **Suffolk**

skurr fishing ground near the shore with a hard bottom **Shetland**

slogger sucking sound made by waves against a ship's side (Gerard Manley Hopkins) **poetic**

soft general term for a fishing ground with a sandy bottom **North Sea coast**

swad fine green weed that grows on ropes, etc. **North Sea coast**

thwart seat across a boat **nautical**

tommy small crab, thrown back **North Sea coast**

trim the most advantageous set of a ship in the water, and/or the most advantageous adjustment of a ship's sails **nautical**

wow-tin fisherman's lunch tin **North Sea coast**

Lights, Hazes, Mists and Fogs

aggy-jaggers mist that forms along the sea edge **north Kent coast**

bar'ber haze which rises from the surface of sea water when the air is very cold **Shetland**

briming marine phosphorescence **Cornwall**

brim'skud smoke-like haze which rises from the breaking waves **Shetland**

fret mist or fog coming in from the sea **eastern and southern England**

glimro phosphorescent glimmer **Orkney**

haar misty rain that drifts in from the sea, often reaching several miles inland **Cornwall, north-east England, eastern Scotland**

hag light said to appear at night on horses' manes and men's hair **nautical**

maril'd sparkling luminous substance seen in the sea on autumn nights, and on fish in the dark **Shetland**

milk sea water made phosphorescent by shoals of herring **Suffolk**

rime fog coming in from the sea; also hoar frost **Galloway**

rouk sea mist **Scots**

siaban sand-blow and sea-froth **Gaelic**

sun-scald   patch of bright sunlight on the surface of water **Sussex**

water-burn   marine phosphorescence **Kent**

woor   low-hanging sea mist that dims the light and chills the air **Manx**

The Sea

brabble   ruffle on the sea's surface **East Anglia**

brimfus'ter   sea-froth **Shetland**

coulpress   continued breaking of the sea **North Sea coast**

endragoned   of a sea: raging (Gerard Manley Hopkins) **poetic**

flint-flaked   of a sea: white-topped (Gerard Manley Hopkins) **poetic**

freith   foam on the sea **Scots**

glacio-eustasy   changes in sea level caused by the waxing and waning of ice sheets **geological**

haaf   the deep sea as distinguished from that close to shore; deep-sea fishing ground or station **Orkney, Shetland**

hobbles   choppy, short waves roused by wind **North Sea coast**

hob-gob   nasty, choppy sea **Suffolk**

jap   choppy sea **Shetland**

limon   sea-foam **Jèrriais (Jersey Norman)**

lippers   white caps on sea **North Sea coast**

luragub   sea-froth churned into a lather in crevices of rocks by the action of the sea **Shetland**

marshum   balls of sea-scum or sea-foam **Shetland**

roost   tidal race or whirlpool caused by inequalities on the sea bottom or the meeting of tides **Orkney, Shetland**

selkie, silkie   seal; in folklore, a spirit that assumes the form of a seal in water and of a human on land **Scots**

skeer   stone patch on the sea floor in shallow water **north Lancashire**

sweep, swipe   to recover anchors from the seabed **Suffolk**

wart   small bank near the coast **Manx**

Shores and Strands

air   shingly beach **Shetland**

baa   sea-rock which may be seen at low tide; sunken rock, breaking in bad weather only **Shetland**

ballisten'   round sea-worn stone of such size as may be easily handled **Shetland**

ballow   shoal, sandbank **East Anglia**

bentalls   low sandy flattish land on the coast **East Anglia**

bold of a coast: rising steeply from deep water
nautical

brim'tud sound of the sea breaking on the shore **Shetland**

bus seaweed-covered rock **North Sea coast**

cladach stony beach **Gaelic**

dene bare sandy tract by the sea **Suffolk**

eid isthmus, strip of land between two waters;
sandbank cast up by the sea across the head of a
bay **Shetland**

êtchièrviéthe rock frequented by cormorants (toponym)
Jèrriais (Jersey Norman)

faoilinn strand between a shingle beach and a loch
Gaelic

frotting examining the beach or broken cliff for coins or
other valuables (i.e. beachcombing) **Suffolk**

intertidal zone area of the shore between the highest and
lowest tides **geographical**

kane water left at the ebb of tide between an outer
sandbank and the beach, which is easily
sun-warmed and therefore offers good bathing
East Anglia

klett low-lying earth-fast rock on the seashore
Shetland

kythin worm-casts on beach sand **North Sea coast**

littoral existing or taking place on or near the shore
geographical

managed retreat form of coastal management where the shoreline is allowed to move inland in a controlled way (i.e. due to the abandoning of previously used hard sea defences) **conservation**

merse pastureland beside the sea **Galloway**

ore-stone rock covered with seaweed **south-west England**

sho and 'im she (the sea) and him (land) **Shetland**

slack hollow in sand- or mudbanks on a shore **northern England, Scotland**

slake stretch of muddy ground left exposed by the tide; mudflat **northern England**

sleck mud at a river where the tide comes in and out **North Sea coast**

sparrow-beaks fossilized sharks' teeth **Northamptonshire**

tiùrr beach out of reach of the sea; high-water mark; sea-ware cast up on the high-water mark **Gaelic**

tombolo ridge of sand built by wave action, connecting an island to the mainland **geographical**

towan dune, coastal sandhill **Cornish**

wæter-gewæsc land formed by the washing up of earth **Old English**

6

The Tunnel of Swords and Axes

I

Haugr – Old Norse noun meaning 'hill, fell, burial mound or entrance to the world of the departed'.

The night before I first met Richard Skelton and we ended up going into the hill together, I read a story taken from the great Finnish folk epic, the *Kalevala*. The story's title caught my eye on a contents page: 'Vainamoinen Finds the Lost-Words'. Its hero, Vainamoinen, is trying to build an enchanted ship of oak wood in which he will be able to sail to safety over the 'rough sea-billows'. But he is unable to conclude his shipbuilding for want of three magic words, the utterance of each of which will perform a task: speaking the first will 'complete the stern', the second will 'fasten the ledges' and the third will 'finish the forecastle'. Synonyms are no use: the power of each word is specific to its form, and only the utterance of all three will render the ship seaworthy. So Vainamoinen – whose name comes from the Finnish *vaina*, meaning 'stream-pool' – sets out in search of the 'lost-words'.

He looks for them first in 'the brains of countless swallows', then 'the heads of dying swans' and then 'the plumage of the grey duck', but does not find them. He looks on 'the tongues of summer-reindeer' and in 'the mouths of squirrels', but still without success. So he travels to the Deathland of Tuoni, a perilous island that is reached by passing through fen, forest, mead and marsh, then by a week's walking through brambles, a week through hazel and a week through juniper. At last he reaches the island, where he almost succumbs to an evil enchantment intended to lull him to sleep and into lifelong imprisonment. He escapes from Tuoni, but is still without the words. He is sitting on a hillside, wondering where he should next seek them, when he is approached by a shepherd. The shepherd tells him that he must enter the underworld and find the dead hero Wipunen, on whose tongue can be found 'a thousand words of wisdom'. He offers to show Vainamoinen the road that leads to Wipunen's grave, deep within the earth – but warns him that to reach it he will have to 'journey over the points of needles, the edges of swords and the blades of axes'.

Wary of this warning, Vainamoinen goes to Ilmarinen the smith and asks him how to pass over swords and axes unharmed. The smith answers by stoking his furnace and forging a pair of copper soles for Vainamoinen's shoes. Wearing these, he approaches the place where Wipunen is buried. It is marked by a cleft in the hillside, guarded by a tree. There, Vainamoinen sings a song to bring Wipunen back to life, and as Wipunen opens his vast mouth – the cleft in the hillside – Vainamoinen steps through it and into the tunnel of Wipunen's throat. The floor of the tunnel is, as the shepherd had foreseen, lined with the blades of axes and swords. But they cannot pierce Vainamoinen's copper soles. He reaches the 'spacious caverns' of Wipunen's vitals – and once he is there Wipunen begins to sing.

Wipunen sings for three days and three nights, telling his knowledge and reciting each of his spells. At the end of this time, Vainamoinen has learnt 'all the wisdom of the great magician'. He returns along the tunnel of swords and axes, and emerges into the sunlight of the outer world. Ilmarinen is waiting for him, and asks if he will now be able to finish his vessel. 'I have learnt a thousand magic words,' Vainamoinen replies, 'and among them are the lost-words that I sought.'

II

Ulpha – Cumbrian place-name, also *Ulfhou*, *Wolfhou*; meaning 'wolf-fell', from *ulfr* (Old Norse for 'wolf') and *haugr* ('hill, burial mound').

The morning after reading the story of Vainamoinen, I left my parents' house in the north-western Lake District, where I was staying, and drove out to the Cumbrian coast near Whitehaven, before turning south along the sea road. It was 30 October and a westerly gale was sweeping squalls off the Irish Sea. I saw the nuclear power station at Sellafield in silhouette, backlit against a sky of storm. Dome, pylon, stacks, chimneys, ash, beech, wind-shorn hawthorns, two firs, a cemetery and its crosses, all struck in black, and then the land dipping away and down to meet the silver sea. Clouds as big as islands rushed inland overhead, rain-bearing.

I had a strong sense of darkness rising, of the winter solstice not far distant, and of the world as disturbed. Cows with pale hides galloped behind barbed-wire fences, tossing their heads uneasily, and trembling in the gold light when they stopped. Water was rife from a fortnight of steady rain and a night of torrent. The asphalt showed silver, and in towns the drains bubbled over. A tall monkey-puzzle tree shivered in the wind.

At Ravenglass I turned north-east along the Esk Valley, and just past Muncaster Fell I went up and over to reach the plateau of low crags, moor, bracken and beck known as Birker Fell. Birker is a scarce place, and lonely. Once well wooded – its name is from the Norse *birkr*, meaning 'birch' – barely a tree still stands there now. There are two fragments of pine plantation, one of which shelters a Quaker burial ground from the eighteenth century, in which none of the dead are named or known.

Steeply then down the south slope of Birker Fell to Ulpha and Dunnerdale, and at Seathwaite I left the car and set off on foot, up a path that followed a beck-line and led me first through birch and larch woods, the stones gold with the millions of larch needles dropped from the trees by the wind and rain. Then I passed out of the trees and onto the bare stone-slopes of a conical mountain called Caw. A mile led to a pass between the shoulder of Caw and a lumpy low crag called Brock Barrow. This was the path's high point before it dropped again into the Lickle Valley. The pass was a brief but sharp-sided gorge, the sides boulder-strewn, and among the boulders was a jungle of juniper, which lent the scent of gin to the air.

I scrambled up between the boulders to the top of Brock Barrow. A summit stone was stained purple and white, with a black feather snagged by its vanes in the bilberry at its base. In the shelter of this ravens' perch I hunkered down to wait for Richard – for this was the place he had suggested we meet (no street corners or house addresses for Richard: just a grid reference and a crag name). Clear cloud layers, the shine of the estuary to the west, mudflats shimming the scant light, and the metalled sea beyond. A couple of ravens cursing and cawing. The rocks slick with the night's rain; the wind hefty.

From the pass two old tracks diverged across this hard country: one leading south-east to the Lickle Valley, and one due south towards the tiny settlement of Hoses and the fells of Dunnerdale. Ulpha Fell was to the north, and in that wild weather it was possible to imagine a wolf pack running there, through bracken and copse, past crag and over ghyll.

I watched the southerly path, getting colder, eyes rheumy in the wind. After half an hour, I was too cold to wait any longer. I dropped off the south slope of Brock Barrow and followed a high drystone wall towards Hoses, grateful for the wall's lee. A high stile crossed it. I climbed steps to the stile's summit and there at last was Richard, coming towards me over reedy ground, stalky and thin, moving with a shepherd's gait and in shepherd's garb too: a full stride, gumboots clacking against his shins, a flat cap, a long black coat, hands jammed into pockets to pull the coat tighter around. We met each other, grinned, shook hands, hugged. Years of letters, and now meeting here at last, with Dunnerdale suddenly patched green by sun to the north, and to the south the silver of moor-glisk.

III

Glisk – Cumbrian dialect verb, meaning 'to glitter, shine, sparkle, glisten'.

Richard Skelton is a keeper of lost words, and I had come to see him to learn some of his language, in its place. He is – what else is he? A musician, a writer, a glossarian, an archivist. Landscape, language and loss are the three great subjects of his work, and they are at its heart because of a tragedy.

In 2004 Richard's wife Louise died. I don't know how she died; I have never asked and he has never told. She was in her late twenties; he also. Richard, born and brought up in Lancashire, retreated to the West Pennine Moors of that county, close to his birthplace. There, struggling with grief, he began to walk the moors of the nearby parish of Anglezarke. His walking soon took on the status of ritual: a pilgrimage-like beating of the moor's bounds, a labyrinth-like exploration of its interior. In his own words, he 'limned the edges of its streams and rivers, followed the contours of its hills, the eaves of its woods'. The purpose of the walking was unclear even to him, perhaps especially to him: some mixture of distraction, diversion, expiation and commemoration. He began also to note the moor's phenomena, to record its languages (natural and human), and to explore its history in the relatively few archives that documented it.

His existence at this time of his life was solitary, tending to spectral. A haunted man, he was drawn to haunted places: ruined steadings, abandoned mine-workings. He came to know the moor's fall-lines, its adits and its hags. He reached and counted the 'seventeen thresholds that grant access to the moor'. He made hundreds of hours of field recordings of its sounds, and he also began to make music about and upon the moor. Some of this music was fugitive in composition and performance, played once on violin at the crook of a stream or the mouth of a swale. Some of it he recorded. Some of these sites he returned to repeatedly, playing music at them over and over again. He restrung his violin with heavier and heavier gauges of wire, until it possessed the reverberatory power of a small cello, and trembled his body as he played. Gradually, over five years of walking and working, a major body of music – echoic, repetitive, faded and fading; a minimalist sound-palette; shades of Arvo Pärt or Brian Eno – emerged, itself ghosted by missing partner-pieces: all those compositions that had been played to no audience but air and the moor grass.

There also emerged a book, eventually titled *Landings*, published in its first form in 2009. Like the music that accompanies it, *Landings'* acoustics are shaped by dearth. Both sound and text are devoted to a kind of echo-location, used to measure the relations of distanced entities. The terrible absence of Louise is compensated for in *Landings* by means of a pained record-keeping of the Anglezarke moor – a textual summoning-back of its lost and forgotten. The book possesses an archival intensity: long lists of the names of farms once active on the moor, retrieved from historical maps; or lexicons of Lancashire dialect terms, presented as litanies spoken against loss:

Hare-gate: an opening in a hedge sufficient for the passage of hares.

Slack: a hollow between sand-hills on the coast. Also a depression between hills.

Water-gait: a gully or rift in the rock, which in summer is the bed of a streamlet, but in winter is filled with a torrent.

Landings is a work appalled by amnesia, by the torrent of daily forgetting – the black noise that pours always over the world's edge. In *Landings*, all omissions are losses: it aspires to a completion of memory that is impossible. Nature is sometimes seen as fabulously memorious (pollen records that archive the species composition of forests that vanished 3,000 years ago) and sometimes as rife with loss (the bodies of creatures mulching unseen into the moor). The book's knowingly hopeless wager is that if a moor's memories might somehow be retrieved in full and perfectly preserved, then so might those of a person. 'Could I reconstruct the landscape from its stress pattern? From the rhythm, the cadence, of its utterance? . . . Is there a clue within each subtle voicing, which, when gathered together, provides a key with which to sound the landscape?' Completion is the work's futile ideal, and a deep sorrow seeps through it, sprung from the knowledge that no place can be fully mapped, and that the dead can never return to us. Simultaneously it longs for that power of utterance also sought by Vainamoinen: the magic words that might finish the forecastle, or entreat the vanished back to sight.

Slight signs of hope are present, though, in both the music and the text that Richard produced in the course of those sad years. Among the obscure private rituals he developed on Anglezarke was the burial of objects in unmarked places on the moor: boxes, photographs, notebooks. He gave these items to the landscape as future relics, finding in that act a means to mitigate the erosion of memory. Something desperately dear had been taken from him without his consent, and he responded to this by giving: in the face of disappearance, offering; in the face of theft, gift.

And this was how I first came to know Richard: as a giver of gifts. Packages would arrive through the post: a tiny glass phial with granules of quartz-sand in it; an ash-box containing found items. Books, chapbooks, pamphlets, all exquisitely printed, containing poems and prose-poems, rich with words – glossaries of place-terms, lists of place-names, threaded through with dialect quotations, lexical relics from Gaelic, Icelandic, Old English or Manx. 'Where before I collected fragments found on . . . the moor,' Richard had written near the end of *Landings*, 'I now gather words that were once used to call upon the landscape.' I liked that phrase 'call upon', with its two contrasting senses: one magical, grand, powerful (to summon the forces or spirits of); the other homely, intimate (to visit a friend, to drop in or drop by).

We shared a passion for word-hoards, dictionaries, etymology and precise place-language. Both of us felt that this largely lost vocabulary of landscape was obscure but not obsolete, and that its retrieval might be of value. 'Perhaps there is a glimpse of something behind such words,' Richard had written:

a hint at a way of looking at the world that is now also lost, an attention to the form of things and a care, a generosity in the bestowing of names. *Brog* is not simply a branch, but a broken branch. *Lum* is not just a pool, but a deep pool . . . Each word has its own feel on the tongue, its own sound, an inherent poetry. Moreover, each word tells us something subtly different about its referent, and our attitudes to it . . . Could these old forms vivify and invigorate contemporary language, by virtue of their difference, their strangeness?

IV

Breast-hee – north Lancashire dialect noun, meaning 'the mouth of a tunnel which has been made into the side of a hill, the shaft being horizontal rather than vertical'.

From our meeting point at the stile, Richard and I turned back up towards the summit of Brock Barrow, talking as we walked. I wanted to show Richard the ravens' perch where I had waited, and he to show me an old tuff quarry on the barrow's west shoulder. We climbed a zigzag path up a slope of tailings and clitter, then dropped down into the depression of the quarry itself. Cleaved and riven stone lay about, chaotic on the quarry floor, but stacked neatly as shelved books at its edges. Stone structures of uncertain purpose stood at the site's perimeter: shelters in which to carry out the riving, perhaps. They had once been well built with the stone that lay amply to hand; now their walls had slumped and splayed to reveal flares of flat-faced tuff slabs.

The source of all this worked stone was clear: a bare cliff, twenty-five feet high or so, the lower face of which had been hollowed out in blocky chunks by fire or explosion, back when the quarry was active. The tuff had formed around 450 million years ago, during the Ordovician. Though densely welded, it split cleanly and this made it a desirable building stone, worth the vast human effort – for a few years at least – to blast it, rive it and dress it into slabs. The whole quarry zone had undergone a complex dilapidation, and it had about it now, unused, something of the air of a reliquary.

In the wind shelter of the quarry, we looked seawards. Richard pointed out the fold of fell that hid his cottage, and other landmarks that were familiar to him and new to me. 'So many kinds of mist and cloud come in off the sea here,' he said. 'Haars creep in low, thicker mists rush over us. Some mornings we pull back the curtains and it's just blank white beyond.'

He talked a little about the years after Anglezarke, when he had begun to re-emerge into the world. He had met a Canadian called Autumn Richardson, like him gentle of manner and fascinated by what she called 'place-name poetry', 'word-list poetry', and 'the economy and beauty of certain lexicons'. He and Autumn began to collaborate – and they also fell in love. While travelling in England in 2008, they passed through the spare landscape of the western

Cumbrian uplands, and both found themselves strongly drawn to the region. So they moved there, to a cottage in Ulpha, and began to close-map the area around their cottage and further up the Dunnerdale valley, making new works out of this old place. They delved into its natural histories and constructed lists of the grasses and flowers likely to have flourished in the area once the glacial ice had retreated, at the end of the Pleistocene. 'Ulpha is still inhabited by the ghosts of lost flora and fauna,' Autumn wrote; 'these are the echoes left in its place-names, traces that even now, centuries later, can be uncovered and celebrated.' They learnt to navigate the linguistic-historical complexities of toponymy and language in Cumbria, heavily influenced as it was by the Scandinavian settlement that took place in the late eighth to eleventh centuries, but also by Gaelic and Old English: a mixture brought about by the impacts of trade, exploration and colonization on the region.

They moved to the Burren in the west of Ireland for eighteen months, and then in 2011 they returned to the Ulpha area to complete work they felt to be unfinished. They found a tiny cottage of three rooms, tuff-walled and slate-roofed, in a cluster of farm buildings high under Stickle Pike, on the south slopes of Caw. The first winter they were there the snow lay until May. After six months of snow came six months of rain. But the work poured from them in spite of or because of the weather: beautiful work in collaboration or individually, work that seemed unhurried and unshaped by the demands of anything but their own fascinations. Together they had made a booklet called *Wolfhou*, gathering text fragments and place-name poems about the Ulpha valley; and another called *Relics*, each page of which showed the cross-section of a different tree (ash, alder, birch, elm, hazel, juniper) printed white onto black pages, in which each growth-ring was a circle of increasingly ancient words for that species, such that dendrochronology and etymology came to overlay one another. Richard also made a sequence of 'text-rivers' and 'myth-poems' called *Limnology*, through which flowed the terms in English and its commingled languages for rivers, streams, lakes and other inland water-forms. *Limnology* began life with water-words found in the Cumbrian dialect, and then, as Richard put it, 'gathered pace, taking in tributaries from Icelandic, Old English, Gaelic, Manx, Irish, Welsh, Old Welsh and Proto-Celtic (a hypothetical, reconstructed language thought to have been spoken in the Late Bronze Age)'.

~

It began to rain again, a spittery smirr, as we left the Brock Barrow quarry and picked our way south towards Hoses and the cottage.

'I want to show you a raven's nest on the way home,' said Richard. 'It's in another quarry, a bigger one. Just a short diversion. There's a tunnel there too you might like to see.'

The path was quick with running water, still rushing off the fells from the night's soaking. '*Limnology* came about,' Richard said, as we splashed down the track, 'because of all the rain in our first year here. The summer and autumn were so wet that the tracks became streams, and the paths became rivers.'

A few hundred yards from the cottage, he led us up a rising side track that curved under the flank of a fell called Fox Haw. It ran to an area of old workings, much bigger than the Brock Barrow quarry. Every slope and shoulder of ground was covered with small shining shards of tuff: chain-mail for the terrain. Sound echoed sharply off the stone surface, the shards clinking and ringing as we shifted them underfoot.

The path led us into a tiny valley, its side-slopes shining with clitter and slip, that narrowed into the hillside. And the valley ended in a black hole, four feet high and two across. It was the mouth of a tunnel. Two great guard stones flanked it, and a thick-trunked holly grew across it, as if to bar the way. The holly rose to ten feet, and among its glossy leaves were berry clusters. From the lintel of the tunnel mouth ran a ragged fringe of water.

I felt an eerie tremor of recognition.

'Have you been in?' I asked.

'Only to the entrance, never further.'

We reached the guard stones. I turned sideways and squeezed past the holly and under the fringe of water that ran icy down my neck. I shivered, but not only from the cold. Away from me stretched the tunnel, arch-roofed and shapely. I could see perhaps twenty feet along it; beyond that, blackness. It was flooded with clear water to the depth of twelve inches or so, and I could see that in the water lay hundreds of blades of tuff – sharp like the edges of swords, or the heads of axes.

The invitation to enter this intimidating place could not be refused. But neither of us had a torch or matches, let alone copper-soled shoes. We decided to go back to Richard and Autumn's cottage, and then return to the tunnel with full bellies and green wellies.

Autumn saw us approaching along the road, and she came out to greet us, smiling warmly, instantly welcoming. The cottage had fresh-painted eaves. A pan of potato soup was bubbling on the stove, and a loaf of fresh bread made by Richard was on the table. I had wondered if their home would possess some of the austere spectrality of their preoccupations, but it was a busy, happy space: snug and sheltered, quickly full of laughter and kindness. A cello leaned in the corner, two violins were held upright by hooks on a white wall, and next to them had been fixed three piebald oystercatcher feathers, decreasing in size from left to right. Everywhere were books, many of them glossaries, thesauruses and dictionaries. The wind flung rain against the windows with a fat clatter.

'It's getting even wilder out there,' said Richard.

We sat on the floor, drinking tea, and words and stories spilled out of them both: about people we had in common, discoveries they had made, projects they had underway.

'We don't normally talk to anyone except each other!' said Autumn, apologetically.

But I loved their company, and I admired their self-reliance: the nettle patch they cultivated for tea and soup, the tiny vegetable plot fenced off for them in the corner of a field by the farmer from whom they rented the cottage, in which they grew carrots and beetroot.

'We eat well in the summer, at least,' said Autumn.

And I admired the commitment needed to work together and produce such original texts. They pulled books from the shelves, told stories. I scribbled down etymologies, titles, words.

'There's a word I'm fascinated by at the moment,' Richard said. '*Hummadruz*. It means a noise in the air that you can't identify, or a sound in the landscape whose source is unlocatable.' It was good to have a word for that: the white noise of a place, an ambient murmur that lacked referent or source.

They talked a little about their years in Ulpha, and about lonely Devoke Water, a lake that lay on the far west of Birker Fell, and the circuit of whose tear-shaped shoreline I had once walked. 'If you keep going westwards from the tip of Devoke,' Richard said, 'you'll find a scatter of cairns, not there for waymarking. A similar scatter lies at the east of Birker, between Rough Crag and Great Worm Crag. No one's been able to date them for certain, but they're clearly of sepulchral origin, maybe Bronze Age. Birker is a funerary landscape.'

I thought about all the barrows, the borrans, the bields and the burial cairns I knew here in Cumbria. I thought, too, about the quarries Richard and I had seen that day, and how across Birker, as across Cumbria and so much British upland, the landscape is riddled with abandoned mines and quarries – copper, lead, slate, gold, iron, tuff – and their associated tunnels, adits, levels, scaurs and workings. The Lake District landscape had been dug into since the Neolithic, for the two main reasons that people ever enter the underland: to leave something within it (bodies, ashes, ritual objects) and to fetch something out of it (stone, mineral, metal, memory, metaphor).

I also recalled something Richard had written about the acoustics of landscapes: how, in certain places, sounds subside rather than vanish, 'receding below the threshold of hearing to commingle with the residual undersong – the map . . . of all melodies'. I liked that idea of 'undersong', and as the sound of the falling rain outside the cottage got louder and louder, I imagined the water finding its way along the paths and the gaits and the bournes, and down into the hills, through cracks, seams and runnels.

V

Eawl-leet – north Lancashire noun, variant pronunciation of *owl-light*, meaning 'twilight, dusk'.

Late in the afternoon, as dark was falling, Richard and I left the cottage and walked back up towards the quarries and the tunnel. The rain was drenching now, the heaviest rain I had been in for months, and within minutes we were wet through. I could feel rain streaming down the inside of my trousers and into my shoes. Richard had only found one pair of wellingtons, and they had holes in the soles. He was wearing the holey wellies. I was in trainers.

'At least we don't need to worry about getting our feet wet,' I said.

We walked on up the quarry track, which was also a stream. I wondered if the tunnel would be so flooded as to be unenterable.

'All Hallow's Eve is the time when the veil between the two worlds is at its thinnest,' said Richard.

'Does that make this a good time or a bad time to explore abandoned mine-workings?' I asked.

We reached the clitter valley. *Ting, ting*, the sounds of the stone as high as coin on glass. There at its end was the mouth of the tunnel of swords and axes, black and intimidating. There were the guard stones and the holly. I had a torch with a weak beam. I flashed it down the tunnel. Water was coursing through the roof, showing silver in the beam, like silk. The walls streamed with water – but the level on the tunnel floor had risen only by a few inches.

I slipped between the guard stones and stepped down onto the blades. Richard followed me. Quickly the outer world was left behind, as if a door had been closed, and we were in a space of darkness and new noises: an echo chamber reverberating with the sounds of moving water. I felt the prickle in the neck that signals risk. I sloshed onwards into the darkness, the blades rucking beneath my feet.

The tunnel led deeper into the hill. After a minute or two its route kinked to the right, and the acoustics altered. The further in we got, the less water came through the roof of the tunnel, until it slowed to a trickle, then to drops. Richard lit a tea candle, cupping it in his hand, though the wax ran onto his palm and set there. I switched off my torch, preferring the flame light, which flickered warmly on the walls.

'There's a breeze coming towards us,' Richard said.

We stopped, and he held the candle still. Its flame leaned back towards him, and now I could feel the breeze too, fresh and white on my face.

Suddenly, out of the darkness, I could see that the tunnel roof had collapsed. Slabs and hunks of tuff crammed the passage. There was no way through. So we sat on the rubble of the ruckle, lifted our feet from the blades and the water, and waited there silently, listening, far into the hill.

'Look at the candle,' said Richard. The flame was behaving curiously again: now it was being sucked towards the collapse, then held at a slant for a second, and then released, so that it sprang back to the upright and flickered there, before leaning again, as if something vast were inhaling, then exhaling, out beyond the collapse. *Lean, release, flicker; lean, release, flicker*.

'Can you hear that?' I asked. Richard could; a sound that was not water, a high murmur or note, whose source we could not identify – an undersong, a hummadruz.

We stayed for perhaps five minutes at the collapse and then returned as we had come, emerging at last between the guard stones and into the owl-light, the still-heavy rain, and a white mist that was thick enough to stop sight at a few yards. Sounds came from the mist: a raven croak, the hiss of raindrops striking heather stalks, the rush and rickle of stream over gravel. We left the quarry and walked back down the path which had become a rill, a strife, a strint, and a thousand other magic words for water.

GLOSSARY V

Underlands

Chambers and Burial Sites

barrow burial mound of earth or stones raised over a grave (Neolithic barrows tend to be lozenge-shaped; Bronze Age barrows tend to be round) **English, especially southern and eastern England**

càirn burial mound of stones raised over a grave **Gaelic**

catacomb underground cemetery, usually galleried and with recesses for tombs **English**

ciste burial chamber or coffin made of stone or a hollowed-out tree **Gaelic**

creeg burial mound **Cornish**

cromlech megalithic tomb consisting of a large flat stone laid on upright ones **Welsh**

dolmen megalithic tomb consisting of a large flat stone laid on upright ones **Breton**

fogou artificial cave, earth-house or covered tunnel **Cornwall**

kirkasukken buried dead (as distinguished from those who have a watery grave – those drowned at sea) **Shetland**

lowe grave-mound **Midlands**

mole-country graveyard **Suffolk**

quoit flat capstone or covering stone topping a *cromlech* or *dolmen* **Cornwall**

souterrain underground chamber or passage **archaeological**

tuaim   burial mound **Irish**

tumulus   burial mound, usually of earth; sepulchral hillock or knoll **Middle English**

undercroft   crypt, vault or subterraneum, especially one beneath a church or chapel **southern England**

Mines and Quarries

adit   roughly horizontal passage introduced into a mine for the purpose of access or drainage **mining**

arse-loop   rope chair used when repairing shafts **Pitmatical (north-east England)**

bell-pit   bell-shaped shaft **mining**

breast-hee   mouth of a tunnel which has been made into the side of a hill, the shaft being horizontal rather than vertical **Lancashire**

bunny hole   entrance to a mine **Cornwall**

camouflet   subterranean cavity formed by a bomb exploding beneath the surface of the earth **military**

canch   stone that is above or below a seam of coal and that has to be removed to reach the coal **Pitmatical (north-east England)**

coffen, mungler   open mine, quarry **Cornish**

dumble-hole   derelict clay-pit or quarry **north Herefordshire** *flash*   water body, often large, formed in areas where coal mining took place and subsidence has since occurred **geographical**

fossick   to search for something by rummaging, to prospect for minerals (from Cornish *feusik*, meaning 'fortunate') **Cornwall**

grass   ground level for a mine **Cornwall**

gruff   mine **south-west England**

gruffy ground   remnant landscape of former lead mining **Somerset**

gwag   hollow space in a mine (from Cornish *gwag*, meaning 'empty') **Cornwall**

horod   Irish navvy slang for the path leading to a tunnel or mine mouth **Somerset**

hull   underground shed **Cornwall**

hushing   process of damming water and releasing it to assist with the extraction of minerals, especially lead ores, in the uplands. *Hushes* are the small V-shaped valleys, remains of dams and heaps of spoil that this process leaves behind **mining**

leat   open watercourse in or near a mine **Cornwall, Devon**

monek   mineral-rich ground **Cornish**

scumfished   feeling suffocated at depth in a mine **Pitmatical (north-east England)**

stenak   tin-rich terrain **Cornish**

sump dip in the floor of a mine or cave in which water collects **mining**

wheal mine-works **Cornwall**

yeo a stream or drain (in mining) **south-west England**

Pits, Caves, Holes

berry group of rabbit holes having internal communication **Exmoor**

cave-pearls pearl-like pebbles of calcium carbonate that form around flecks or specks of grit **speleological**

choke jumble of boulders requiring careful negotiation **speleological**

cladd trench, pit, place where anything is hidden or buried **Welsh**

crundle thicket in a hollow through which a stream leads **Hampshire, Sussex**

doline depression or basin, often funnel-shaped, in a limestone landscape **geological**

dripstone calcium carbonate deposited by dripping water, often in elaborate 'melted-wax' formations **speleological**

dúlaoisc sea-level cave **Irish**

ear-dipper cavers' slang for a passage that is low and almost full of water **speleological**

flowstone   calcium carbonate deposited by running water, often in elaborate 'drapery' formations **speleological**

gaur   terrace-like formation of *flowstone* that traps miniature lagoons of water within its banks **speleological**

gew   hollow, cleft **Cornish**

gloup, glupe   opening in the roof of a sea cave through which the pressure of incoming waves may force air to rush upwards, or water to jet and spout **Hebrides, Orkney, Shetland**

helictite   coral-like stalactite that grows in a curved and twisted lateral formation, seeming to defy gravity **speleological**

helier   cave into which the tide flows **Shetland**

hell-kettle   deep black gulf or abyss; a name locally applied to holes or pools popularly supposed to be bottomless **northern England**

hwamp   hollow in the ground **Shetland**

jaw-hole   gaping fissure, abyss **Yorkshire**

jook-hole   hare hole in a dyke **Galloway**

katavothron   subterranean channel or deep chasm formed by the action of water **geological**

lunky   gap in a fence or dyke (big enough to let sheep through but not cattle) **Galloway**

pluais   underground hollow; cave; den **Irish**

plunge-basin   deep hollow or cavity excavated at the foot of a waterfall by the action of the falling water **geological**

ruckle   maze of stacked boulders in a cave passage, often dangerously loose **speleological**

scailp   cleft or fissure; sheltering place beneath rock **Irish**

swale, swallet, swallow   hole where a stream enters the earth **southern England**

talamh-toll   opening in the ground, sometimes over an underground burn **Gaelic**

thorough-shutts   hole burrowed by a rabbit through a hedge **Suffolk**

vuggy   of rock: full of cavities **Cornwall**

weem   inhabited cave or underground dwelling place **Scots**

wholve   short arched or covered drain under a path **Essex**

Tracks and Paths

BOAT   Byway Open to All Traffic: in England and Wales a (category of) public right of way open to all types of vehicle on the basis of historical evidence of vehicular use, but used chiefly as a footpath or bridleway **official**

boreen   small, seldom-used road, usually with grass growing up the middle **Hiberno-English**

bostal pathway up a hill, generally very steep **Kent, Sussex**

cahsy, cahzy raised road or footway at a place liable to flood **Essex**

cansey, cawnie causeway, raised path **Suffolk**

carpet-way smooth grass road or lane **Kent**

ceuffordd holloway, narrow sunken road **Welsh**

ceum known path, often out to moorland shielings **Gaelic**

chase green lane **East Anglia**

ciseach improvised bridge or path across a stream **Irish**

cooms high ridges in muddy tracks, which rise between wheel-ruts **East Anglia**

drong narrow path between hedges **south-west England**

foylings deer tracks through a thicket **Northamptonshire**

ginnel long, narrow passage between houses, either roofed or unroofed **northern England**

holloway lane or path that has been grooved down into the surrounding landscape due to the erosive power of, variously, feet, wheels and rainwater **Dorset**

lagger broad, green lane **Herefordshire**

lich-way, lych way corpse-way, way of the dead: path along which bodies are carried to burial **Devon**

lopeway footpath not adapted to wheeled vehicles **East Anglia**

lyste-way green way on the edge of a field **Kent**

muxy-rout deep muddy wheel-rut **Exmoor**

perquage sanctuary path leading from church to sea by the shortest route **Jèrriais (Jersey Norman)**

popey stretch of road or lane allowed to become derelict, overgrown and unused **Kent**

prickings footprints of a rabbit **Northamptonshire**

pukkering kosh signpost **Anglo-Romani**

rack path made by hares or rabbits **Cotswolds**

ramper raised pathway through muddy ground **Fenland**

rudge deep wheel-rut **Northamptonshire**

sarn causeway, paved way of long usage **Welsh**

scort footprints of horses, cattle or deer **Cotswolds**

sheer-way bridle path or permissive way through private land **Kent**

strodi lane between two walls **Shetland**

tacks zigzag way up a cliff or hillside **Isle of Man**

twitchel narrow path between hedges **Midlands**

twycene fork in a road, a forked way **Old English**

walks unenclosed lands and commons **Suffolk**

wattery-lonnin neglected lane where water is allowed to run undrained **Cumbria** *wence*   centre of a crossroads **Kent**

wilsome   of a way or path: leading through wild and desolate regions **Scots**

Ways of Walking

bamble   to walk unsteadily and awry, to shamble **East Anglia**

beetle-scrunchers   large feet **Suffolk**

bonnleac   sore on the sole of the foot, often caused by walking barefoot **Irish**

buks   to walk with difficulty, as if walking through water **Shetland**

crabhsganach   awkward on one's feet, owing to their being sore **Gaelic**

currick   cairn of stones to guide travellers **Cumbria, Durham, Northumberland**

dander   to stroll leisurely **Ireland**

dew-beater   trail-blazer, pioneer **East Anglia, Hampshire**

dobbles   hard snow or mud collected under the heels of boots **Suffolk**

doddle   to walk slowly and pleasurably **Northern Ireland**

fleggin, lampin   walking with big steps **Galloway**

flinks   to ramble in a rompish manner, as a frolicsome girl might **Shetland**

fuddle	to potter around **Herefordshire**
haik, hake	to tramp, trudge or otherwise effortfully wend one's way **Yorkshire**
hansper	pain in the muscles of the legs after long walking **Shetland**
harl	to drag or trail oneself, to go with dragging feet **northern England, Scotland**
hippit	stiff in the hips **Scots**
hirple	to hobble, walk with a limp **Northern Ireland**
hit the grit	to start a journey on the road **Suffolk**
hochle	to walk in a slovenly way **Northern Ireland**
honky donks	heavy boots **Suffolk**
milestone inspector	tramp, gentleman of the road **Herefordshire**
nuddle	to walk in a dreamy manner with head down, as if preoccupied **Suffolk**
pad	to make a path by walking on a surface before untracked, as in new-fallen snow or land lately ploughed **East Anglia**
peddel	to walk in a hesitating manner, as a child **Shetland**
plutsh	to flap with the feet in walking, as seafowl do **Shetland**
poche	to tread ground when wet **Herefordshire**
prole	stroll, pleasurable short walk **Kent**

scimaunder to wander about, take a devious or winding course **Yorkshire**

scrambly of rough terrain: necessitating scrambling or clambering **hill-walking**

shulve to saunter with extreme laziness **East Anglia**

slomp to walk heavily, noisily **Essex**

soodle to walk in a slow or leisurely manner, stroll, saunter (John Clare) **poetic**

spandle to leave marks of wet feet or shoes on a floor, as a dog does with its pawprints **Kent**

spangin' walking vigorously **Scots**

spurring following the track of a wild animal **Exmoor**

stravaig to wander aimlessly, unguided by outcome or destination **Scots**

striddle to walk uncomfortably, with an unusual gait **Northern Ireland**

talmraich noise of footsteps on the ground **Gaelic**

troll to ramble, walk **Cambridgeshire**

vanquishin aimless visiting around on foot **Galloway**

yew-yaw to walk crookedly **Suffolk**

yomp to march with heavy equipment across difficult terrain **military**

7
North-Minded

In certain regions of the far north, where the dust content of the atmosphere is close to zero, light is able to move unscattered through the air. In such places, under such conditions, faraway objects can often appear uncannily close at hand to the observer. The lichen patterns on a boulder can be seen from a hundred yards; cormorants on a sea-stack seem within reach of touch. Distance enables miracles of scrutiny; remoteness is a medium of clarification.

I am, and have been for as long as I know, north-minded: drawn to high latitudes and high altitudes, and drawn also to those writers and artists for whom northerliness is a mode of perception as well as a geographical position: Matsuo Bashō's *Narrow Road to the Deep North* (1689); Philip Pullman's *Northern Lights* (1995), with its armoured bears and cold that bites to the bones; Farley Mowat's *Never Cry Wolf* (1963); Ezra Pound's translations of classical Chinese frontier poems; the boreal phases of Eric Ravilious's art; the maps and type-works of Alec Finlay; the fiction of the Hebridean sailor and storyteller Ian Stephen; Margaret Atwood's explorations of 'the malevolent north'; W. H. Auden's poems of jetties, night-sailings and the *simmer-dim* . . . Most powerfully, though, and for years now, I have been drawn to the northern prose of Barry Lopez, which I first met in 1997, the year I turned twenty-one.

That summer I spent several weeks in north-west Canada,

climbing in the Rockies and hiking the wilderness trails of the Pacific coast. I was alone for long periods of time, with many hours to kill in tents, so I got through a lot of books. Whenever I came back to cities between trips, I would head for the nearest bookstore to restock. I was browsing shelves in Vancouver when I found a copy of Lopez's *Arctic Dreams*. There were good reasons not to buy it. One: I had never heard of Lopez. Two: the book's subtitle – 'Imagination and Desire in a Northern Landscape' – struck me as Mills & Boony. Three: it was expensive for my budget. Four, and above all: it was *heavy* – almost 500 pages long and printed on thick paper. Because I had to carry everything I read, I'd taken to assessing my books according to a pemmican logic: maximum intellectual calorie content per ounce.

But for some now-forgotten reason I disregarded these objections, bought the book, and read it while I walked the Pacific Rim path on the east coast of Vancouver Island, camping on surf-crashed beaches, and suspending my food from trees in compliance with the bear-safety code. I read it then, and it amazed me. I read it again, lost my copy somewhere near Banff, bought another copy, gave it to my father as a present, borrowed it back off him and read it again, and again, and again. I still have that copy (with a red-ink inscription from me to my father, dated 18 August 1997): the spine is cracked, the uppers ripped, the margins dense with annotations, and the pages are held together with Sellotape, now brown.

Arctic Dreams changed the course of my life: it showed me how to write. Its combination of natural science, anthropology, cultural history, philosophy, reportage and lyrical observation revealed that non-fiction could be as experimental in form and beautiful in its language as any novel. Its gyres from the phenomenal to the philosophical proved to me that first-hand experience could be related to broader questions of place-consciousness. And the other lesson that it taught me – though it would take me longer to understand it – was that while writing about landscape often begins in the aesthetic, it must always tend to the ethical. Lopez's intense attentiveness was, I came later to realize, a form of moral gaze, born of his belief that if we attend more closely to something then we are less likely to act selfishly towards it. To exercise a care of attention towards a place – as towards a person – is to achieve a sympathetic intimacy with it. His prose – priestly, intense, grace-noted – is driven by the belief that 'it is possible to live wisely on the land, and to live well', and by a conviction that the real achievement of place-writing might be to help incorporate nature into the moral realm of human community.

Before writing *Arctic Dreams*, Lopez had travelled for several years in the Canadian north. He passed through the diverse territories of the region: the orange-and-ochre badlands of Melville Island; the deep-cut canyons of the Hood River; Baffin Bay, where big bergs jostle slowly; and Pingok Island in the Beaufort Sea, where the tides are so slight that one can 'stand toe-to at the water's edge, and, if one has the patience, see it gain only the heels of one's boots in six hours'. His sustained contact with these places brought him to a subtle understanding of the region. It also produced his austerely particular style as a writer. The Arctic, Lopez observes early on, has 'the classic lines of a desert landscape: spare, balanced, extended, and quiet' (one notes with admiration the adjectival balance – short-long-long-short – of that second clause). The same is true of Lopez's prose. Of all the great modern landscape writers, his style seems most purely to enact the terrain it describes.

When he began to write about the Arctic, Lopez was faced with the challenge of making language grip a landscape that is both huge and 'monotonic'. How was he to depict a realm of immensities and repetitions: 'unrelieved stretches of snow and ice' and 'plains of open water'? How was he to bring this stark and enigmatic landscape within reach of words, without trivializing or compromising it? Northern regions possess surfaces – stone, light, snow, ice, bright air – to which words will not easily cleave.

What Lopez understood was that detail anchors perception in a context of vastness. It is perhaps the defining habit of his style to make sudden shifts between the panoramic and the specific. Again and again, he evokes the reach and clarity of an Arctic vista – and then zooms in on the 'chitinous shell of an insect' lodged in a tuffet of grass, a glinting tracery of 'broken spider-webs', or 'the bones of a lemming' whose form resembles that of the 'strand of staghorn lichen next to them'. The effect for the reader of these abrupt perspectival jumps is exhilarating – as though Lopez has gripped you by the shoulder and pressed his binoculars to your eyes.

So many great northern artists and writers are, like Lopez, distinguished by what Robert Lowell called 'the grace of accuracy'. Thinking across their work, it becomes possible to deduce a shared metaphysics of northerliness: an exactness of sight; lyricism as a function of precision; an attraction to the crystalline image; shivers of longing, aurora-bursts of vision, and elegies of twilight. In the northern writers and artists to whose work I consistently return, the north represents not a retreat to an imagined distance, but rather a means of seeing more clearly and thinking more lucidly. Looking from afar – from present to past, from exile to homeland, from island back at mainland, mountain-top down at lowland – results not in vision's diffusion but in its sharpening; not in memory's dispersal but in its plenishment.

~

Lopez has long been vital to my understanding of the Arctic north. Vital to my understanding of the north of my own country has been the work of Nan Shepherd, and also that of the essayist and poet Peter Davidson. Davidson lives in what he calls a 'removed and exceptional part of Scotland': the wedge of land bounded to its south by the mountains of the Cairngorms, to its north by the waters of the Moray Firth, and that stretches eastwards to meet the North Sea between Peterhead and Aberdeen. A few miles from his house in the town of Turriff rises the five-toothed peak of Bennachie, on the slopes of which Agricola's auxiliaries fought and defeated the Caledonians – the northernmost Roman action undertaken during the centuries of occupation. Further west are the Ruthven Barracks, that lonely outpost – a Camp Bastion of its day – built by Hanoverian soldiers after the Jacobean rising of 1715. Davidson's latitude is a frontier latitude, then: around and beyond him issue the true 'northlands', whose cultures and landscapes have inspired his poetry, essays, scholarship and dreams for more than thirty years.

This is an 'exceptional part' of Scotland in that it has excepted itself from many of the conventions of British history and geography. Beaker inhumation is thought to have been practised there for two centuries longer than anywhere else in Europe. Catholicism thrived and was fomented there after the Reformation; loyalty to the House of Stuart persisted after the Revolution of 1688. It is a dissident region: not renegade, exactly, but fond of being able to mind its own business.

Like the landscapes out of which they chiefly arise, Davidson's poems and essays – *The Idea of North* (2005), *The Palace of Oblivion* (2008) and *Distance and Memory* (2013) – are bound together by a tight web of qualities (reticence, allusiveness, unshowiness); by a repertoire of moods (elegiac, desirous); by a cluster of tropes (shadows, gleams, light and its gradations, ice, cusps, thresholds); and by a palette of colours (the green-gold of summer, the silver-blues of winter, the bronzes of autumn). Davidson writes in a northern vernacular, exactly responsive to its regions, in which the specifics of terrain and weather are internalized as a kind of grammar. It is a style fine in its granulation, subtle in its shadings – and tinged throughout with a gentle melancholy.

Davidson, like Lopez, practises an acute attentiveness to the shifts and flux of landscape. He is observant – both in the devotional sense of regular habits adhered to, and the phenological sense of recording natural details. Paragraph after paragraph of his prose about the northlands glint with details born of long acquaintance and repeated seeing: in May there is 'a pencil-stripe of light beyond the pine trees on the northern horizon, the reflection of the brightness over Sutherland, relentless daylight over Norway'; a June evening brings 'green silence'; on October afternoons 'bright kingdoms . . . open in the Cairngorms'; soon afterwards 'brilliant depths of frost and the returning cold' signal winter's ascent. Such observations seem at first like jottings, but on examination turn out to be images of intricate faceting, as in this single-sentence description of a lake: 'A little stone jetty in still water: water like pewter, extraordinary water.' The extreme stillness of the sentence is in part a function of its verblessness, but is due also to the reflection of water within itself ('water: water'), an effect doubled again as the word *pewter* catches and supplely returns – with a ripple – the word *water*.

The artist Eric Ravilious 'noticed everything', Davidson writes. The same might be said of him. Ravilious saw 'the gradations of rust and soot on a tar-engine put away for the winter'. Davidson notices the '[f]ine gradations' that:

> mark this turn of the year to spring: the glass of the lake rising a little with the snow melt; steel drifts of ice on water like mercury. The first wood-anemones on the scrubbed table which runs the length of the room.

The 'rising' 'glass' of the lake suggests first a thermometric change, the temperature-creep of the coming spring; but it is also – and foremost – 'glass' as water-surface, rising in level as the snow-melt joins the winter water. 'Mercury' draws us back into the thermometer, but is at once an image of the ice's hard silver gleam. The intricacy of language here is a version of the intricacy of the handover of winter to spring – overlapped and shifting. Such careful slivering-out – the ability to discriminate without finicking – is one of the signatures of Davidson's style and sensibility. It results in a lyricism as delicate in its structures as an ash-frail. He is, like Lopez, a connoisseur of degrees; but like Lopez he also acknowledges those aspects of landscape that refuse such slivering-out – those infinitely subdivisible increments of change, such that one cannot say when a day becomes dark, only that it is so.

~

One August I visited Davidson at his high-halled, white-walled, hunkered-down house in a wooded fold of valley near the Aberdonian town of Turriff. After we had eaten, he took me up to a south-facing room that was thick with summer light, and there he opened the two pale-blue doors of a large wooden cabinet that stood against the back wall. It was, he explained, a cabinet of curiosities of his own devising, in homage to the great *Wunderkammern* or 'wonder-rooms' of the Renaissance and the Baroque, in which examples of natural history (*naturalia*), precious artefacts (*arteficialia*), scientific instruments (*scientifica*), findings from distant realms (*exotica*) and items of inexplicable origin and form (*mirabilia*) were gathered and displayed.

He reached into the cabinet and retrieved object after object, explaining to me the skein of stories that each drew behind it. For the individual compartments of the cabinet held remarkable things, among them a little dog modelled in unfired clay, Babylonian in origin; a sixteenth-century armourer's trial piece of a long face framed by a helmet in the form of a wolf's head with open jaws; an engraved brass box of seventeenth-century Low Countries manufacture, which once held one of the straws on which fell drops of the blood of the Jesuit Henry Garnet, executed in London on 3 May 1606, bloodstains which were said to have formed a likeness of his face; a slice of marble from a quarry near Bristol, in which the veinery had, by geological chance, formed into a perfect facsimile of a sad Victorian landscape of misty ploughlands at evening; and the oval case of an original Claude glass, the small, blackened pocket mirror designed to reproduce in its reflection of any landscape the softened tones and single focal point characteristic of the art of Claude Lorrain.

As the day dimmed, Peter spoke of these objects with a loving care and a sadness. His preoccupation with the *Wunderkammer* was, I saw that afternoon, temperamental as well as art-historical, and indeed his essays and poems often themselves resemble these curatorial cabinets – rich with discrete images but shot through with sadness (for the fragment always grieves for its whole).

Davidson's writing often aspires 'to capture the moment, lost and yet preserved forever'. His sentences devote themselves to the record of volatile subjects – textures of weather, tones of colour, a fall of light 'which dies even as the hand attempts to catch its likeness' – but they do so in foreknowledge of the failure of their task. The relationship between the fixed and the fugitive is at the heart of his work, and at the source of its melancholy. The inestimable value of the instant is proved by its perishability. The paragraphs of his essays, the verses of his poems: these act as what Thomas Browne in *Urne-Buriall* – his great 1658 meditation on corruption, pristination and retrieval – beautifully calls a 'conservatorie'. Yet none of these 'conservatories' is quite reliable, none fully sealed. All leak a little light. All are vulnerable to what Davidson calls 'the predatory loss that shadows all human pleasure'. Walking the coast of Arctic Finland in summer, he comes upon a cove:

> basalt rocks bordering the Baltic, with the dazzling track of the sun coming straight through the sandbar which sheltered the bay. A young man was swimming there, quietly and alone, swimming breaststroke with barely a ripple – until he moved out of the shadowed waters and his tow-fair head vanished in an instant into the brilliance of the high sun on the sea.

Here, the completion of the scene is also its annihilation: the swimmer cannot stay still, however tranquil his motion, and must move on from the shadows and into the irradiating 'high sun', which both illuminates and abolishes him.

Yes, melancholy steeps Davidson's language, and melancholy

differs from grief in its chronic nature: it is an ache not a wound, it lies deeper down, is longer lasting, is lived with rather than died of. We might perhaps imagine melancholy hydrologically, as a kind of groundwater – seeping darkly onwards, occasionally surfacing as depression or anguish. It is clear, reading Davidson's work, that he is someone for whom melancholy has been an enduring companion. When in an essay he writes that a 'black dog flickers in and out of the shadows at the edge of the lawns', this is at once a Labrador and a metaphor. His writing has the power to strike its readers with sorrow also, which is among the reasons why, although his essays often emerge out of the impulse to account for art, they are art themselves.

'We have gathered things about us which are of the place where we live,' Davidson remarks of the contents of his house and its garden. So many images in his work are of 'gatherings': gatherings of people who must perforce disperse, the gathering up of last things, lost things, late lustres. The 'moony silver' of a 'double-handed silver cup' on a table 'gathers the reflections of the garden and the summer and the bright sky into itself'. A bend in the stream 'breaks forward into the sunlight and the water draws the light into itself'. High tarns among peat and bracken 'hold the dimming sky', 'last light hangs reflected in mirrors inside the house', a 'pale yacht steers through the long dusk to far islands in the archipelago'. The act of 'gleaning' (a word which carries a shimmer of gleaming) occurs often in his writing – a fossicking after items of value, a gathering that is both a refusal of time's claims and a dark counting of losses.

Davidson's relationship with loss also explains the what-ifs, the returns-from-the-dead and the hypothetical dreams that recur in his essays and poems. One of these, the finest of them, concerns Eric Ravilious, who disappeared in 1942 off the coast of Iceland while flying a search-and-rescue mission for another downed plane. Radar ceased to register the plane's presence, radio contact was lost, and no trace was ever found of craft or crew. 'All the years I have been writing about Ravilious,' Davidson recalls in a late essay:

> I have occasionally dreamed about him: that he will come into the cold hall of a house which does not exist, a house smelling of coal fires; that he will begin to talk at once, shaking the Arctic Ocean off his dark hair as if it were only rainwater after all, as if he had been caught in the storm on a headland, benighted, laughing, painting out of doors.

Optical physics refers to a phenomenon known as the 'duct'. A duct is an atmospheric structure, born of a thermal inversion, which takes the form of a channel that traps light rays within a few minutes of the arc of the astronomical horizon. Because the curvature performed within a thermal inversion is stronger than the curvature of the earth's surface, light rays can be continuously guided along the duct, following the earth's own curvature, without ever diffusing up into space. In theory, therefore, if your eyes were strong enough to see that far, a duct would allow you to gaze around the whole earth and witness your own back and shoulders turned towards you. The existence of ducts has been theorized since the eighteenth century, but their science became more fully understood during the Second World War, when radar operators began observing returns from objects far beyond the normal horizon-limit. I think of Davidson's what-ifs as versions of the duct: strange spaces in which time's claims are stilled – and through which one might see so far into the future that it becomes the past.

~

Both Lopez and Davidson are north-minded – and both are topographic humanists. They see landscape not as a static diorama against which human action plays itself out, but rather as an active and shaping force in our imagination, our ethics, and our relations with each other and the world. In the work of both, place invests consciousness and geography is inseparable from morality. Throughout their writings recurs the idea that certain landscapes are capable of bestowing a grace upon those who pass through them or live within them. The stern curve of a mountain slope, a nest of wet stones on a beach, the bent trunk of a wind-blown tree: such forms can call out in us a goodness we might not have known we possessed. 'In a winter-hammered landscape,' writes Lopez, 'the light creates a feeling of compassion . . . it is possible to imagine a stifling ignorance falling away from us.' The north is, to both men, especially powerful in this regard. Its severities bring us to witness the transgression of our own limits; its austere beauties induce both modesty and heart-lift. 'The sharpness of the morning frost had cleared the air into a magnifying lens,' recalls Davidson of a pin-bright Cairngorm dawn. In wind-washed Arctic air that is 'depthlessly clear', observes Lopez, both terrain and mind stand revealed.

GLOSSARY VI

Northlands

Dusk, Dawn, Night and Light

aurora borealis Northern Lights: the phenomenon whereby bright streamers and curtains of coloured (reddish, greenish) light dance and swirl in the atmosphere, caused by charged particles from the sun interacting with atoms of the upper atmosphere **meteorological**

benighted overtaken by darkness while walking or climbing **mountaineering**

blinter dazzle, but with a particular sense of cold dazzle: winter stars or ice splinters catching low midwinter sunlight **Scots**

burr mistiness over and around the moon, a moon-halo **East Anglia**

dark hour interval between the time of sufficient light to work or read by and the lighting of candles – therefore a time of social domestic conversation ('We will talk that over at the dark hour') **East Anglia**

dimmity twilight **Devon**

doomfire sunset-light which has the appearance of apocalypse to it (Gerard Manley Hopkins) **poetic**

eawl-leet twilight, dusk (literally 'owl-light') **north Lancashire**

faoilleach last three weeks of winter and first three weeks of spring **Gaelic** *fireflacht* lightning without thunder; a flash of light which is seen in the sky, near the horizon, on autumn nights **Shetland**

glouse strong gleam of heat from sunshine **East Anglia**

goldfoil fork lightning that illuminates the sky with 'zigzag dints and creasings and networks of small many-cornered facets' (Gerard Manley Hopkins) **poetic**

green flash optical phenomenon occurring just after sunset or just before sunrise, in which a green spot is briefly visible above the upper rim of the sun's disc **optics**

grey morning twilight, early dawn **Exmoor**

grey-licht dusk; shortly before dawn **Galloway**

grimlins night hours around midsummer when dusk blends into dawn and it is hard to say if day is ending or beginning **Orkney**

haggering distortion of objects by atmospheric refraction **North Sea coast**

hjalta dance, different names for the peculiar dancing *simmer kloks,* appearance of the light on the horizon, along *simmer ree,* the tops of the hills, which is seen in sunny *simmermal brim,* summer weather **Shetland** *simmermal ton, titbow dance*

hoarlight 'burnished or embossed forehead of sky over the sundown, beautifully clear' (Gerard Manley Hopkins) **poetic**

hornlight   yellowish moonlight resembling the light emitted through a lantern's horn window (Gerard Manley Hopkins) **poetic**

mathionnettes   Northern Lights **Jèrriais (Jersey Norman)**

mirkshut   twilight **Herefordshire**

pink   of a candle, star, etc.: to shine with a faint or wavering light, to glimmer, to twinkle **southern England**

plathadh grèine   sudden temporary glimpse of the sun between passing clouds **Gaelic**

shepherd's lamp   first star that rises after sunset (John Clare) **Cambridgeshire, Northamptonshire**

shivelights   splinters of light (Gerard Manley Hopkins) **poetic**

shreep   of mist: to clear away partially **East Anglia**

Frost and Cold

aingealach   acute numbness in great frost **Gaelic**

atteri   bitterly cold **Shetland**

clumst   benumbed with cold **northern England**

crool   to huddle miserably together from cold **Herefordshire**

dis   not able to stand cold well **Gaelic**

dùbhlachd   depth of winter **Gaelic**

finger-cold cold that is not bitter, but enough to make the fingers tingle **Kent**

fresh of weather: the breaking of a spell of frost **Scots**

geal-cauld ice-cold **Scots**

glince, glincey slippery, icy **Kent**

haari cold that is hard and piercing **Shetland**

horripilation erection of the hairs on the skin by contraction of the cutaneous muscles, often caused by cold **medical**

hovvery, kivvery very shivery, numb with cold **Kent**

hussy to chafe or rub the hands when they are cold **Kent**

jeel frost **Scots**

knit up of a bird: to fluff up feathers as a response to cold **Herefordshire**

kreemee shivery with cold **Exmoor**

nurped freezing **Herefordshire**

peart cold **Devon**

pinjy cold **Galloway**

pinnish to shrink from the effect of cold **Shetland**

plucky of earth: broken and rigid following a hard frost **Essex**

skinner cold day **North Sea coast**

stirn to tremble from the effect of cold **Shetland**

wurr   hoar frost **Herefordshire**

yark   cold; wild, stormy weather **Exmoor**

Wind, Storm and Cloud

aigrish   of wind: sharp, cutting **Essex**

black-east,   cold, dry east wind **Galloway**
black-easter

blackthorn winter   winter that turns very cold late in the season **Herefordshire**

blae   of wind: cold, cutting, harsh **Galloway**

boff   to blow back: used only of wind blowing smoke back down a chimney **Staffordshire**

bright-borough   area of the night sky thickly strewn with stars (Gerard Manley Hopkins) **poetic**

bruach   ring or halo around the moon, presaging unsettled weather **Irish**

carry   drift or movement of clouds **English**

cherribim   sky **Anglo-Romani**

ciabhar   slight breeze, just enough to stir the hair **Gaelic**

dim-wood   area of the night sky where few stars can be seen (Gerard Manley Hopkins) **poetic**

dintless   of a sky: cloudless **poetic**

duvla's pani   rainbow **Anglo-Romani**

eeroch	pains thought to be caused by the east wind in winter **Northern Ireland**
fell	sudden drop in wind **Galloway**
flam	sudden light breeze **North Sea coast**
flan	sudden gust of wind **Shetland**
flinchin	deceitful promise of better weather **Scots**
fuaradh-froise	cool breeze preceding a rain-shower **Gaelic**
garbhshíon	unseasonably cold and windy weather **Irish**
greann-gaoth	piercing wind **Gaelic**
gurl	howl of the wind **Scots**
gurley	cold, threatening wind **Galloway**
gussock	strong and sudden gust of wind **East Anglia**
hefty	of weather: rough, boisterous, wild **Ireland**
hot-spong	sudden power of heat felt when the sun comes from under a wind-shifted cloud **East Anglia**
huffling	wind blowing up in sudden gusts **Exmoor**
hulder	the roar in the air after a great noise (e.g. thunder) **Exmoor**
katabatic	wind that blows from high ground to low ground, its force being aided by gravity; sometimes known as a 'fall wind' **meteorological**
lambin' storm	gale which usually happens in mid March **North Sea coast**

lythe calm or absence of wind **Fenland**

mackerel-sky sky mottled with light, striped cirrus clouds **Exmoor**

meal-drift high, wispy clouds **poetic**

moor-gallop wind and rain moving across high ground **Cornwall, Cumbria**

Noah's ark cloud that widens upwards from the horizon, in the shape of an ark, and signals an approaching storm **Essex**

noctilucent cloud high and rare cloud type (literally 'night-shining') that drifts in the upper atmosphere, is made of ice crystals and is so high as to be invisible except when, after sunset around midsummer, 'the tilt of the earth allows it to catch the last light of the sun' (Amy Liptrot) **meteorological**

oiteag wisp of wind **Gaelic**

osag gust of wind **Gaelic**

piner penetrating, cold south-easterly wind **North Sea coast**

roarie-bummlers fast-moving storm clouds (literally 'noisy blunderers') **Scots**

shepherd's flock white fleecy clouds indicating fine weather **Suffolk**

skub hazy clouds driven by the wind **Shetland**

thraw of sky, sea or wind: threatening **Galloway**

twitchy   of wind: blowing unsteadily **East Anglia**

ultaichean   strong, rolling gusts of wind **Hebridean Gaelic**

up'tak   rising of the wind, usually signalling a fresh outbreak of bad weather **Shetland**

urp   cloud; 'urpy' means cloudy with very large clouds **Kent**

wadder-head   clouds standing in columns or streaks from the horizon upwards **Shetland**

water-carts   small clouds **Suffolk**

whiffle   of a wind: to come in unpredictable gusts **Kent**

wimpling   rippling motion induced in a bird's wing feathers by the passage of wind (Gerard Manley Hopkins) **poetic**

windin'   rooks circling in the air and thereby indicating stormy weather **Suffolk**

8

Bastard Countryside

The zone goes by different names, few of them complimentary. The landscape theorist Alan Berger calls it 'drosscape'. The activist and writer Marion Shoard calls it 'edgeland'. The American artist Philip Guston called it 'crapola'. In *Les Misérables*, Victor Hugo christened it 'bastard countryside', or '*terrain vague*', by which he meant the debatable realm, 'somewhat ugly but bizarre, made up of two different natures, which surrounds certain great cities':

> To observe the city edge is to observe an amphibian. End of trees, beginning of roofs, end of grass, beginning of paving stones, end of ploughed fields, beginning of shops, the end of the beaten track, the beginning of the passions, the end of the murmur of things divine, the beginning of the noise of humankind.

The decades since the Second World War have seen a surging literary and artistic interest in this 'amphibian' and hotchpotch terrain. In 1949 Kenneth Allsop published an experimental work of nature writing, *Adventure Lit Their Star*, which described the attempts of a rare species of wader, the little ringed plover, to breed by a gravel pit near Staines, Middlesex – in what Allsop called 'the messy limbo which is neither town nor country', a 'scrappy bit of outer-Outer London'. A quarter-century later came Richard

Mabey's prescient book *The Unofficial Countryside* (1973), in which Mabey documented the nature that existed opportunistically and exuberantly in scrubby bombsites, crumbling docks and litter-strewn canal banks. A quarter-century after Mabey, Iain Sinclair set off to walk the 'asphalt . . . noose' of the M25, recording the extruded suburbia that he found out there on the capital's rim, and publishing an account of his penitential circuit as *London Orbital* (2002).

Sinclair and Mabey's brilliant examples inspired hundreds of other chroniclers to take to Britain's edgelands: urb-exers, psycho-geographers, biopsychogeographers, autobiopsychogeographers, deep topographers and other theoretically constituted lovers of the detrital and neglected, cramming their notebooks with sketches of brownfield sites and crypto-cartographies of pylon lines, sewage outfalls, culverted rivers and the 'soft estate' of the British road network and its verges. The edgelands have sprawled all over late-twentieth-century English painting, photography, film (the *Robinson* trilogy of Patrick Keiller, the work of Chris Petit and Andrew Kötting) and children's literature (*Stig of the Dump* (1963), *The Turbulent Term of Tyke Tiler* (1977)). So modish have the edge-lands become that in 2011 a short-film festival was held in London dedicated to Britain's 'urban outskirts', and a book of essays called *Edgelands* appeared, which was animated by the conjoined beauty and banality to be discovered amid the pallet yards and car parks of cities' fringes.

Long before all of these, though, the edgelands of London were being documented by the journalist and nature writer Richard Jef-feries, in a series of essays and sketches collected as *Nature near London*, first published in 1883. It is a book fascinated by the strange braidings of the human and the natural that occur where city and country fray into one another, at what Jefferies called the 'frontier line to civilisation'. Jefferies was a countryman by upbringing, attracted by London's energies but repelled by its voracity and greed, and wishing – by means of his writing – to alert the city's inhabitants to the 'wild life' that existed alongside their own. 'Why, we must have been blind,' declared Walter Besant in 1888 about the experience of reading Jefferies: 'here were the most wonderful things possible going on under our very noses, but we saw them not!'

~

In 1877 Jefferies moved from Swindon in Wiltshire to Surbiton in Surrey. Surbiton was then at the limit-line of London's growth: a high-Victorian edgeland. Jefferies had been born and raised in the countryside at Coate, a village near Swindon. His father was a farmer, and from a young age Jefferies was free to explore the landscape around his home. He hunted with snare and gun, he fished, swam, built boats and rafts, and became something of a minor local eccentric, known for his long hair, swift stride and hunched posture. In 1866 he started as a reporter at local Wiltshire and Gloucestershire papers, for which his work might be described as right-wing populist, but he had different ambitions – both literary and political – and it was in the hope of securing work as an essayist and writer of fiction that he, his wife Jessie and their young son Harold moved to Surbiton.

London's edgelands today comprise jittery, jumbled ground: utilities infrastructure and haulage depots, crackling substations and allotments, scrub forests and sluggish canals, slackened regulatory frameworks and guerrilla ecologies. The Surbiton to which Jefferies moved was less disrupted, and therefore sharper in its main contrasts: fields began where suburban streets ran to their end; footpaths led quickly into copses and woodlands; streams and rivers ran under stone bridges and between houses. Nevertheless, it was still recognizably a marginal zone, intersected by roads and railways, and travelled through both by Londoners escaping the city and by itinerant workers seeking it out.

London was, when Jefferies reached it, the world's maximum city. By 1870 someone died there every eight minutes, and someone was born every five minutes. London had a population of 1 million in 1800, 5 million a century later and would have 7 million by 1911. In the course of the nineteenth century, Britain was the country that 'broke most radically with all previous ages of human history', in Eric Hobsbawm's memorable phrase, and its industrialization was so drastic that in 1850 it became the first nation in the world with more urban than rural inhabitants (a tipping point that the planet is thought to have reached only in 2010). A massive migration of people was underway from fields and villages into towns and cities – and the towns and cities were themselves sprawling out into the fields and villages. In a charismatic reversal of terms, London came itself to be figured as a wild place: 'be-wildering' in its fierce seethe of humanity. 'Wilderness!' cries a poor, elderly Londoner in Dickens's *Nicholas Nickleby* (1839). 'Yes it is, it is. It *is* a wilderness. It was a wilderness to me once. I came here barefoot. I have never forgotten it.' 'London looks so large,' thinks Little Dorrit, 'so barren and so wild.'

Jefferies, too, was awed by the 'wilderness' of London, and he sensed its 'unseen influence' upon him even when he was outside its perimeter. 'The strong life of the vast city magnetised me,' he wrote, 'and I felt it under the calm oaks.' One of the distinctive tensions of his prose about the capital is between the centripetal pull he experiences towards its centre, and the centrifugal efforts he makes to escape it. The decisive motion of *Nature near London*, though, is outwards and away: nearly every chapter starts with Jefferies 'quitting the suburb', in his phrase, by following field-path or stream-side on foot.

Jefferies came to know Surrey, as he came to know all his landscapes, chiefly by walking. He became, on foot, a connoisseur of the capital's marginalia – alert to the unexpected ecologies of the fringes: how 'rubbish heaps' were the 'haunts of the London crow', say, or how 'thrushes . . . build their nests' in suburban shrubberies, or how London honey tastes different from country honey because of the flavours imparted to it by 'the immense quantity of garden flowers about the metropolis'. Railway cuttings caught his eye – as they had caught the eye of Henry David Thoreau (who writes about them in the 'thawing sandbank' section of *Walden*), and as they would catch the eye of Edward Thomas, Jefferies' disciple and biographer – because on their tangled banks grew weeds and 'coloured' wild flowers, 'seen for a moment in swiftly passing', 'border[ing] the line like a continuous garden'. Repeatedly, Jefferies finds London not to have suppressed nature, but rather to have provoked it to odd improvisations. One winter, he watches a 'very large cinder and dust heap' that has been dumped 'upon a piece of waste land', and delightedly records how it has become 'the resort of almost every species of bird – sparrows, starlings, greenfinches, and rooks searching for any stray morsels of food'.

The published text of *Nature near London* draws on journal entries and field notes gathered over years of walking and looking. The simplest way to read the book is as an almanac or diary, as intimate and accidental as White's accounts of Selborne or Roger's *Notes from Walnut Tree Farm*. Jefferies was alert to the nuances of both climate and season, and the details of the book bring old weather back to life. He records the great snow of October 1880, heavy enough to shatter the oak trees that carried its weight (a snow that recurs in his other writings of the 1880s, much as the bitter winter of 1962–3 exerts a keen climatic influence on *The Peregrine*). We learn that the haw-berry harvest in the autumn of 1881 was profuse, and that it was a 'berry year' more generally, with blackberries 'thick' in the hedges and 'prickly-coated nuts hang[ing] up in bunches' on the horse chestnuts, 'as many as eight in a stalk'. On 14 February 1882 a yellowhammer sings, brambles 'put forth green buds', 'two wasps buzz in the sunshine', and Jefferies listens to a songbird's mellifluously unpredictable notes coming 'like wild flowers not sown in order'. On 1 January 1882 he sees 'fully two thousand' lapwings settled on a field, and then watches amazed as they take flight – the sudden upwards snowfall of 'a vast body of whitebreasted birds uprising as one from the dark ploughed earth', before turning and descending, 'all so regular that their very wings seem to flap together'.

~

I am an edgelander. Like Jefferies, I grew up in the country, at the end of a lane in rural Nottinghamshire. And, like Jefferies, I moved in my late twenties, newly a father, to live in a house at a city's fringe. A few hundred yards from that house, in which I still live, the southern edge of Cambridge gives way to arable fields that are split by B-roads and hedgerows, and scattered with copses and spinneys. The landscape rises to a pair of low-lying chalk hills – the Gog Magogs, named after the hyperborean giants whose prostrate forms the hills were once thought to resemble when seen in profile. By Scottish standards, the Gogs are molehills. By Cambridgeshire standards, they are Himalayas. Cambridge is, unmistakably, a curious place for someone who loves mountains to have ended up. I live in a county so flat (as the old joke goes) you could fax it; a county so flat (as the older joke goes) you can stand on a chair and see into Norfolk. Up in the Fens, near the village of Pidley, there is a roadside collection box for 'The Fenland Mountain Rescue Service', to which I give generously whenever I pass, on the superstitious basis that I might somehow be paying forwards to the day when I do need an airlift out of a corrie or off a crag.

When I first came to live in south Cambridge, I barely registered the bastard countryside on my doorstep. Why would I have? My eyes and dreams were all for the Highlands, Snowdonia, the Lake District, the Peak – the places I would quit Cambridge to reach. The edgelands were there to be travelled through and left behind: a pure transit zone. The notion of developing a relationship with this mixed-up, messed-up terrain did not occur to me. Disruptive of the picturesque, dismissive of the sublime, this was a landscape that required a literacy I didn't then possess: an aesthetic flexible enough to accommodate fly-tipping, dog shit, the night-glare of arc lights at the park-and-ride, and the *pock-pock-pock* of golf balls being struck up the driving range by architects and fund managers – as well as the yapping laugh of green woodpeckers through beech trees.

Slowly, though, I have acquired that literacy. I have learnt to read the edgelands, and have come, if not quite to love them, at least to arrive at an intimacy with them. Proximity and time have helped: I have lived here a decade now, and in that period I have walked and run thousands of miles back and forth over the few hundred hectares of edgeland between my home and the Gogs. Just past the last house on the road that leads up towards the chalk tops, there is a hole in the hedge through which you can duck to reach a quiet field-path rich with bird and plant life. Grey partridge, sparrowhawks, wood-peckers, charms of goldfinch; foxes, rabbits, big golden hares; scabious, cowslips, a rare orchid. The hedgerows that flank it are of dogwood, hawthorn and dog rose mostly; each autumn they are thick with haws and hips, which bring the birds: fieldfares and red-wings by the dozen, a gang of waxwings, all powder-puff pinks and hipster hairstyles, and – unforgettably – the peregrine I saw the day I went to Baker's archive. I have also gained a sense of the deeply layered history of the area: the Roman road that runs to the north-east of the hills, the causewayed enclosure of Magog's open down, the Bronze Age burial mounds here and there, the Neolithic trackway that probably underlies the Roman road, and the wooded and mysteriously earth-worked summit of Gog.

My children have also helped me explore the edgelands. Becoming a father altered my focal length and adjusted my depth of field. Children are generally uninterested in grandeur, and rapt by the miniature and the close at hand (a teeming ants' nest, a chalk pit, moss jungles, lichen continents, a low-branched climbing tree). From them – among countless other lessons – I have learnt that magnitude of scale is no metric by which to judge natural spectacle, and that wonder is now, more than ever, an essential survival skill.

I have also come to 'see' the edgelands thanks to the art and literature of what contemporary conservation calls 'nearby nature': the work of English hedge-visionaries and foot-philosophers including Samuel Palmer, Edward Thomas, Roger Deakin, Dorothy Wordsworth, Virginia Woolf – and Richard Jefferies. Jefferies was absorbed by what lay hidden in plain view. 'It would be very easy,' he noted of his favoured Surrey haunts, 'to pass any of these places and see nothing, or but little.' His engagement with the landscape was not prescriptive but exemplary, offering what he called – with an epistemological flourish – a 'method of knowing'. 'Everyone must find their own locality. I find a favourite wild-flower here, and the spot is dear to me; you find yours yonder.' His method was based on long-term and patient acquaintance, and on careful observation. It involved 'keep[ing] an eye' on one's locale 'from year's end to year's end', and in this manner coming 'to see the land as it really is': the creaturely bustle of hedge, copse, sky and field.

'Unseen' is a word that recurs discreetly in his writing: the 'blue-bells in th[e] hedge' that are 'unseen, except by the rabbits'; the plump trout that wavers gently in the current, holding its place in the shadow under the bridge – 'unseen' save by Jefferies. His use of the word anticipates that of the artist Paul Nash, who in 1938 wrote of the 'unseen landscapes' of England. 'The landscapes I have in mind,' said Nash:

> are not part of the unseen world in a psychic sense, nor are they part of the Unconscious. They belong to the world that lies, visibly, about us. They are unseen merely because they are not perceived; only in that way can they be regarded as invisible.

Unseen people preoccupied Jefferies, as well as unseen landscapes. Throughout his writing he was drawn to those who worked the land as well as those who watched it. Out in the Surrey edgelands, he found and wrote about hedgers and ditchers, hay-tyers, mouchers, drovers, shepherds with 'pastoral crooks', Irish harvesters, tinkers, tramps, gravel-dredgers toiling with hand-scoops, carters, reapers and others. These people – the rural poor – never speak to Jefferies and seem hardly to notice him (Jefferies himself being another of the 'unseen' presences in the book), but he observes them sympathetically rather than voyeuristically, recording the 'hard hand-play' and 'ceaseless toil' of their labour. 'The few [workers] that wear bright colours are seen,' he remarks, 'the many who do not are unnoticed.'

Optics and perception fascinated Jefferies, and *Nature near London* – like his late essay collection *The Life of the Fields* (1884) – contains some premonitory investigations not just into what we see, but how we see. As Richard Mabey has pointed out, Jefferies was decades ahead of his time as an ethologist, intuiting his way to an understanding of animal instinct that pre-dated the breakthroughs of Darling and Lorenz in the 1940s and 1950s. He was also pioneering as a philosopher of vision: his work foresaw the discoveries of phenomenology in the twentieth century concerning intersubjectivity. Thus it is that landscape, in Jefferies, often refuses to act as a flat frieze that yields its content stably to the viewer. Rather, it is volatile and unruly – dynamically disobedient to the eye. Often Jefferies wobbles our sense of reliable vision, showing the impossibility of achieving a privileged position of perception: 'Even trees which have some semblance of balance in form are not really so, and as you walk round them so their outline changes.' If you 'walk all round [a] meadow . . . still no vantage point can be found where the herbage groups itself, whence a scheme of colour is perceivable'. Repeatedly, phenomena refuse to resolve into order: a wind blowing across water makes 'wavelets' that 'form no design; watch the sheeny maze as long as one will, the eye cannot get at the clue, and so unwind the pattern'.

The cumulative result of these seemingly idle adventures into optics is radical: they demonstrate a decentred eye and a centreless nature. Walking becomes a means to a certain kind of knowledge – one of the constituents of which is an awareness of ignorance.

Moments such as these recall Shepherd's brilliant observations about observation in *The Living Mountain*:

> This changing of focus in the eye, moving the eye itself when look-ing at things that do not move, deepens one's sense of outer reality. Then static things may be caught in the very act of becoming. By so simple a matter, too, as altering the position of one's head, a differ-ent kind of world may be made to appear . . . Details are no longer part of a grouping in a picture of which I am the focal point, the focal point is everywhere. Nothing has reference to me, the looker.

Jefferies, too, aspires to catch things 'in the very act of becoming'; thus the present participles that gang and roister in his prose: 'the leaves are enlarging, and the sap rising, and the hard trunks of the trees swelling with its flow; the grass blades pushing upwards; the seeds completing their shape; the tinted petals uncurling'.

Jefferies was alarmed by scarcity and exhilarated by excess. Nature's surplus – its gratuity of gift – often thrillingly exceeds his ability to record it: 'a thousand thousand buds and leaves and flowers and blades of grass, things to note day by day, increasing so rapidly that no pencil can put them down and no book hold them, not even to number them'. Just beyond the city fringe, he finds a profusion of life: 'Sparrows crowd every hedge and field, their numbers are incredible; chaffinches are not to be counted; of greenfinches there must be thousands.' During his first spring in Surbiton, he is 'aston-ished and delighted' to discover the bird life which proclaimed itself everywhere:

> The bevies of chiffchaffs and willow wrens which came to the thickets in the furze, the chorus of thrushes and blackbirds, the

chaffinches in the elms, the greenfinches in the hedges, wood-pigeons and turtle-doves in the copses, tree-pipits about the oaks in the cornfields; every bush, every tree, almost every clod, for the larks were so many, seemed to have its songster. As for nightingales, I never knew so many in the most secluded country.

What a stark, sad contrast this teeming bird life makes with the contemporary countryside. Over the past half-century, Britain has lost more than 44 million breeding birds, including an average of more than fifty house sparrows every hour for those fifty years. Over the past twenty years, farmland bird populations in particular have plummeted: the turtle dove has suffered a 95 per cent decline in numbers, the cuckoo population has halved, lapwings have lost 41 per cent of their numbers. Jefferies would hardly recognize London's edgelands today: they would look and sound so very different.

Jefferies' eye for flowers was at least as sharp as his eye for birds. He wandered the verges of Surbiton's suburban lanes, finding them to be ruderal idylls of astonishing diversity. 'There are about sixty wild flowers,' he writes wonderfully of one road, 'which grow freely along [it], namely':

yellow agrimony, amphibious persicaria, arum, avens, bindweed, bird's foot lotus, bittersweet, blackberry, black and white bryony, brooklime, burdock, buttercups, wild camomile, wild carrot, celandine (the great and lesser), cinquefoil, cleavers, corn buttercup, corn mint, corn sowthistle, and spurrey, cowslip, cow-parsnip, wild parsley, daisy, dandelion, dead nettle, and white dog rose, and trailing rose, violets (the sweet and the scentless), figwort, veronica, ground ivy, willowherb (two sorts), herb Robert, honeysuckle, lady's smock, purple loosestrife, mallow, meadow-orchis, meadow-sweet, yarrow, moon daisy, St John's wort, pimpernel, water plantain, poppy, rattles, scabious, self-heal, silverweed, sowthistle, stitchwort, teazles, tormentil, vetches, and yellow vetch.

What riches in a single verge! Echoes here of MacDiarmid on the intricacies of heather, and Finlay and Anne teasing such variety out of the peat-lands of Lewis. Jefferies' list celebrates profusion, but it should also be heard as an elegy-in-waiting. He saw *Nature near London*, like much of his late writing, as fulfilling an archival function. It was clear to him that London would keep spreading, and that the countryside would be engulfed by the city's mobile margins. The image of the archive occurs explicitly in Jefferies' chapter on Kew Gardens, where he praises the 'great green book' that grows there. The garden 'restores the ancient knowledge of the monks and the witches', he writes approvingly; it prompts him also to regret that modernity has led to 'the lore of herbs [being] in great measure decayed and . . . lost'. 'The names of many of the commonest herbs,' he notes sadly, 'are quite forgotten.' He elected himself a recording angel for landscape and knowledge that was to be lost, and he wrote in the certainty of its future destruction – rather as Eugène Atget set out to photograph old Paris in the 1890s, aware that its abolition approached, or as Baker tasked himself with evoking the Essex peregrines and their territory: 'Before it is too late, I have tried to recapture the extraordinary beauty of this bird and to convey the wonder of the land he lived in . . . It is a dying world, like Mars, but glowing still.'

~

'The heart from the moment of its first beat instinctively longs for the beautiful,' declares Jefferies in a late essay, 'Hours of Spring'.

At his most movingly and innocently optimistic, he saw nature as a redeeming force, and his writing worked as what might now be called a consciousness-raising exercise – an attempt to bring urbanites and suburbanites to a fresh awareness of natural beauty, and thereby to a heightened sense of 'joy in life' and the collective nature of identity:

> [T]he goldfinches and the tiny caterpillars, the brilliant sun, if looked at lovingly and thoughtfully, will lift the soul out of the smaller life of human care that is of selfish aims . . . into the greater, the limitless life which has been going on over universal space from endless ages past, which is going on now, and which will for ever and for ever, in one form or another, continue to proceed.

It is true that at times, when striving to evoke the joy he felt in nature, Jefferies can sound too much like Molesworth's sissyish classmate, Basil Fotherington-Thomas, who wanders round the grounds of St Custard's school in a late-Romantic rapture, trilling his greetings to the world. But Jefferies' cries of wonder are ballasted by his cries of despair. Often he writes of his sense of the material world's terrible indifference to human presence. 'The earth is all in all to me,' he says bleakly in 'Hours of Spring', 'but I am nothing to the earth: it is bitter to know this before you are dead.' He acknowledges as an 'old, old error' the proposition that 'I love the earth, therefore the earth loves me – I am her child – I am Man, the favoured of all creatures.' And he writes blackly of the lack of the world's answer to his calls: 'Dull-surfaced matter, like a polished mirror, reflects back thought to thought's self within.' A similar veering between hope and hopelessness would characterize Edward Thomas's relations with nature. 'I am not a part of nature,' wrote Thomas desperately in 1913. 'I am alone. There is nothing else in my world but my dead heart and brain within me and the rain without.'

Sunlight was the substance Jefferies associated most with life; dust the substance that most often triggered his dismayed materialism and his thoughts of death. Sunlight prompts him to his famous deliquescence in the opening pages of his autobiography, *The Story of My Heart* (1883), and sunlight falls through many pages of *Nature near London*. But dust – comminuted matter, collateral of ruin – settles upon them too: ripped handfuls of 'delicate grasses' and 'dandelion stalks' that lie 'sprinkled with dust' on a roadside verge, the 'passing feet' that crush 'silverweed . . . into the dust'. The source of this morbid dust is almost always London. Dust is the metropolis's scurf. Like the 'white granular powder' that gathers lethally upon a thriving landscape in the opening pages of Rachel Carson's *Silent Spring* (1962), Jefferies' dust contaminates both body and soul:

> The dust of London fills the eyes and blurs the vision; but it penetrates deeper than that. There is a dust that chokes the spirit, and it is this that makes the streets so long, the stones so stony, the desk so wooden; the very rustiness of the iron railings about the offices sets the teeth on edge, the sooty blackened walls (yet without shadow) thrust back the sympathies which are ever trying to cling to the inanimate things around us.

At some point, probably in the late 1860s, Jefferies had contracted tuberculosis and he came increasingly to blame London for his affliction, which he figured as a kind of 'dust' that 'settles on the heart as well as that which falls on a ledge'. Repeatedly in *Nature near London*, the 'immense City' is the source of poison and pollution. On one hot July day, Jefferies writes, 'the atmosphere of London . . .

came bodily and undiluted out into the cornfields' – a toxic miasma that shifts and shimmers in the air. Elsewhere he conjures a vision of London as a city with its own *Götterdämmerung* building above it:

> the aurora of dark vapour, streamers extending from the thicker masses, slowly moves and yet does not go away; it is just such a sky as a painter might give to some tremendous historical event, a sky big with presage, gloom, tragedy.

In another late essay, written when he was severely ill, even nature will not serve as salve: he wonders aloud if all of existence has been a dream, and whether 'in course of time I shall find out also, when I pass away, physically, that as a matter of fact there never was any earth'.

~

If the suburbs, as J. G. Ballard observed, are places where the future waits to happen, then the edgelands might be where the future is already underway. In 1884, a year after the publication of *Nature near London*, John Ruskin delivered two minatory lectures under the title 'The Storm-Cloud of the Nineteenth Century'. Since the early 1870s Ruskin had become anxious that the weather in Britain had 'decisively worsened', becoming 'darker and stormier, possessed of an animate threat'. His 'Storm-Cloud' lectures explicitly connected this deteriorating climate with physical and moral pollution, and they are rife with images of airborne toxicity, plague-winds, pollution and moral 'gloom'. The year following Ruskin's lectures, Jefferies published a counterfactual novella entitled *After London; Or, Wild England*, which realized in hypothetical form both his and Ruskin's senses of impending 'tragedy'. *After London* is set in a post-apocalyptic southern England in which, as a result of an unspecified catastrophe, the landscape has been dramatically re-wilded. Its opening paragraph assumes the matter-of-fact tone of a chronicle:

> The old men say their fathers told them that soon after the fields were left to themselves a change began to be visible. It became green everywhere in the first spring, after London ended, so that all the country looked alike . . . No fields, indeed, remained, for where the ground was dry, the thorns, briars, brambles, and saplings already mentioned filled the space, and these thickets and the young trees had converted most part of the country into an immense forest . . . By the thirtieth year there was not one single open place, the hills only excepted, where a man could walk, unless he followed the tracks of wild creatures or cut himself a path.

Grass here – as so often in eco-apocalyptic literature – is the concealer and healer, greenly unwounding the damaged earth. Only a few humans have survived the scarification of their species. Mad-Maxish tribes of 'gypsies' and 'Bushmen' roam the land, divided along ethnic as well as self-interested lines. Jefferies' book follows its lone hero, Sir Felix Aquila, as he navigates the landscape and tries to find a way to re-establish a viable community that might mature into a worthwhile civilization. Early in the novel, Aquila crosses a vast inland lake to reach a noxious swamp, which he eventually realizes is the site of 'the deserted and utterly extinct city of London', now lying under his feet. The capital is granted no reprieve by the punitive Jefferies; Aquila is present to witness its total vanquishing by nature.

Nature near London contains the seeds of *After London*. As he wandered his edgelands, Jefferies' eye was often caught by signs of nature's irrepressibility: the desirable ease and swiftness with which it might return to absorb human structures. He notices a ruined barn, on whose 'old red brick wall . . . mosses have grown . . . following the lines of the mortar', and on which 'bunches of wall grasses flourish'. He writes approvingly of 'the great nature which comes pressing up so closely to the metropolis'. Nature near London is waiting patiently for its chance to claim back its territory – the humanized landscape predicting its coming obliteration.

In 1887, a decade after moving to Surbiton, Jefferies died of tuberculosis at the age of thirty-eight. He was buried in the Broadwater cemetery in Goring, then a suburb of the Sussex town of Worthing. At the time of Jefferies' burial the cemetery was in open country, but Worthing has since spread and its edgelands have converged around the site, which now looks on to a car park, a flyover and two schools. Trees – yews, hawthorn, ash, sycamore and oak – grow thickly over the cemetery's thirty-four acres, though, and the area retains – at least in daylight – an atmosphere of calmness and natural life.

Jefferies' grave is marked by a ziggurat headstone of white marble, set into a marble-bordered plot. The inscription on the border reads, in heavily serifed black lettering: 'To the honoured memory of the prose poet of England's fields and woodlands'. The interior of the plot has been filled with earth, in which now grows a profusion of weeds and wild flowers: ox-eye daisies, daffodils, agrimony, lady's bed-straw, wild mignonette . . .

GLOSSARY VII

Edgelands

Edges, Hedges and Boundaries

bar-slap   temporary gate in a gap in a drystone wall **Galloway**

boodge   to stuff bushes into a hedge to confine livestock **Herefordshire**

buckhead   to cut the top off a hedge to within about two or three feet of the ground **Suffolk**

bullfinch   hedge that is allowed to grow high without laying **Northamptonshire**

buttil   to fix boundaries **Suffolk**

carvet   thick hedgerow **Kent**

cop   bank of earth on which a hedge grows **Cumbria**

cuasnóg   wild bees' nest **Irish**

glat   gap in a hedge **Herefordshire**

grounders   bottom stones in a hedge **Cornwall**

hangstreet   upright part of a gate, to which the hinges are attached **Herefordshire**

hare-gate   opening in a hedge sufficient for the passage of hares **Lancashire**

hedgers, soldiers, toppers   top stones in a hedge or wall **Cornwall**

kes, kess   build-up of soil and stone along the base of a very old hedge **Cumbria**

lunkie	hole deliberately left in a wall for an animal to pass through **Scots**
May-mess	profusion of hedge blossom in full spring (Gerard Manley Hopkins) **poetic**
outshifts	fringes, boundaries and least-regarded parts of a town **East Anglia**
prick-nickle	dry hedge of thorns set to protect a newly planted fence **Northamptonshire**
round-about	boundary hedge of a coppice **Northamptonshire**
selvedge	field boundary; also the edge of a piece of woven material finished so as to prevent unravelling **agricultural**
shard	gap in a hedge **south-west England**
shattles, shettles	bars of a five-barred gate **Exmoor**
smeuse	gap in the base of a hedge made by the regular passage of a small animal **Sussex**
smout	hole in a hedge used by a hare **Derbyshire, Lincolnshire, northern England, Somerset**
soft estate	natural habitats that have evolved along the borders and verges of motorways and trunk roads **Highways Agency**
squiggle	to wriggle through a hedge **Essex**
stoop	gatepost **Cumbria**
thru'-ban, thrubin, truban	long stones for building a dyke **Galloway**

Farming

arrest harvest **Exmoor**

ass-upping of hoeing: to turn the docks and thistles end upwards, or to cause the posterior to be the superior part of the body while stooping in the act of hoeing **East Anglia**

bing a passage in a cowhouse, along the heads of the stalls **Herefordshire**

BMV of agricultural land: Best and Most Versatile **official**

bog to burn dead grass **Staffordshire**

boon party of men, usually neighbouring farmers, helping each other out during harvests **Ireland**

brake field after the corn has been reaped **Northamptonshire**

bray hay spread to dry in long rows **Cotswolds**

combar sharing of work or equipment between neighbours; mutual assistance **Irish**

cropmark light and dark marks visible in growing and ripening crops, especially via aerial photography **agricultural**

crow stone shed **west Cornwall**

feather pie hole in the ground, filled with feathers fixed on strings and kept in motion by the wind, as a device to scare birds **East Anglia**

fid portion of straw pulled out and arranged for thatching **Kent**

fochann corn beginning to blade **Gaelic**

fozie of turnips: not good, spongy **Northern Ireland**

franion, frem of a crop: luxuriant, thriving **Northamptonshire**

gort field **Irish**

gurracag heap of hay or corn not yet made into stacks **Gaelic**

hain to leave a meadow ungrazed to allow cutting later **Northamptonshire**

hallo bundle of straw made up for laying before cattle for fodder **Shetland**

headland strip of land at the edge of a field where agricultural machinery turns back into work **agricultural**

howk to dig, as in 'tattie-howking' **Scots**

jogget small load of hay **Cotswolds**

malkin, mawkin scarecrow **Northamptonshire**

maumble moist soil that clings to the spade in digging **Northamptonshire**

meat-earth good and fertile soil, as distinguished from clay, gravel or sand **Exmoor**

mommet scarecrow **Yorkshire**

moocher potato, left in the ground, which sprouts again **Herefordshire**

ollands pasture **Fenland**

pannage fattening of domestic pigs on acorns **agricultural**

pook heap of new-mown hay that has been cut and turned and is awaiting baling **West Country**

prink of crops or seedling plants: to emerge from the ground **East Anglia**

risk to cut grass with a sickle **Shetland**

sock liquid manure **Staffordshire**

swarf line or row of cut grass as left by the harvester **Kent**

swedeland countryside as perceived by someone from a town or city **English (urban slang)**

swipe to beat down bracken with rotating flails from the back of a tractor **Exmoor**

ted to turn over hay **Staffordshire**

walter of corn: to roil and twist about in heavy wind and rain **East Anglia**

wharve to turn over mown grass with a rake **Shetland**

wind-rows hay raked together in rows, so that the wind may dry it **Northamptonshire**

zwar crop of grass to be mown for hay **Exmoor**

Fields and Ploughing

addle headland of a field **Northamptonshire**

balk ridge between two furrows, or strip of ground left unploughed as a boundary line between two ploughed portions **agricultural**

berhog sterile piece of ground **Shetland**

browings cleared areas that were formerly brambled **East Anglia**

bukli tan waste-ground by the roadside **Anglo-Romani**

cant corner of a field **Sussex**

capper crust formed on recently harrowed land by heavy rain **Suffolk**

centroid point in a field from which the Rural Payments Agency takes the Ordnance Survey references **official**

chart rough wasteland or common **Kent**

cockshot, cockshut glade where woodcock were netted as they flew through **Herefordshire**

cowlease unmown meadow **Exmoor**

dallop patch of ground among growing corn that the plough has missed **East Anglia**

dwarf money old coins turned up in ploughing **Herefordshire**

eddish second crop of grass; also lattermath, aftermath **Northamptonshire**

elting-moulds soft ridges of fresh-ploughed land
Northamptonshire

end-rigg last row of the plough **Scots**

fairy darts, prehistoric arrowheads/coins turned up in
fairy money ploughing **Herefordshire**

first-earth first ploughing **Suffolk**

flinket long, narrow strip of land, whether arable or
pasture **Northamptonshire**

fog poor-quality grassland on which cattle could
fend for themselves in the winter months
Derbyshire

hawmell small paddock **Kent**

intack enclosed piece of common **Lancashire**

konsas areas or corners of land suitable for making
camp on **Anglo-Romani**

ley-field grass field ploughed for the first time **Galloway**

marsk high, rough pasture **Cumbria**

okrigjert stubble field **Shetland**

pightle small grass field near a house **Essex**

pingle enclosure of low shrubs or brushwood **Fenland**

plough-pan compacted layer in cultivated soil resulting
from repeated ploughing **agricultural**

queach unploughable, overgrown land
Northamptonshire

sillion	shining, curved face of earth recently turned by the plough **poetic**
strip lynchet	bank of earth that builds up on the downslope of a field ploughed for a long period of time **agricultural**
vores	furrows **Devon**
warp	soil between two furrows **Sussex**

Livestock

after; afterings	to extract the last milk from a cow; last milk drawn from a cow **Staffordshire**
al'mark	animal that cannot be restrained from trespassing on crop-land; sheep that jumps over dykes or breaks through fences **Shetland**
antony	runt of a litter of pigs **Northamptonshire**
báini-báini	used to call pigs to eat **Irish**
beestings	first milk from a cow after calving **Staffordshire**
beezlings	third or fourth milk from a cow after calving, said to be particularly rich **Suffolk**
belsh	to cut the dung away from around a sheep's tail **Exmoor**
billy-lamb	lamb reared by hand **Northamptonshire**
bishop	over-large heap of manure **Herefordshire**
buttons	sheep dung **Exmoor**

caoirnan globule of sheep dung **Gaelic**

chook-chook-chook call to chickens **Herefordshire**

ciorag pet sheep **Gaelic**

clart clot of wool or manure on an animal
Galloway

crew-yard winter yard for cattle **Fenland**

crottle hare dung **hunting**

dilly-dilly-dilly call to ducks **Herefordshire**

doofers horse dung **Scots**

dottle sheep dung **Scots**

eksben thigh bone of a slaughtered animal
Shetland

faing enclosure for holding sheep **Gaelic**

flop cow dung on pasture **Suffolk**

fumes deer dung **hunting**

gibby child's name for a sheep **Exmoor**

gimmer ewe between the first and second shearing
northern England, Scotland

grit-ewe ewe in lamb **Galloway**

heft; hefting herd of sheep that have learnt their particular
boundaries and stick to those areas throughout
their lives (thus doing away with the need for
fences); the skill by which sheep are taught to
do this **agricultural**

hefting skill by which sheep are familiarized with and thus stay within one territory on hills or fells, without resorting to fences or walls to pen them in **agricultural**

hogg, hogget young sheep of either sex from nine to eighteen months (until it cuts two teeth) **agricultural**

ho-ho-ho call to cattle **Herefordshire**

hummer gentle murmuring neigh a horse makes when it hears someone it likes approaching or the fodder being brought **Suffolk**

kepp-kepp-kepp call to poultry **Herefordshire**

koop-koop-koop call to horses **Herefordshire**

krog to crook or crouch when taking shelter from the weather under some high overhanging thing, as cattle do **Shetland**

lamb-storms storms near the vernal equinox, often hurtful to new-weaned lambs **East Anglia**

langle to tie the forelegs of an animal to prevent it leaping **Galloway**

licking last meal given to cattle before milking **Staffordshire**

maxon heap of dung **Sussex**

oo wool **Galloway**

pirl single globule of sheep's dung **Shetland**

plat cow dung **Scots**

riggwelter	sheep that has fallen onto its back and can't get up because of the weight of its fleece **Cumbria**
scalps	rinds of turnips, left by the sheep in the fields **Northamptonshire**
scrave	bench for cleaning a fresh-killed pig **Essex**
sharn	cow dung for spreading on the fields **Shetland**
sheep-hurk	permanent winter fold **Northamptonshire**
si-ew-si-ew-si-ew	call to pigs **Herefordshire**
skelloping	of cattle: rushing around the field **Herefordshire**
spancel	rope used to tie up goats **Northern Ireland**
sussing	noise made by pigs when feeding **Suffolk**
teg	sheep in its second year **Cumbria**
ting	to cause a swarm of bees to settle by means of 'tinging' a house key against glass or metal **East Anglia**
transhumance	seasonal movement of grazing animals to and from pasture **agricultural**
turdstool	very substantial cowpat **south-west England**
twinter	two-year-old cow, ox, horse or sheep **northern England, Scotland**
ujller	unctuous filth that runs from a dunghill **Shetland**
wigging	removal of wool from around a sheep's eyes to prevent wool blindness **Cumbria**

9
Stone-Books

I first met Jacquetta Hawkes's name as the author of an approving quotation on the cover of Clarence Ellis's *The Pebbles on the Beach* (1954). 'Mr Ellis writes simply and well about the natural processes which compose, shape and transport pebbles . . . he is a most excellent guide,' said Hawkes – and she was right. Ellis's was the book that we took as a family when we went treasure-hunting for stones on the coasts of Britain: wandering bent at the waist, eyes peeled for rough orbs of agate, quartz prisms, purple jasper and elusive amber, hard to tell in its unpolished form from the flints among which it usually lay. I pored over Ellis's book as a child, especially the colour plates that carried glossy close-up photographs of stones – 'fragment of gabbro', 'ovoid of quartz-veined grit' – arrayed on sand. I appreciated the calm teacherliness with which he approached his subject from first principles ('What is a pebble?' 'How have raised beaches come about?') and the hint of moral duty with which he infused the study of geology ('We paid some attention to sandstone in the last chapter, but we must examine it more closely'). I prized the insider tips he offered: that serpentine discloses its identity by means of its 'wax-like lustre', or that if you break a quartzite pebble 'into two pieces and strike one against the other in darkness' there will be an 'orange-coloured flash' and a 'difficult to describe' smell.

Ellis also broke open the language of stones for me. He struck names against roots to produce flashes and smells: 'Gneiss (pro-nounced "nice") is a word of German origin, derived from an Old High German verb *gneistan*, "to sparkle". In sunshine, especially after rain, it certainly does sparkle, as it is a highly crystalline rock.' 'Schist (pronounced "shist") is derived from a Greek word *schistos*, meaning "easily split".' I began to collect stone-words as well as stones: the axe-knock syllables of *quartz, jet, chert, onyx* and *agate*, the classical complexities of *carnelian* and *citrine*. Ellis clearly loved language for its capacity to grade and sort perception, but also for the poetry it carried. As an ordinary-looking pebble could be sliced and polished to reveal dazzling patterns, so could a word. Ellis taught me *swash, backwash* and *fetch* as the terms necessary to help understand 'the rudiments of wave action . . . upon the movement, the shaping and the smoothing of pebbles'; he noted *swales* and *fulls* as being respectively the ridges and hollows of shingle formation on the seaward-side of long shingle banks. He gave me *crinoid* and *calyx, piriform, foliation* and *erratics*: the last denoting those stones that have been transported by glacial action far from their origin, often identifiable by the striations (Latin *stria*, 'a groove') that showed where they had been scraped along by a glacier while 'frozen into its underside'.

About the only sentence of his book that I didn't understand was its third: 'Collectors of pebbles are rare.' Really? For as long as I could remember, my parents and I had picked things up as we walked. Surfaces in our house were covered in shells, pebbles, twists of driftwood from rivers and sea. We weren't the only ones. Every-one I knew seemed to gather pebbles, and line them up on window ledges and mantelpieces, performing a humdrum rite of happiness and memory-making. *Spot, stoop, hold in the hand, slip in the pocket*: a kind of karmic kleptomania. In their Cairngorms house my grandparents kept special stones in glass bowls that they filled with water to keep the stones shining. They even constructed a makeshift *Wunderkammer*: a wall-mounted cabinet, the white-wood compartments of which held a pine cone, a rupee, cowries, a dried shepherd's purse, a geographic cone-snail shell with its map-like patterns, and polished pebbles of chalcedony and onyx.

Ellis helped turn me into a petrophile; he also helped turn me into a logophile, and when he wrote of nineteenth-century pebble-hunters who 'combed the beaches with painstaking zeal . . . and compiled glittering collections', he might have been describing my own subsequent dictionary-fossicking and word-list-making. 'All I know is that at the very early stage of a book's development,' wrote Vladimir Nabokov, 'I get this urge to gather bits of straw and fluff, and eat pebbles.' Like Nabokov, I am a pebble-eater and a straw-gatherer: my own books have begun as gleaned images, single words and fragment-phrases, scribbled onto file cards or jotted in journals. They have also emerged from actual stones, gathered while walking. These stones – among them a heart-sized stone of blue basalt from Ynys Enlli, an eyeball of quartz taken from the black peat of Rannoch Moor, a pierced flint from Chesil Bank (*Chesil* from the Old English *ceosol* or *cisel*, meaning 'shingle'), a clutch of fossilized polyps from the Palestinian West Bank, a rounded boulder of zebra-striped gneiss from the Isle of Harris – have served as triggers when I have begun to write: a means of summoning back memories of a landscape at the instant of finding (the scents and temperatures of the air, the nature of the light, the ambient sounds). Each stone is a souvenir in the old sense of the word; collection spurs recollection.

~

Ellis's *The Pebbles on the Beach* was the stone-book of my childhood; Jacquetta Hawkes's *A Land* (1951) that of my twenties. 'I have used the findings of the two sciences of geology and archaeology,' Hawkes declares at the opening of *A Land*, 'for purposes altogether unscientific.' So – candidly, audaciously – starts her strange book, a deep-time dream of 4 billion years of earth-history, whose 'purposes' are to demonstrate that we are all 'creatures of the land', substantively produced by the terrain on which we live, and to advance a synthetic cosmogony of consciousness, culture and geology. Passionate and personal, *A Land* became a best-seller upon publication in May 1951 and remains one of the defining British books of the post-war decade. It reads now, sixty years on, like a missing link in the tradition of British writing about landscape, but also as prophetic of contemporary environmental attitudes and anxieties. It feels both a period piece – as of its year as the Festival of Britain, the Austin A30 and *The Goon Show* – and Delphically out-of-time in its ecstatic holism. 'The image I have sought to evoke,' Hawkes declares in her Preface, 'is of an entity, the land of Britain, in which past and present, nature, man and art appear all in one piece.'

Hawkes knew she had written an unclassifiable work. It is, she observed in 1953, 'an uncommon type of book, one very difficult to place in any of our recognized categories'. The difficulty of 'placing' it arises in part because it dons and discards its disguises with such rapidity. It appears, at different points, to be a short history of Planet England; a Cretaceous cosmi-comedy; a patriotic hymn of love to Terra Britannica; a neo-Romantic vision of the countryside as a vast and inadvertent work of land art; a speculative account of human identity as chthonic in origin and collective in nature; a homily aimed at rousing us from spiritual torpor; a lusty pagan lullaby of longing; and a jeremiad against centralization, industrialization and our severance from the 'land'. It is all of these things at times, and none of them for long. Its tonal range is vast. There are echoes of the saga, shades of the epic, and tassels of the New Age. It is tagged throughout with poetry (Wordsworth, Hardy, Lawrence, Norman Nicholson). It is flamboyant enough that I can imagine it re-performed as a rock opera. It brinks at times on the bonkers. Hawkes disarmingly refers to the book as a memoir, but if so it is one in which she investigates her past with reference to the whole of planetary history. It is a work of back-to-nature writing that advocates a return not just to the soil but right down to the core. In its obsession with clear and firm forms, *A Land* reads like Roger Fry on rocks; in its preoccupation with synchronicities, like Gurdjieff on geology; and in its fascination with the particularities of stone, like Adrian Stokes on acid. Its politics are occasionally troubling, but mostly animated by a federate vision of the nation as a union of loosely linked locales. It is not a jumble, exactly, for out of its contradictions arise its charisma. It is not wise, exactly, but its intensity approaches the visionary.

A Land's apparent solipsism and its disciplinary waywardness dismayed academic specialists when it was published, especially pure archaeologists, who reacted to Hawkes's projection of self into her prose either with foot-shuffling embarrassment or with intellectual aggression. But such responses misunderstood Hawkes's ambitions. Harold Nicolson, whose rave review of *A Land* in the *Observer* helped turn the book into a best-seller, knew straight away what he was dealing with. 'There is,' he noted with awe, 'a weird beauty in this prophetic book . . . it is written with a passion of love and hate.' H. J. Massingham compared Hawkes's prose to that of Donne's sermons, possessing 'something of their imaginative range, their recondite knowledge, their passion of exploration, their

visionary sense of integration'. *A Land* was, he concluded, 'a germin-
al book and may well herald a change in cultural orientation that
bitter experience has made tragically overdue'.

Hawkes later attributed that 'passion' to the flux of her emotional
life at the time of writing. *A Land* was composed between the spring
of 1949 and the autumn of 1950. Her marriage to her first husband,
the archaeologist Christopher Hawkes, was breaking up; she had
recently met the man who was to become her second husband, the
writer and broadcaster J. B. Priestley; and she had three years previously lost to sudden death her lover, the poet and music critic Walter
Turner, to whom she had been devoted. By her own account, she
was at a 'highly emotional pitch', which expressed itself as a 'vital
energy' in the prose. *A Land*, she later recalled, came 'directly out
of my being': 'Wars can stir up personal lives to revolutionary
effect . . . life took hold of me, and quite suddenly, my imagination
was opened and my sensibility roused.' She sat down to write out of
a wish to contribute something 'to our understanding of being and
the overwhelming beauty and mystery of its manifestations'.

The book was an eccentric move for her to make in terms of its
register. Hawkes had from 'an absurdly tender age' wanted to
become an archaeologist. Born in Cambridge in 1910, her childhood
home was located on the site of both a Roman road and an
Anglo-Saxon cemetery. She grew up in an 'extraordinarily reserved'
family, who were 'as silent as trees in our emotional lives', but intellectually dedicated (her father was a Nobel Prize-winning
biochemist, Sir Frederick Gowland Hopkins). At nine, she wrote an
essay declaring that she would be an archaeologist; at eighteen she
was duly admitted to Cambridge University to read archaeology,
graduated with a first-class degree and travelled to Palestine – then
under the British Mandate – to take part in the excavation of a

Palaeolithic-era cave dwelling on Mount Carmel. In 1933 she married Hawkes, then an Assistant Keeper at the British Museum, later to become Professor of European Archaeology at Oxford, and for the next seven years she worked as an independent archaeological researcher, writing 'only the most severely technical of articles and books'. But the upheavals of the Second World War and her love affair with Turner caused Hawkes to become distrustful of academic archaeology's distrust of the imagination. She decided to use her 'scientific archaeology' for 'more imaginative purposes'. The success of *A Land* launched her as a public intellectual, and she remained well known for the rest of her long life as a broadcaster, writer and culture broker.

In person, Hawkes was a distinctive mixture of austerity and ardour. Priestley, early in their acquaintance, described her as 'ice without and fire within'. 'Mostly, people apprehended the ice,' remembered her son, Nicolas. She spoke slowly and deliberately; 'daunting' was a word often used of her by those who did not know her well. But Hawkes was also transgressive. Aged sixteen, she founded a 'Trespassers Society', dedicated to the disregard on foot of private property. While an undergraduate, she organized what was then the first ever rugby-football match between teams from the all-female Girton and Newnham colleges. The university proctors resisted, she pushed, they yielded – but insisted that the match be held at dawn. Despite the early kick-off, several hundred male spectators turned up. She was bisexual throughout the 1930s, wrote a controversial and sexually frank memoir in the 1970s, was friends with Henry Moore, Paul Nash and Graham Sutherland, and visited Robert Graves in Mallorca to sit in swimsuits upon the beach and discuss Graves's theory of the White Goddess mother-myth. She was someone for whom the feeling human body was the first principle of the thinking human mind, and who – as her son put it – had a 'great capacity for physical response not only to people, but also to nature and the land'.

~

It is with a feeling human body that the first chapter of *A Land* begins: 'When I have been working late on a summer night, I like to go out and lie on the patch of grass in our back garden . . . this hard ground presses my flesh against my bones and makes me agreeably conscious of my body.' From that patch of grass – on Primrose Hill in north London – Hawkes sends her mind out journeying. Her mind moves downwards, as if the soil were continuous with her skin, through humus and topsoil, into the London clay and the sedimentary bed-rocks, formed during the Palaeogene between 34 and 56 million years ago, at the bottom of oceans. Her mind also moves upwards, as if the air were continuous with her skin, through the 'fine silhouettes of the leaves immediately overhead', past the 'black lines of neigh-bouring chimney pots' and upwards at last to 'stray among the stars'. And her mind also moves sideways, across 'the huge city spreading for miles on all sides', along 'the railways, roads and canals rayed out towards all the extremities of Britain'. It is a brilliantly managed scene, quaquaversal in its geometries, simultaneously expanding pres-ent space and deepening past time. It also allows her to return to the book's true origin (and implicitly her own), the birth of the earth: 'I must begin with a white-hot young earth dropping into its place like a fly into an unseen four-dimensional cobweb, caught up in a delicate tissue of forces where it assumed its own inevitable place, following the only path, the only orbit that was open to it.'

Reading of Hawkes lying down on the 'hard ground' near the top of Primrose Hill, I think of Nan Shepherd lying down on the granite of the Cairngorm summits: another woman for whom 'flesh' and 'bones' were means to thought, and for whom, just as the mountain 'does not come to an end with its rock and its soil', so the body does not come to an end with its skin. 'There I lie on the plateau,' writes Shepherd near the end of *The Living Mountain*:

> under me the central core of fire from which was thrust this grumbling grinding mass of plutonic rock, over me blue air, and between the fire of the rock and the fire of the sun, scree, soil and water, moss, grass, flower and tree, insect, bird and beast, wind, rain and snow – the total mountain.

Shepherd's 'total' is of course totally distinct from the 'total' of 'totalizing' or 'totalitarian'. Her mountain, like Hawkes's 'earth', is 'total' insofar as it exceeds the possibility of our capacity ever to know it entirely.

Hawkes's prose also recalls the opening of Jefferies' *The Story of My Heart*, in which he lies on the 'sweet short turf' of a Wiltshire hill in high summer – warmed by 'the great sun', 'rapt and carried away'. He senses himself 'absorbed into the being or existence of the universe', and senses 'down deep into the earth under and high above into the sky and farther still to the sun and stars . . . losing thus my separateness of being'. 'Full to the brim of the wondrous past,' he concludes, 'I felt the wondrous present.' Hawkes inverts Jefferies' terms. Full to the brim of the wondrous present, she feels the wondrous past. And where he is abolished, she is extended. 'I imagine,' she writes later in *A Land*, 'that I can feel all the particles of the universe nourishing my consciousness just as my consciousness informs all the particles of the universe.'

Those who suspected Hawkes of solipsism were guilty of mis-
reading: she in fact offers an account of selfhood in which,
molecularly and emotionally, 'every being is united both inwardly
and outwardly with the beginning of life in time and with the
simplest forms of contemporary life'. The 'individual' (from the
Latin *individuus*, meaning 'indivisible') is not unique but soluble,
particulate, fluid. Her book is dedicated to proving that 'inside this
delicate membrane of my skin, this outline of an individual, I carry
the whole history of life'; she is merely one of the outcrops or
features of the 'land'. 'Consciousness must surely be traced back to
the rocks,' she argues. *A Land* should be read, she suggests at its
close, as 'the simple reaction of a consciousness exposed at a particular point in time and space. I display its arguments, its posturings, as
imprints of a moment of being as specific and as limited as the
imprint of its body left by a herring in Cretaceous slime.' Her book
is itself a geological formation, no more or less extraordinary than
a fossil or a pebble.

To Hawkes, stone did not only prompt thought – it constituted it.
Our 'affinity with rock' was so profound that she understood us to
be mineral-memoried, stone-sensed. Often in *A Land* she writes
geologically of the mind's structures: thoughts are 'rocks . . . silently
forming', memory is 'the Blue Lias' of the fossil-filled strata around
Lyme Regis. She admires Henry Moore because while 'Rodin pursued the idea of conscious, spiritual man emerging from the rock',
'Moore sees him rather as always a part of it'. Admittedly, the sections of *A Land* in which Hawkes advances her thesis of collective
consciousness – she would later, under Priestley's influence, read
widely in Jung, whose complete works formed part of their shared
library – have dated least well. Partly because no one writing today

would think of proposing such a grand unified theory of existence, and partly because Hawkes becomes most breathless and least careful when she is expounding these complex ideas. 'It is hardly possible to express in prose,' she reflects, 'the extraordinary awareness of the unity of past and present, of mind and matter, of man and man's origin which these thoughts bring to me.' True enough.

Written with ardour and supercharged with sensitivity, *A Land* often finds itself on the edge of melodrama. Hawkes was aware that she had 'just . . . escape[d] disaster' in terms of her style, but felt too that the risks had been necessary. The history of the earth 'has to be told in words', she notes early, and 'the senses must be fed'. This was the challenge she set herself: to administer 'a continual whipping of the vitality' in order 'to keep the words as true expressions of consciousness, to prevent them from turning into some dead march of the intellect'. Mostly, she laid on the lash with panache, succeeding in bringing prehistory alive. She brought the distant past and the living present into vibrant contact: the Old Red Sandstone of Herefordshire has 'the glow of desert suns' invested in its grain; the little island of Ailsa Craig, formerly the plug of a volcano, is now a gannetry in which 'pale-eyed birds press their warm feathers against the once boiling granite'. As her biographer Christine Finn nicely puts it, to Hawkes:

> the [Neanderthal] skeleton, lying asprawl on the slopes of Mount Carmel, was a human being not so dissimilar to those excavating it. The rooms at Skara Brae were still alive with Neolithic voices. The Lascaux cave paintings anticipated a Palaeolithic hunter returning to complete another image. The marks left by antler-picks in Grimes Graves were fresh with chalk-dust.

Hawkes's book is filled with odd rhymes and elective affinities: she explains how 'Jurassic water snails' helped 'medieval Christians to praise their God', how ammonites influenced the plate armour of fifteenth-century knights, and why the hypertrophied antler of an early species of deer offers a precise analogy with twentieth-century western European consciousness. She possessed the synecdochic imagination of the gifted archaeologist, able to reconstruct whole beings from relict parts, and the sharp sight of the crime-scene investigator, able to attribute complex cause to simple sign.

Hawkes was one of the writers – the quarryman-devout Hugh Miller was another, and John Ruskin a third – who taught me to see through geological eyes, and gave me trilobite-sight, as it were: the urge to read a landscape backwards and perceive something of the violent earth-history that has brought it to its present appearance. I do not know my eras and epochs in order, I would be pressed to distinguish dolerite from rhyolite in the field, and the real geologists I know are rightly in contempt of my ignorance, but I am nevertheless consistently excited by the drama of deep time. In the Scottish Highlands, I find it easy for thousands or millions of years to fall away in a glance. Out on the prow of one of the rock buttresses that lean over the great valley of Lairig Ghru, I can envisage some version of the glen as it was in the Pleistocene: filled with creased grey glacial ice that surges slowly northwards, leaving raw pink granite where its blue belly and flanks scour the rock. But it took Hawkes to help me see southern England icily:

Stand at Moreton-in-the-Marsh, in that sweet, mild, agricultural country of the Cotswolds, and imagine it as the meeting place of two gigantic glaciers, one thrusting eastward from Wales, the other advancing against it from the Midlands. Or stand where the traffic roars down Finchley Road and see it instead filled by the ragged tip of the most southerly of the glaciers: from desolation to desolation.

~

The oddest contradiction of *A Land* is between its island patriotism and its planetary holism. On the one hand, Hawkes compelled her readers to imagine themselves in ways which make mockery of the idea of individual beings, let alone of nations. Seen from the perspective of the Cretaceous, the notion of the nation seems ridiculous, and fighting for a 'country' as ludicrous as going to war on behalf of a raindrop. She writes sardonically of 'our composed Britain', and her (now outdated) geological maps show the migrations and divisions of the world's land masses over billions of years. She seems less a 'European' – as she at one point proclaims herself to be – and more an inhabitant of the supercontinent of Gondwanaland. Again and again she reminds us of the extreme contingency of human existence: volcanoes 'speak of insecurity', are reminders of 'our participation in process'. The idea of the individual is 'a fiction', and we are part of a group of fictional individuals who by chance happen to inhabit 'that small part of the earth's crust known to us as the British Isles'.

On the other hand, *A Land* was triumphantly the story of 'Great Britain'. It was published in the damp summer of the Festival of Britain, that great post-war carnival of backslapping and chin-upping, with its well-intentioned rhetoric of 'the land' and 'the people', its mobilizing of a 'blessed heritage of farmers, sailors, poets, bravely advancing into the age of radar and jet propulsion'. On London's South Bank, the Skylon pointed its space-age finger skywards above the Dome of Discovery, and the Oyster Creek Branch Railway clattered up and down on its tiny track near the Telekinema. The festival's aim was to provoke recovery and promote progress in a war-battered nation. It was a rebuke to ruin, a tonic for the nation, and the regenerative patriotism of the festival, to which Hawkes was a key advisor, rings out often in *A Land*: there in her insistence that Britain become self-sufficient again agriculturally, there in her vaunting of 'regional difference', and there most audibly in her declaration that '[t]he people of this island should put their hearts, their hands, and all the spare energy which science has given them into the restoration of their country'. The dream-tour that ends the book – taking the reader over the South Downs, across the East Anglian wheat-bowl, up through West Riding and the Yorkshire Moors, which sniffs the Pennines 'for a faint but palpable tang of wildness', and then passes on up to the 'mountain regions' – concludes with (of course) a close-up of the long line of chalk cliffs: Britain's Cretaceous bastion, its white shield raised against invaders, its symbol of pride and of insularity.

So the 'land' of the book's title is in part the same 'land' that Arthur is fighting for in T. H. White's *The Book of Merlyn*, an allegory for the wartime defence of England: 'the land under him', which he loves 'with a fierce longing'. And it is a similar 'land' to the one that J. B. Priestley invoked in his wartime radio broadcasts: the 'sense of community' and the 'feeling of deep continuity' that he experienced out in the 'English hills and fields', alongside 'ploughman and parson, shepherd and clerk'.

The patriotism of *A Land* leads to some awkward moments: there are queasy-making allusions to 'the racial stock' of Britain, which feel especially odd given Hawkes's demonstration elsewhere in the book of what nonsense the ideas of 'stock' and 'race' seem when viewed from a prehistoric perspective. One can see why Henry Williamson, the troubled author of *Tarka the Otter*, might have written Hawkes the fan letter he did, composed in his writing hut in Georgeham, north Devon. For while the book would certainly have appealed to the pacifist Williamson of the 1910s and 1920s – who was longing for a theory of human identity that might transcend nationalism and dissolve war – aspects of it would also have spoken to the Williamson of the 1930s to 1950s: admirer of the Hitler Youth, member of the British Union of Fascists, regular contributor to the Mosley-sponsored periodical *The European*, for whom engagement with the land had curdled into a version of *Blut und Boden* belonging.

Williamson wrote to Hawkes in February 1952, having had to wait 'for months' to get hold of a copy of *A Land* due to its popularity. He read it, he told her, 'during a fortnight of pre-midnights by the copper oil lamp of this hut', and reacted with 'enthusiasm and delight & indeed wonder' to her 'sentences, paragraphs and chapters'. Flattering to the point of unctuousness, he acclaimed it a 'perfect book': 'You indeed have married poetry with science, and . . . revealed what wonder there is in the seed of the poppy and the luminous seed of the Milky Way.' He thought that both the Lawrences (T. E. and D. H.) would have 'loved' *A Land*, before bowing and scraping his way backwards out of the letter: 'Is this presumption on the part of a minor "nature writer"? . . . You surely have had such praise and fame that I feel I must not obtrude upon your consciousness any further, having rendered my tribute unto Caesar, Yours faithfully, Henry Williamson.'

It is a muddled and uneasy letter, but Williamson was right to settle on 'wonder' as both the source of the book's energies, and its effect upon him. Hawkes was enthused by the earth's past in the original Greek sense of the word (*entheos*, meaning 'divinely inspired, rapt, in ecstasy') and her enthusiasm leapt and arced from page to reader. She esteemed Moore for choosing to sculpt in Liassic-era 'Hornton' stone, 'a rock . . . full of fossils, all of which make their statement when exposed by his chisel', rather than in 'the white silence of marble'. In this way, she wrote, he allowed 'stone to speak'.

So did Hawkes. Nabokov, in his novel *Transparent Things*, reflects on the temporal vertigo that can come from the contemplation of the earth's substance. 'When we concentrate on a material object,' he wrote, 'whatever its situation, the very act of attention may lead to our involuntarily sinking into the history of that object,' such that we become 'not of the now'. Hawkes knew how to become not of the now – how to break the surface tension of the world, and sink into the deep-time dream-life of debris.

GLOSSARY VIII

Earthlands

Minerals and Rocks

anaclinal of a valley or river: descending in a direction opposite to the dip of the underlying rocks **geological**

arenaceous sandy **geological**

cank hard sandstone **Midlands**

carraig rugged rock with stones jutting out from it **Gaelic**

cataclastic exhibiting a structural character due to intense crushing and pressure **geological**

chucky small, flat stone **Galloway**

clastic consisting of broken pieces of older rocks **geological**

clint hard, bare surface of limestone showing at ground level **Yorkshire**

clitter rock rubble that accumulates around the tops of tors **south-west England**

cludderach pile of stones in a river **Galloway**

coccoliths individual plates of calcium carbonate formed by certain single-celled algae **geological**

creach thin lamina of limestone **Northamptonshire**

dappy stones small pebbles **Exmoor**

dilapidation falling of stones or masses of rock from mountains or cliffs by natural agency **geological**

dòirneag round stone that fills the fist when held **Gaelic**

dyke sheet-like body of igneous rock that cuts across the bedding or structural planes of the host (older) rock **geological**

eoliths name given to the earliest worked stones **archaeological**

erratic stray mass of rock, foreign to the surrounding strata, that has been transported from its original site, apparently by glacial action **geological**

esker elongated and often flat-topped mounds of post-glacial gravel that occur in large river valleys, probably formed as depositions within ice-walled tunnels carved by meltwater through the bellies of glaciers **geological**

feldspar name given to a group of minerals, usually white or flesh-red in colour, occurring in crystalline masses (granite is often composed of feldspar, quartz and mica) **geological**

garbhlach stony place **Gaelic**

geode rock body or nodule having an internal cavity lined with mineral crystals growing inwards **geological**

geodiversity natural diversity of geological (rocks, minerals, fossils), geomorphological (land form, processes) and soil features of a landscape or region **ecological**

gneiss metamorphic rock composed, like granite, of quartz, feldspar or orthoclase, and mica, but distinguished from granite by its foliated structure **geological**

grey wethers, sarsens boulders of sandstone found lying on the surface of the chalk downs in Devon and Wiltshire **Devon, Wiltshire**

gritstone sedimentary rock composed of coarse sand grains with inclusions of small pebbles **geological**

gryke vertical cleft or crack in a *clint* **Yorkshire**

hagstone flint pierced by a hole, traditionally thought to bring luck or ward off ill-fortune **Suffolk**

haltadans stone circle (literally 'limping dance') **Shetland**

hamar, hammer large masses of earth-fast rock on the side of a hill **Orkney, Shetland**

hoarhusk debris left by the frost-weathering of stones and boulders (Gerard Manley Hopkins) **poetic**

hoodoo tall thin spire of rock **geological**

karst limestone landscape marked by abrupt ridges, fissures, sinkholes and caverns **geological**

lias blue limestone rock, rich in fossils **geological**

lithic of or pertaining to stone **geological**

lizzen split or cleft in a rock **Herefordshire**

loess deposit of wind-blown dust **geological**

marian   gravelly bank; *moraine* **Welsh**

megalith   large stone forming all or part of a prehistoric monument **archaeological**

moraine   mound or ridge of debris carried and deposited by a glacier at its sides or extremity **geological**

orogeny   process by which mountains are formed **geological**

ortholith   stone that has been raised by human effort into an upright position **archaeological**

runi   prominent rock on a hillside **Shetland**

rupestral   living among or occupying rocks or cliffs **ecological**

scowles   surface remains of iron-ore deposits **geological**

selfquained   rocks that have, by the natural action of weathering and erosion, formed into quains or cornerstones (Gerard Manley Hopkins) **poetic**

sheepy silver   flakes of mica in a stone **Cairngorms**

sinter   of particulate materials: to coalesce into a solid mass under the influence of heat without liquefaction **geological**

skálm   cleft, fissure **Old Norse**

snake-stones   ammonites **southern England**

stenloppm   bruised by stone **Shetland**

tuff   light, porous rock formed by consolidation of volcanic ash **geological** urraghag pile of large boulders left by glaciation **Gaelic**

ventifact faceted stone shaped in texture and form by
           wind-blown sand **geological**

Mud, Humus

claggy lumpy, muddy, as in heavy clay **Exmoor**

clairt mud **Scots**

clogsum heavy, wet land **Suffolk**

glaur muddy mess **Galloway**

gullion stinking mud-hole **Galloway**

gutters wet mud on the surface of the ground made by
         the continued treading of folk or animals
         Shetland

jaupie, platchie splashy, muddy **Scots**

lick-ups clay clods dropped from wheels passing
          through heavy land **Suffolk**

mizzy quagmire **North Sea coast**

muxy miry and muddy **Exmoor**

puxy miry and muddy (more so than *muxy*, at least
      ankle-deep) **Exmoor**

slabby muddy, miry **Northamptonshire**

slappy slippery, wet **Kent**

slosh, slush dirty water; a muddy wash **Kent**

slotter	muddy slush **Exmoor**
slub, slud, slup	sludge, soft mud **Fenland**
slub-slab	noise of an animal splashing through mud and water **Gaelic**
sore	mud **Cheshire, Yorkshire**
squatted, squat-up	splashed with mud by a passing vehicle **Kent, north Staffordshire**

Soil and Earth

brash	light, stony soil **Cotswolds**
bruckle	easily crumbled, stony soil **Galloway**
cats' brains	rough, clayey ground **Herefordshire**
chaps	fissures into which the land is broken after a long period of hot weather **Northamptonshire**
chawm	crack in the ground caused by dry weather **Herefordshire**
chizzelly	land that breaks into small hard fragments when it is turned up by the plough **Northamptonshire**
clarty	of earth: sticky, boot-clingy **Scots**
creech land	light, marly soil containing stones **Fenland**
dough	thick clay **Kent**
frush	easily crumbled, stony **Galloway**

gall vein of sand in a stiff soil through which water oozes out or is drained off **East Anglia**

jingly warm, easily crumbled, stony soil **Galloway**

klevi patch of ground where the sward is worn away and the subsoil is exposed **Shetland**

live-earth common vegetable mould **Northamptonshire**

milly warm, stony soil **Galloway**

moil sticky, wet dirt **Herefordshire**

moory-land black, light, loose earth, without any stones **Northamptonshire**

mould soil scratched from a rabbit hole **Cambridgeshire**

ognel land that is wet, heavy, difficult to work **Herefordshire**

pellum, pillom dust of a cobwebby and straw-like nature **Exmoor**

soilmark area of soil that differs as a result of archaeological features and can be visible in aerial photography **archaeological**

The Black Locust and
the Silver Pine

Two of the greatest twentieth-century English poets of place, Ted Hughes and W. H. Auden, came late in their lives to resemble the landscapes they loved. One thinks of Hughes's great granitic head, more tor than skull, and the Auden of the 1960s, his face creased and grooved like the limestone pavements of northern England, where so much of his early verse is grounded.

John Muir (1838–1914) also grew into likeness with his chosen terrain. One of the best-known photographs of the elder Muir – guardian of Yosemite, family man, influential essayist and memoirist – is a black-and-white image taken in 1907 that shows him perched on a boulder of Californian granite at the base of a rockfall, gripping a twisted staff of pale pinewood. In the background the curled branches and silver trunks of fallen trees can be seen among the rocks. Sunlight falls dappled through foliage. Muir – long-limbed, root-thin – has twists of grey hair that reach his collar, and a white beard that reaches his chest. His legs are crossed, his arms are folded, his hands are gnarled as timber, and his eyes are raised towards the canopy. He is part patriarch, part granite – and mostly tree.

Muir himself never knew quite what he was, and it delighted him not to know. 'I am a poetico-trampo-geologist-bot and ornith-natural, etc.!' he wrote gleefully to a friend in 1889. Looking back over his long life, one sees why he had to weld together this compound description of himself, for there are many John Muirs. There is Muir the long-distance tramp, vagabondizing a thousand miles from Indianapolis to the Gulf of Mexico. There is Muir the pioneering mountaineer, stalking the high country of the Sierra Nevada and making first ascents of several of its biggest peaks. There is Muir the geologist, decoding the glacial origins of the Yosemite Valley. There is Muir the explorer, opening up unmapped regions of Alaska in his fifties. There is Muir the botanist, striding through the pollinous bee-meadows of the Sierra and counting the 10,000 flower-heads in a square yard of subalpine pasture. There is Muir the woodsman, worshipping in the crypt light of the sequoia groves. There is Muir the activist, successfully lobbying Congress for federal protection of the Yosemite region. And there is Muir the writer, honing his skill at epigrams:

> The world is big, and I want to have a good look at it before it gets dark.

> Everybody needs beauty as well as bread.

> The clearest way into the Universe is through a forest wilderness.

> Writing . . . is like the life of a glacier; one eternal grind.

Muir expertly disguised the 'grind' of writing. His books prefer immediacy to reflection. They are lit by sunshine and starlight, and they ringingly communicate the joy of being outside. The chill air of the mountains and the resin-reek of conifer woods lift from his pages. I can think of no other writer as astonished by nature as Muir. He lived, as he put it, in 'an infinite storm of beauty', and to read him is also to be stormed.

In North America, Muir has achieved the status of sage. He is conventionally referred to as the 'Father of the National Parks'. *Time* magazine elected him as one of the hundred Men of the Millennium for the revolution he brought about in environmental thought, for the inspiration he continues to offer to conservation, and for his founding of the Sierra Club. So many peaks, lakes and glaciers have been named after Muir that the U.S. Geological Survey has been obliged to issue a statement declaring that they would be unlikely to approve any further such commemorations. Three plants, a butterfly and a mineral have been christened in his honour, as well as a touring musical and – less expectedly – the John Muir Parkway, a four-lane freeway in Martinez, California, off which tired travellers can pull into the Best Western John Muir Inn. Apparently the beds there are not constructed according to Muir's preferred specifications: gale-felled branches for a frame, pine needles for a mattress and a rock for a pillow.

'Wildness is a necessity,' wrote Muir, 'and . . . mountain parks and reservations are useful not only as fountains of timber and irrigating rivers, but as fountains of life.' He showed that certain landscapes might be precious not in terms of the economic or agrarian resources they provide, but in terms – far harder to measure, far harder to prove – of their effects upon the spirit and the mind.

~

Like all those who survive posterity's prolific deletions, Muir's life has the outline of a parable. At least as Muir told it, he underwent as a young man a 'glorious . . . conversion' that transformed him from son of a preacher to child of the universe.

Muir was born in Dunbar in Scotland, the third child of a fiercely Presbyterian farmer and lay preacher called Daniel Muir, who obliged his children to memorize the Bible in its entirety, and who thrashed them in the belief that he was beating the devil out. In 1849, when Muir was eleven, the family moved from Scotland to Wisconsin, where his father hoped to establish a new life as a farmer and homesteader. Trying to ripen arable land out of the Wisconsin earth was arduous work. Time was rigidly managed by Muir's father – the family rose early, worked all day and went to sleep after evening prayers. When he was fifteen, Muir was set the task of excavating a well in the sandstone on which the farm stood. For several months, every day except Sundays, Muir was lowered alone in a bucket, with a single candle for light, to continue the digging work. At a depth of eighty feet, Muir passed out for want of oxygen and was hauled up barely alive. The next morning his father lowered him to the bottom again. Muir did not hit water until he was ninety feet down.

Muir left home at twenty-one, and soon afterwards enrolled at the University of Wisconsin-Madison, where he studied irregularly for several years. It was under a black locust tree on campus that Muir was given his first botany lesson: a fellow student picked a flower from the tree and explained to Muir how the towering locust was a member of the same family as the lowly pea plant. 'This fine lesson charmed me and sent me flying to the woods and meadows in wild enthusiasm,' Muir remembered later.

After heading to Canada in 1864 to avoid the draft, he returned to America in 1866 and found work as a sawyer in a factory in Indianapolis. In March 1867 he slipped while using a sharp cutting tool, and drove its point into his eye. Cupping a hand to his eye in agony, he felt the aqueous humour trickling through his fingers. When he took his hand away he could see only blackness. Hours later, the vision of his left eye also vanished in sympathetic reaction to the injury. For six weeks Muir lay bandaged in a darkened room, having been told he was unlikely ever to see again. But at last he recovered his sight, felt his eyes had been 'opened to . . . inner beauty', and decided to dedicate himself to the study of trees and plants, and to the exploration of nature.

In this way, Muir's childhood of labour made him at last a loafer. The virtues of diligence and time-hoarding drubbed into him during his adolescence – what he came to call his 'old bondage days' – would be unlearnt during a summer of ecstatic idleness in the Californian mountains. In 1868, aged twenty-nine, he arrived in San Francisco. He disliked the city and stopped a passer-by to enquire the nearest way out of town. '"But where do you want to go?" asked the man to whom I had applied for this important information. "To any place that is wild," I said.' So off Muir was sent to the Sierra Nevada, the range of mountains that spines central California.

The following May he took a job in the Sierra as a shepherd. He was to move a sheep flock 'gradually higher through the successive forest belts as the snow melted, stopping for a few weeks at the best places we came to'. *My First Summer in the Sierra* (1911) is Muir's account of this time – exploring, sleeping out, botanizing, climbing – and certainly his finest book, based on the journal he kept from June to September that year. Reading it now, one is rushed back to those first months of ecstatic freedom, and to Muir's drastic re-imagining of himself. This is his entry for 6 June:

> We are now in the mountains and they are in us . . . making every
> nerve quiver, filling every pore and cell of us. Our flesh-and-bone

tabernacle seems transparent as glass to the beauty about us, as if truly an inseparable part of it, thrilling with the air and trees, streams and rocks, in the waves of the sun, – a part of all nature, neither old nor young, sick nor well, but immortal . . . In this newness of life we seem to have been so always.

'I' has turned into 'we': the singleton of the Presbyterian soul has dissolved into the plurality of the pantheist's. The 'tabernacle' of the chapel is now the tabernacle of the body, 'transparent' to beauty and sympathetic in the strongest sense of the word. Muir has become the mountains – and they have become him.

Muir's commitment to sympathy was part of his broader enmity to egotism: 'Most people are *on* the world, not in it – having no conscious sympathy or relationship to anything about them – undiffused, separate, and rigidly alone like marbles of polished stone, touching but separate.' His own experiences of 'diffusion' came close to the Greek concept of 'metempsychosis', the transmigration of the spirit – or, to give it its beautiful German name, *Seelenwanderung*, 'soul-wandering'. 'One's body seems homogeneous throughout, sound as a crystal,' he records in a journal entry: the mountains were mineralizing him. In a letter to a friend, Muir put his address down as 'Squirrelville, Sequoia Co., Nut time'. 'I'm in the woods woods woods,' the letter began, '& they are in *me-ee-ee.*'

~

The Sierra Nevada is home to some of the most remarkable woods in the world: it is 'indeed . . . the tree-lover's paradise', as Muir put it. From the dwarf willow that makes a 'silky gray carpet, not a single stem or branch more than three inches high', to the giant sequoia, the 'forest kings' whose crowns can reach 'over 300 feet in height', Muir studied them all. His writing about mountaineering inspires me in its commitment to action; his writing about trees amazes me in its commitment to attention. He sketched trees as well as describing them: some of these sketches are tiny, set among the words on the pages of his notebook, such that the branches of the trees reach out and join the serifs and descenders of his handwriting.

For true 'knowledge' of trees, Muir noted in an essay called 'The Forests', 'one must dwell with the trees and grow with them, without any reference to time in the almanac sense'. He did so, living in Yosemite for years after his first summer there. Arboreal study was for Muir a full-body experience. He touched, tasted and smelt the trees he met, in an effort to distinguish the character of each species. He pried apart pine cones, noting the 'silvery luster' of the 'fine down' that coats the cone of *Abies magnifica*, the 'Silver Pine', and the 'rosy purple' tints of its scales and bracts. He tore 'long ribbon-like strips' of 'cinnamon-colored' and 'satiny' bark off the Sierra juniper. He tried to interpret the 'wind-history' and 'storm story' of individual trees, based upon their growth and form. He liked to sleep 'beneath the interlacing arches' of the 'Dwarf Pine', *Pinus albicaulis*, the needles of which 'have accumulated for centuries, [and] make fine beds, a fact well-known to other mountaineers, such as deer and wild sheep, who paw out oval hollows'. And he loved tree-climbing both as sport and as research. When a big winter storm hit the valley in December 1874, Muir clambered to the top of a hundred-foot-high Douglas spruce in order to experience the wind as a tree might. The 'lithe, brushy top' of the tree was 'rocking and swirling' in the gale's 'passionate torrent'. Muir 'clung with muscles firm braced, like a bobolink on a reed', taking 'the wind into my pulses' as the spruce bent and swirled 'backward and forward, round and round, tracing indescribable combinations of . . . curves'. From that 'superb outlook' he could 'enjoy the excited forest':

> Young Sugar Pines, light and feathery as squirrel-tails, were bowing almost to the ground; while the grand old patriarchs, whose massive boles had been tried in a hundred storms, waved solemnly above them, their long . . . branches streaming fluently on the gale and every needle thrilling and ringing and shedding off keen lances of light like a diamond . . . But the Silver Pines were the most impressively beautiful of all. Colossal spires 200 feet in height waved like supple goldenrods chanting and bowing low as if in worship, while the whole mass of their long, tremulous foliage was kindled into one continuous blaze of white sun-fire.

This delicate discrimination between species is typical of Muir. He was a distinctive looker, who always discovered miscellany where others would see uniformity. Up on Mount Hoffman he found a 'broad gray summit' that seemed 'barren and desolate-looking in general views'. But on 'looking at the surface in detail, one finds it covered by thousands and millions of charming plants with leaves and flowers so small they form no mass of color . . . Beds of azure daisies smile confidingly in moist hollows, and along the banks of small rills, with several species of eriogonum, silky-leaved ivesia, pentstemon, orthocarpus, and patches of *Primula suffruticosa*, a beautiful shrubby species.' His books are full of word-lists, embedded glossaries whose language records natural richness with relish. One of my favourite passages of Muir comes when he turns his attention to the trousers of his fellow shepherd, during his first summer in the Sierra. The shepherd is an old-timer, and his trousers have seen decades of wear. Muir notices that they carry a sheen of grease and tree-sap, which causes them to:

> become so adhesive . . . that pine needles, thin flakes and fibers of bark, hair, mica scales and minute grains of quartz, hornblende, etc., feathers, seed wings, moth and butterfly wings, legs and antennae of innumerable insects . . . flower petals, pollen dust and indeed bits of all plants, animals and minerals of the region adhere to them and are safely imbedded.

Brilliant! Where anyone else would see greasy trousers, Muir sees an archive of the Sierra. He concludes his riff with a flourish: 'Instead of wearing thin they wear thick, and in their stratification have no small geological significance.'

There is little Muir does not perceive as significant – except the Native Americans of the Sierra Nevada, whom he is disturbingly unwilling to include in his vision of the wilderness. Otherwise, his prose is rich in generosity and precise of image. He sees a snowfield 'as trackless as the sky' (an image that tellingly pre-dates aviation), he exults in 'the wild gala-day of the north wind', and he describes squirrels in their pines as 'fiery, peppery, full of brag and fight and show, with movements so quick and keen they almost sting the onlooker'. He enjoys existing technical language, especially dendrological ('pistillate', 'bract', 'bole', 'taper', 'axis'), but delights also in his own coinages. He often refers to the sky as 'cloudland', a terrain in its own right that contains 'hills and domes of cloud', and the topography of which is re-made every hour.

Muir's joyfulness can, like Jefferies', spill over into effusion. 'How fine the weather is!' he cries; 'Nothing more celestial can I conceive! How gently the winds blow! Scarcely can these air-currents be called winds! They seem the very breath of Nature, whispering peace to every living thing!' E. M. Forster once compared the use of exclamation marks to laughing at one's own jokes, but for Muir the exclamation mark was a means of notating rapture. The thousands of pages of his published prose demonstrate scant self-regard – the landscape is never tilted flatteringly to reflect his own image. One of his favourite adjectives was 'showy' – the 'showy and fragrant' azalea – but he used the word in its innocent form: to suggest gleeful extravagance rather than immodesty. Muir the writer was 'showy' in the best sense of the word.

Muir the man was exceptionally intrepid. Iain M. Banks once speculated on the leisure activities of the future: they would include, he imagined, lava-rafting and avalanche-surfing. He should have read Muir, who, a hundred years earlier, was already inhabiting Banks's alternative future. In 1873 Muir surfed his first avalanche:

> I was swished down to the foot of the canyon as if by enchantment. The wallowing ascent had taken nearly all day, the descent only about a minute. When the avalanche started I threw myself on my back and spread my arms to try to keep from sinking. Fortunately, though the grade of the canyon is very steep, it is not interrupted by precipices large enough to cause outbounding or free-plunging. On no part of the rush was I buried. I was only moderately imbedded on the surface or at times a little below it, and covered with a veil of back-streaming dust particles; and as the whole mass beneath and about me joined in the flight there was no friction, though I was tossed here and there and lurched from side to side. When the avalanche swedged and came to rest I found myself on top of the crumpled pile without bruise or scar. This was

a fine experience. Hawthorne says somewhere that steam has spiritu-
alized travel; though unspiritual smells, smoke, etc., still attend
steam travel. This flight in what might be called a milky way of
snow-stars was the most spiritual and exhilarating of all the modes
of motion I have ever experienced! Elijah's flight in a chariot of fire
could hardly have been more gloriously exciting!

There is much to admire here, whether it is that 'veil of back-
streaming dust particles', or the 'milky way of snow-stars', or that
trio of peculiar verbs – 'outbound', 'free-plunge' and 'swedge': typically Muirish neologisms for actions. What might, in another's
hands, have become a self-vaunting story of a life nearly lost is for
Muir an experience midway between scientific experiment and sacred
epiphany.

Reading Muir, I feel invulnerable. He gives me seven-league
boots, lets me climb high mountains in a single paragraph. Rockfall,
blizzard and avalanche cannot harm him. Even his metabolism is
superhuman – when he goes off to attempt a big peak, he 'fastens a
hard, durable crust to my belt by way of provision in case I should
be compelled to pass a night on the mountain-top'. When a blizzard
engulfs him at dusk on the summit ridge of the volcanic Mount
Shasta, he survives by locating a fumarole from which 'scalding gas
jets' hiss and sputter. He spends the night trying to avoid being
frozen to death by the blizzard or burnt to death by the vent. And
when an earthquake strikes the Yosemite Valley at night in March
1872, Muir is woken by the shaking, realizes what is happening, and
responds remarkably:

The strange, wild thrilling motion and rumbling could not be mistaken, and I ran out of my cabin, near the Sentinel Rock, both glad

and frightened, shouting, 'A noble earthquake!' feeling sure I was going to learn something. The shocks were so violent and varied, and succeeded one another so closely, one had to balance in walking as if on the deck of a ship among the waves, and it seemed impossible the high cliffs should escape being shattered.

The cliffs escape their shattering, and Muir escapes his. Two years later he would publish his first article about the Sierra Nevada in a journal called the *Overland Monthly*. It was entitled 'Mountain Sculpture', and it began by comparing the form of the range to 'a vast undulated wave'. So started Muir's late-onset writing life.

~

In the final pages of *The Mountains of California* (1894), Muir describes exploring the San Gabriel range to the north of Los Angeles. Having made an afternoon ascent of a 'knife-blade' peak, he returns through the chaparral to a canyon whose lower reaches hold 'boulder pools, clear as crystal, brimming full, and linked together by glistening streamlets', their margins adorned by ten-foot-high lilies in full bloom, as well as larkspur, columbines and ferns. A single old Mountain Live Oak spread its boughs over the pools, and Muir camps beneath it, 'making my bed on smooth cobblestones'. Having evoked this miniature Eden, he ends the book by denouncing the 'destruction of the forests' of California, 'now rapidly falling before fire and the ax'.

Seven years after its publication, a copy of *The Mountains of California* found its way into the hands of Theodore Roosevelt, who in 1901 had been sworn in as President of the United States following the assassination of William McKinley by an anarchist in Buffalo,

New York. Roosevelt was a naturalist, outdoorsman and explorer as well as a politician, and an admirer of Muir's writings. He was in sympathy with Muir's belief in the spiritual value of nature, and his conviction that wild landscapes should be estimated in terms of not only what they might do for us, but also what they might do to us. So he wrote to Muir to see if he would be willing to meet in Yosemite to discuss conservation in person. Muir proposed a three-night camping trip, and on 14 May 1903 Roosevelt arrived in the Sierra Nevada dressed in rough hunting clothes. The next day he and Muir set out, and they camped that first night at the Mariposa Grove, near the south entrance of the valley, among the 500 or so giant sequoias of the grove. The two men had talked as they walked, and their conversation continued around the campfire of 'rosiny logs', which released in their flames 'the light slowly sifted from the sunbeams of centuries of summers'. The next night was spent near Sentinel Dome, during a late-season snowstorm that added five inches of fresh snow to the five feet of lying snow: Roosevelt kept himself warm by burrowing into a pile of forty woollen blankets. The third campsite was under the shelter of the pines that fringe Bridalveil Meadow in the heart of the valley. That night Muir urged the president to take Yosemite Valley under federal control as a national park, and to include within its area the Mariposa Grove.

Muir spoke and Roosevelt listened. Or, as Muir would have had it, the trees spoke and Roosevelt listened. 'Few are altogether deaf to the preaching of pine trees,' Muir had said in 1895. 'Their sermons on the mountains go to our hearts; and if people in general could be got into the woods, even for once, to hear the trees speak for themselves, all difficulties in the way of forest preservation would vanish.' Certainly, this worked with Roosevelt. After leaving Yosemite, he stopped in Sacramento and gave a speech in which he exhorted the citizens of California to preserve the natural wealth of their state, and to use their forests and rivers wisely. Three years after his trip with Muir, he signed the Yosemite Recession Bill, which placed the valley and the sequoias of Mariposa under federal protection. He also legislated decisively to proclaim certain landscapes as monuments in the public interest: in 1908 800,000 acres were set aside as the Grand Canyon National Monument, the first such designation. In the course of his presidency, Roosevelt would sign into existence 5 national parks, 18 national monuments, 55 national bird sanctuaries and 150 national forests.

In her fine *Hope in the Dark* (2007), the Californian writer and activist Rebecca Solnit reflects on the nature of social and political changes, and especially those brought about by literature and art. Hope, she suggests, is a function of uncertainty, of not-knowing. It is a longing for change, experienced in necessary ignorance of when that change will come or what form it will take. 'A lot of activists expect that for every action there is an equal and opposite and *punctual* reaction,' Solnit writes, in a passage to which I find myself often returning:

> and regard the lack of one as failure. But history is shaped by the groundswells and common dreams that single acts and moments only represent. It's a landscape more complicated than commensurate cause and effect . . . Politics is a surface in which transformation comes about as much because of pervasive changes in the depths of the collective imagination as because of visible acts, though both are necessary. And though huge causes sometimes have little effect, tiny ones occasionally have huge consequences . . .
>
> Writers need to understand that action is seldom direct. You write your books. You scatter your seeds. Rats might eat them, or they

might just rot. In California, some seeds lie dormant for decades because they only germinate after fire.

Among those trees whose reproduction is fire-dependent is the lodgepole pine, the cones of which are sealed with a resin that is melted away by fire, releasing the seeds for dispersal. The giant sequoia also requires fire to burn gaps in the canopy, letting in light that allows their seedlings to compete with the shade-tolerant seedlings of other species. But I think that the specific seeds Solnit has in mind are those of the bristlecone pine, whose wood glows orange and gold, and the oldest living specimens of which are nearly 5,000 years old – having begun their growth when the Pyramids were under construction. The seeds of the bristlecone lie dormant in the soil profile until their germination is triggered, usually by the blazing passage of wildfire, which also clears the terrain of competitors. Muir loved the bristlecone for its extravagantly torqued and gnarled form, and for its extreme resilience to the adversities of gale, avalanche and flame that the mountains threw at it. He was a bristlecone himself in that respect, and though his words lay dormant for decades, they would eventually germinate and grow with astonishing consequence.

GLOSSARY IX

Woodlands

Branches, Leaves, Roots and Trunks

atchorn acorn **Herefordshire**

balk cut tree **Kent**

bannut-tree walnut tree **Herefordshire**

beilleag bark of a birch tree **Gaelic**

biests wen-like protuberances on growing trees **East Anglia**

bole main part of the trunk of a tree before it separates into branches **forestry**

bolling permanent trunk left behind after pollarding (pronounced to rhyme with 'rolling') **forestry**

brattlings loppings from felled trees **Northamptonshire**

breakneck, tree whose main stem has been snapped by the
brokeneck wind **forestry**

browse line level above which large herbivores cannot browse woodland foliage **forestry**

burr excrescence on base of tree: some broad-leaved trees with a burr, especially walnut, can be very valuable, the burr being prized for its internal patterning **forestry**

butt lower part of the trunk of a tree **forestry**

cag stump of a branch protruding from the tree **Herefordshire**

cant-mark, stub	pollarded tree used to mark a land boundary **forestry**
celynnog	abounding in holly (place-name element) **Welsh**
chats	dead sticks **Herefordshire**
chissom	first shoots of a newly cut coppice **Cotswolds**
cramble	boughs or branches of crooked and angular growth, used for craft or firewood **Yorkshire**
crank	dead branch of a tree **Cotswolds**
crìonach	rotten tree; brushwood **Gaelic**
daddock	dead wood **Herefordshire**
damage cycle	narrower rings in the stump of the tree, indicating the accidental loss of branches which are gradually replaced. Useful in helping to work out when and at what intervals a tree has been pollarded/coppiced **forestry**
deadfall	dead branch that falls from a tree as a result of wind or its own weight **forestry**
dodder	old *pollard* **Bedfordshire**
dosraich	abundance of branches **Gaelic**
dotard	decaying oak or sizeable single tree **Northamptonshire**
eiry	tall, clean-grown sapling **Cotswolds**
ellern	elder tree **Herefordshire**
flippety	young twig or branch that bends before a hook or clippers **Exmoor**

foxed term applied to an old oak tree, when the centre becomes red and indicates decay **Northamptonshire**

frail leaf skeleton **Banffshire**

griggles small apples left on the tree **south-west England**

interarboration intermixture of the branches of trees on opposite sides (used by Sir Thomas Browne in *The Garden of Cyrus*, 1658) **arboreal**

kosh branch **Anglo-Romani**

Lammas growth second flush of growth in late summer by some species, e.g. oak **forestry**

leafmeal tree's 'cast self', disintegrating as fallen leaves (Gerard Manley Hopkins) **poetic**

lenticel small pore in bark or a leaf for breathing **forestry**

maiden tree which is not a coppice stool nor a *pollard* **forestry**

mute stumps of trees and bushes left in the ground after felling **Exmoor**

nape when laying a hedge, to cut the branch partly through so that it can be bent down **East Anglia**

nubbin stump of a tree after the trunk has been felled **Northamptonshire**

palmate leaves that have lobes arranged like the fingers of a hand, e.g. horse chestnut **forestry**

pank	to knock or shake down apples from the tree **Herefordshire**
pollard	tree cut at eight to twelve feet above ground and allowed to grow again to produce successive crops of wood **forestry**
raaga tree	tree that has been torn up by the roots and drifted by the sea **Shetland**
rammel	small branches or twigs, especially from trees which have been felled and trimmed **Scots**
rootplate	shallow layer of radially arranged roots revealed when a tree has blown over **forestry**
rundle	hollow *pollard* tree **Herefordshire**
scocker	rift in an oak tree caused either by lightning blast or the expansive freezing of water that has soaked down into the heart-wood from an unsound part in the head of the tree **East Anglia**
scrog	stunted bush **northern England, Scotland**
slive	rough edge of a tree stump **northern England, Warwickshire**
spronky	of a plant or tree: having many roots **Kent**
staghead	dead crown of a veteran tree **forestry**
starveling	ailing tree **forestry**
stool	permanent base of a coppiced tree **forestry**
suthering	noise of the wind through the trees (John Clare) **poetic**

tod stump of a tree sawn off and left in the ground; the top of a *pollard* tree **Suffolk**

wash-boughs straggling lower branches of a tree **Suffolk**

wewire to move about as foliage does in wind **Essex**

whip thin tree with a very small crown reaching into the upper canopy **forestry**

wolf bigger than average tree which is dominant in the crop, often removed at first thinning **forestry**

Fallen Wood and Cut Wood

batlings brushwood, too small for timber and too big for faggots **Essex**

biscuity, frow wood which is crumbly, with broken grain **forestry**

brosny dry sticks for lighting a fire **Northern Ireland**

creathach brushwood for fuel **Gaelic**

dharrag log or stump of bog oak **Manx**

droxy of wood: decayed **Cotswolds**

fairy butter, scoom, star jelly, witches' butter yellowish gelatinous substance, found on rotten wood or fallen timber, once reputed to have dropped from the sky **Herefordshire, Northamptonshire**

fox-fire phosphorescent light emitted by decaying timber **Lincolnshire**

musgan dry, rotten wood **Gaelic**

shakes cracks that form in timber as it dries **forestry**

silk-ash flakes of fine grey ash that gather around wood embers that still cover a core of orange heat (Gerard Manley Hopkins) **poetic**

slay pile of cut timber in a wood **Essex**

stob splinter under the skin **Gaelic**

tundey of rotten wood: shining with phosphorescence **East Anglia**

Woods and Woodlands

aldercarr wet place where alder grows **Essex**

bedwos grove of birch trees (usually as a place-name element) **Welsh**

box the fox to raid an orchard **Ireland**

copsy small overgrown woodland **Exmoor**

cyllog abounding in hazels **Welsh**

dene wooded or wood-lined valley with pasturage **Kent**

doire oak wood, oak grove **Irish**

dumble narrow, steep-sided, wooded valley **Nottinghamshire**

dyrys tangled, thorny, wild **Welsh**

fáschoill underwood; grove or bosket **Irish**

frith holy wood; young underwood growing beside hedges **Sussex**

ghost destroyed wood whose outline remains as a hedge, soil-mark or boundary **forestry**

grout small grove **Suffolk**

hagg copse or woodland, especially on a slope or hillside **Yorkshire**

hagginblock wooded area **Northern Ireland**

hake to steal apples **Ireland**

hanger wood on the side of a steep hill or bank **Berkshire, Hampshire**

holt high wood **Cotswolds**

hurst isolated wood, especially one on a hill **forestry**

leaf-whelmed in such dense foliage that sight is extremely limited **poetic**

lēah permanent glade or clearing in woodland **Old English**

overstorey trees forming the upper canopy of a forest **forestry**

perthog abounding in bushes or thickets **Welsh**

pett clump of trees **Kent**

pingle clump of woods, smaller than a *spinney* **Northamptonshire** *plain*   open area in a wooded forest **forestry**

rhedynog   abounding with ferns **Welsh**

ripple   small coppice **Herefordshire**

rosán   brushwood; *understorey* **Irish**

roughet   small wood, containing little or no large timber, comprising chiefly hazel or ash saplings, or both, with a thick bramble undergrowth **Kent**

scrub   young woodland **forestry**

shadowtackle   shifting net-like patterns of shadow formed on woodland floors by the light-filtering action of the canopy in wind (Gerard Manley Hopkins) **poetic**

shelter belt   trees and shrubs planted in a comparatively narrow strip to provide protection, usually of farmland **forestry**

spinney   small wood, often thick with thorns **forestry**

toll   clump or row of trees **Kent**

understorey   trees and shrubs below the canopy **forestry**

wayleave   strip of land either side of power lines in which tall trees are not permitted **forestry**

wildwood   natural woodland unaffected by Neolithic or later civilization **forestry**

Childish

'As you sit on the hillside, or lie prone under the trees of the forest, or sprawl wet-legged by a mountain stream,' wrote the walker Stephen Graham in 1927, 'the great door, that does not look like a door, opens.' Such visionary moments came rarely to Graham – as they come rarely to all adults – though he sought them throughout his life, tramping across America, Russia and Britain in the hope of glimpsing 'the great door' swing open. John Muir, childish by nature, had used the same image some thirty years earlier: 'Between every two pines is a door leading to a new life.'

To young children, of course, nature is full of doors – is nothing but doors, really – and they swing open at every step. A hollow in a tree is the gateway to a castle. An ant hole in dry soil leads to the other side of the world. A stick-den is a palace. A puddle is the portal to an undersea realm. To a three- or four-year-old, 'landscape' is not backdrop or wallpaper, it is a medium, teeming with opportunity and volatile in its textures. Time is fluid and loopy, not made of increment and interval. Time can flow slow enough that a mess of green moss on the leg of a tree can be explored for an age, and fast enough that to run over leaves is to take off and fly. What we bloodlessly call 'place' is to young children a wild compound of dream, spell and substance: place is somewhere they are always *in*, never *on*.

The best children's literature understands this different order of affordance. This is why so many of the greatest children's stories involve thresholds, place-warps, time-slips and doorways: access points that lead to experience and danger, in defiance of standard geometries, and often beyond the guardianship of adults. Virginia Woolf once observed that the most difficult task for a novelist was getting a character out of one room and into another. Children's literature feels no such awkwardness: characters can step out of one room and find themselves – without explanation – in a different epoch, continent or universe. Thus the wardrobe that opens into Narnia, or the flickering border through which Will passes in Philip Pullman's *The Subtle Knife* (1997) to reach the shadowlands. Susan Cooper's *The Dark Is Rising* (1973), the eeriest novel I know, begins in a Buckinghamshire village on Midwinter Eve, four days short of Christmas and one short of the birthday of a boy named Will Stanton. Far to the north a blizzard is brewing, and things are not as they 'normally' are in the land around. Animals are restless, and rooks clatter from the treetops to swirl blackly above the fields. The blizzard strikes in the evening, and Will wakes the next morning to hear strange music, rising loudly and then falling away:

> It had gone again. And when he looked back through the window, he saw that his own world had gone with it. In that flash everything had changed. The snow was there as it had been a moment before, but not piled now on roofs or stretching flat over lawns and fields. There were only trees. Will was looking over a great white forest: a forest of massive trees, sturdy as towers and ancient as rock.
>
> The strange world lay stroked by silence. No birds sang. The garden was no longer there, in this forested land. Nor were the outbuildings nor the old crumbling walls. There lay only a narrow clearing round the house now, hummocked with unbroken snow-

drifts, before the trees began, with a narrow path leading away . . .
As soon as he moved away from the house he felt very much alone,
and he made himself go on without looking back over his shoulder,
because he knew that when he looked, he would find that the house
was gone.

'[H]e saw . . .', 'he knew . . .': These drastic transformations don't
surprise Will, though they scare him, nor does their uncanniness
need explanation – for they pre-exist within his sense of the possible.
He has not yet fallen to the real.

'Children have many more perceptions than they have terms to
translate them,' wrote Henry James, memorably, in his Preface to
What Maisie Knew (1897). But it might be truer to say that 'Children
have many more terms than we have perceptions to translate them.'
For the speech of young children is subtle in its intricacies and rich
in its metaphors. It is not an impoverished dialect of adult speech.
Rather, it is another language altogether; impossible for adults to
speak and arduous for us to understand. We might call that language
'Childish': we have all been fluent in Childish once, and it is a language with a billion or more native speakers today – though all of
those speakers will in time forget they ever knew it.

~

Five or six years ago I met a remarkable person called Deb Wilenski.
Deb understands Childish better than any other adult I have met. In
her thirties she was a researcher specializing in primate behaviour
and psychology. She undertook fieldwork with rhesus macaques in
Cayo Santiago, and with baboons in Namibia, following a pack in
the high orange hills of the country's south-west. She was studying

how the baboons oriented and navigated themselves, and how intent and knowledge were communicated between members of the troop. 'The baboons would meet and mingle in the mornings,' she told me, 'flow their many different ways down into the valleys, and then miraculously coincide, miles away, hours later, as if each knew where the invisible rest of the group was heading.' Up in the Namibian hills, looking out over the landscape, with seventy-four pairs of baboon eyes also looking out over the same relatively simple terrain (slopes, gravel plains, dry riverbeds), she began to realize how she and the baboons were 'seeing different things: the routes and resources, the ways through the land, the landmarks, were all multiple'.

From baboons, Deb turned to young children, but continued her interest in 'multiple' landscapes. She left anthropology and academia behind, and became involved in outdoor pre-school education, inspired in the first instance by the forest kindergartens of Scandinavia, and by Loris Malaguzzi, the founder of the Reggio Emilia approach, who emphasized the need to listen to children rather than to instruct them. Deb wanted to let children lead her into landscapes, rather than the reverse – and to explore their imaginations as they explored places. She began working with groups of children over several months, taking them often to the same areas of forest or wild ground and then letting them find their own ways into the woods. As they discussed their findings with one another, Deb listened – and this was how she began to comprehend at least some of what Malaguzzi once called 'the hundred languages of children'.

One of the first places Deb went was Wandlebury, the area of mixed beech woods and grassland that lies on the chalk uplands south of Cambridge, near to my home. Wandlebury is a child's delight: there is an Iron Age ring-fort with a deep outer ditch, twelve feet deep in places, around which you can run in an endless circle. Beyond it, among the trees, is a network of forking and interlacing paths so complex that it seems impossible to trace the same route twice. At Wandlebury the children led and Deb followed. She was careful not to intervene in their plots and plans, except when safety required it. Slowly, she began to make records of the children's conversations as they explored the area. She mapped the routes they followed, the dens they built out of dead wood and fallen branches, the places of rest and shelter they settled upon and the doorways they found, and the language they used to describe what they discovered each day.

In the winter of 2012, together with an artist called Caroline Wendling, and encouraged by an organization called Cambridge Curiosity and Imagination, Deb began work with a reception class from a primary school in Hinchingbrooke, north Cambridgeshire. For three months, each Monday morning she and Caroline went with around thirty four- and five-year-old children into the country park that bordered the school's grounds. The eve of that first Monday was – echoes of *The Dark Is Rising* – a night of blizzards. Heavy snow lay on the land the next morning, and there ensued one of the harshest winter-springs of recent years in the south of England. 'It was cold when we began in January,' remembered Deb later, 'and it was still cold when we ended in April. What was amazing was that nobody seemed to mind.'

Hinchingbrooke Country Park consists of 170 acres of meadow, lake, wood and marsh, lying a mile or so west of Huntingdon and bounded on one side by a dual carriageway and on another by a hospital car park. It is a landscape of contrasts: tall old pines with dark short sightlines give way to meadows that lead down to the edge of water. The children were free to explore within the park, and the hours they spent there were unstructured by commitment. Each Monday morning was spent in the landscape, each afternoon back in the school further investigating 'the real and fantastical place that the park was becoming'.

Deb watched and listened over the months, and tried to record without distortion how the children 'met' the landscape, and how they used their bodies, senses and voices to explore it 'with imagination and with daring'. She sought to follow how the children navigated and oriented themselves: the 'visible and invisible traces through the forest' that they left, the 'lines drawn on paper' and 'words [and stories] that connect one place to another'.

It was clear that the children perceived a drastically different landscape from Deb and Caroline. They travelled simultaneously in physical, imagined and wholly speculative worlds. With the children as her guides, Deb began to see the park as 'a place of possibility', in which the 'ordinary and the fantastic' – immiscible to adult eyes – melded into a single alloy. No longer constituted by municipal zonings and boundaries, it was instead a limitless universe, wormholed and Möbian, constantly replenished in its novelty. No map of it could ever be complete, for new stories seethed up from its soil, and its surfaces could give way at any moment. The hollows of its trees were routes to other planets, its subterrane flowed with streams of silver, and its woods were threaded through with filaments of magical force. Within it the children could shape-shift into bird, leaf, fish or water.

Each day brought different weather, and each weather different worlds. The snow of the first week was white to Deb's and Caroline's eyes, but to the children it was technicoloured: 'yellow at the edges' and 'green at the top of the trees' to a boy called Filip; a 'pink forest' to Thomas. When the thaw eventually came, it left a world 'of newly made mud'. The smooth snow-sward gave way to new textures and dimensions: slipperiness, sinkholes, ruts and rivulets. The wood became suddenly deep to the children, as the mud sucked and clutched at them. When rain came, the children were drawn to water and waterways. One of the children, Cody, became fascinated by the disappearance and reappearance of running water within the park: how pond connected to lake, stream to puddle. In ways that were in contradiction of gravity, but consistent with the physics of his own imagination, Cody started to account for the existence of visible water by means of an unseen network of what he called 'secret water' that ran unprovably beneath the ground. He took to a kind of dowsing, pacing out on the surface the flow-lines of this secret water, and – as Deb put it – helping her 'realize that the land we are exploring sits on top of a whole other land, subterranean, that shares with ours a single, continuous, touchable surface'.

Cody found entrances to this underworld by reeds and tree roots – as every child found doorways to the realms they named into being. These doors led to dangerous places as well as 'good spots', and the landscape was soon crowded with them, like the beehive cells of the Skelligs. The drawings the children made in the afternoons were also densely doorwayed: mouse holes, tunnel mouths, portals. None of the doors the children drew, Deb noticed, had locks. The doors appeared and disappeared, but always opened both ways.

As well as opening doors, the children made dens: the doors allowing access and adventure, the dens permitting retreat and shelter. Young children are, as all parents know, natural den-makers. Indoors, they curl up in bedclothes, they string sheets between chairs, they prop cushions in corners, they crawl under tables, they shut themselves into cardboard boxes – fashioning nests, bolt-holes, setts and holts. Outside they steal into the hearts of hedges, improvise shelters from packing cases and plastic bags, or make rickety wigwams and lean-tos out of branches. Children's literature is dense with dens: the hollow-tree hideout that becomes the redoubt of the feral siblings in BB's *Brendon Chase* (1944), the scavenged shanty-den of *Stig of the Dump* down at the bottom of the chalk pit, or the piratical stockades founded by Tom Sawyer and Huck Finn.

In the architecture of dens, function is subservient to form: it doesn't matter that a den's loose-ribbed walls would keep out no wind, or that its entrance can be entered only at a crawl. A fallen trunk will serve as a roof ridge, against which sticks and branches can be leaned. Yellowing leaves are gathered and piled to make a heatless fire, around which the children can sit, warming their hands in its light. Old dens are cannibalized to make new dens, and no one structure is built to last more than a season. The woods at Wandlebury hold dozens of dens at any one time, and when I see them there together and in such number, seen between the beeches, there is a curiously ethnographic feel to the encounter: as if the dens are the evidence of a lost tribe, discovered in a region that is barely reachable or known.

Which, of course, is what they are: the tribe being children, the region being childhood, and the ethnographers being adults. Not that we wholly lose our fascination with dens as we age. 'After one of his shipwreckings in the *Odyssey*,' notes Tim Dee:

Odysseus clambers up a hill from a beach and crawls beneath two olive trees, one wild and one domesticated, and makes a nest there from the dropped leaves of both. Samuel Taylor Coleridge, walking in the Lake District in June 1801, found 'a Hollow place in a Rock like a Coffin – exactly my own Length – there I lay and slept. It was quite soft.'

In his classic study of intimate places, *The Poetics of Space* (1958), the French phenomenologist Gaston Bachelard writes at length about our lifelong dream-need for hollows and huts. Traversing ornithology, psychology, architecture and literature, Bachelard discovers a family of den-like recessed spaces – corners, birds' nests, cellars, attics, chests, caverns, walled gardens (the *hortus conclusus*) – that continue to exert a fascination upon the mind even as it ages, because they 'shelter day-dreaming'. He calls the readiness to be astonished by such spaces 'topophilia' (place-love), but I think we might also name it 'wonder', 'innocence', or even just 'happiness'.

~

We live in an era of diminishing childhood contact with nature, and landscapes outside the urban. A 2012 'Natural Childhood' report recorded that between 1970 and 2010, the area in which British children were permitted to play unsupervised shrank by 90 per cent. The proportion of children regularly playing in 'wild' places fell from one in two to one in ten. In another study, participants from three generations were given maps of the places in which they grew up, and asked to mark with crosses where they remembered playing. The spread of the crosses – the so-called 'roaming radius' – tightened from generation to generation, until in the third it was cinched right down to house, garden and pavement. Screen-time has increased dramatically. Environmental literacy has plummeted. Nine out of ten children can identify a Dalek; three out of ten a magpie.

The disconnection from nature is greater now than it has ever been. 'The children out in the woods, out in the fields,' said the naturalist and broadcaster Chris Packham in May 2014, 'enjoying nature on their own – they're extinct.'

Flashes from history mark the contrast with our own. My father, growing up in Malvern in the 1950s, set out at the age of seven each weekday to cycle seven miles to school in the morning, and seven miles home in the evening, along country roads (no helmet); at the age of fourteen he built a canoe in the garage and then paddled it down the River Wye from Upper Breinton to Monmouth, wearing his father's Second World War Mae West life jacket. In the 1930s, schoolchildren from England and Wales were recruited as crowd-cartographers and sent out on foot into the countryside in pairs, tasked with mapping the use of every parcel of land, then 'returning the results to London where they were compiled onto topographic base maps and coloured to reveal national patterns of land use'. In *The Rural Life of England* (1838), William Howitt records how village children would 'use the green lanes as their playgrounds as well as scenes of their earliest employment . . . small children were sent out there to mind big babies, shut lonely gates for horseriders'. Robert Louis Stevenson notes in one of his 'essays of travel' that while out walking in the countryside in the 1880s, he heard a 'bustle' and met 'a great coming and going of school-children upon bypaths'.

These changes in the culture of childhood have huge conse-quences for language: most strikingly apparent in the deletions from the *Oxford Junior Dictionary* that I discussed in the first chapter. And our children's vanishing encounters with nature represent a loss of imagination as well as a loss of primary experience. For, as the nov-elist Michael Chabon writes in an essay subtitled 'The Wilderness of

Childhood', if children abandon 'the sandlots and creek beds, the alleys and woodlands', if 'children are not permitted . . . to be adventurers and explorers as children', then 'what will become of the world of adventure, of stories, of literature itself?'

~

In the early days at Hinchingbrooke, the children stayed among the trees, opening their doors and building their dens. There was plenty to explore in the woods. After several weeks, though, they found their way to the wood's fringe, where it borders grassland that slopes down to a lake. They spotted a gap between two pines: 'A door, a door, can we go through?' The doorway took them to 'an unfamiliar land', sunlit and wide, softer underfoot, light in its colours. Filip 'lay down on the soft spongy ground', wrote Deb of this day, 'meet[ing] the new place like he met the land in the snow – with his whole body'. Filip reminded me of others who had lain down in the landscape to know it better: Shepherd on the Cairngorm plateau, Jefferies on the Wiltshire turf, Muir under the spreading boughs of a mountain oak, and Hawkes on the grass of her London garden.

The profusion of doorways that the children discovered, and the move into the meadows, allowed 'the travelling to reach a new dramatic level', and this in turn helped Deb to comprehend the children's experiences. She realized that they were undertaking a 'kind of fantastic travelling, in which worlds slip easily around each other, where there are soft boundaries between what is real and what is remembered, and each place in front of us is somewhere else too'.

'Childhood is a branch of cartography,' suggests Chabon, but surely – again – we should reverse the terms of his proposition:

'Cartography is a branch of childhood.' Children are intense and intuitive mappers, using story, touch and paper to plot their places. Deb and Caroline listened in the mornings as names were given to places within the park ('The Living Room', 'Snap-land', 'Den-land', 'Spiky Land'), and they watched in the afternoons as the children drew maps of the park that were also documents of realms beyond sight: for in their Hinchingbrooke Country Park wolves lived in tunnels deep within a mountain, dolphins sang below the surface of the lake, there were tree-houses and air-cities, and the sky held cold suns and hot moons. In the final weeks, Caroline drew a huge outline of the park in chalk on brown paper. This was taped to the wall in the corridor, and became a canvas on which the children could place their individual maps, like tiles in a mosaic. In this way a collaged atlas of the park came into existence – a 'map of maps', a 'map of the mind's adventures'.

The children's explorations of place were also, of course, explorations of and in language: they 'weaved words and ways together', creating new terms (playful, specific, personal) to account for the changeable world they were inhabiting. They coined toponyms and nouns: 'honeyfurs', beautifully, for the soft seed-heads that they gathered from the grasses. Their speech was also rich with the magical thinking of early childhood, whereby things imagined true *are* true, and the distinction between the dreamt and the real is shimmery at its strongest. Like Vainamoinen, young children utter words of bidding, confident in their sense that if one points, names, declares, then the terms of the universe are changed by the declaration: 'My name is Kian and I'm going to jump over the whole world!' 'I was born in the climbing tree,' declared a girl who had spent weeks gaining the confidence to climb into the branches of a cherry. 'I was born in space and Mars,' said another, the most confi-dent tree-climber in the group (a natural Cosimo). They told stories of masterful miniaturism, brimming with make-believe: 'This is the mountain, now it's the wolves' home. I wanted to fly – I didn't want to wake the wolves, they just climb up here.' They were narratively at ease with what adults would see as contradiction: paradox was, instead of a tool for collapsing meaning, a means of holding incom-patibilities in rich relation. Gracefully accurate, their utterances rarely required extension.

After they had finished their cold spring at Hinchingbrooke, Deb and Caroline began to try to find a means of recording what they had witnessed. So together they made a slender and beautiful book composed largely of the children's speech, stories and draw-ings. They called it *A Fantastical Guide* in recognition of its subject. Every time I read the *Guide*, I am amazed again. For to open it is to see again through young eyes, and to hear Childish spoken. The *Guide* offers a map to the park's doorways and portals, but also to how all landscapes might be seen childishly, such that a wood – or a field, or a garden, or a house – can 'hold infinite possibilities in a single unfolding place', and to enter a place is – as one of the children put it – to go looking 'for a secret tree, and an invisible door'.

Shortly after first reading the *Guide*, I found myself recalling the story of the T'ang Dynasty artist Wu Tao-Tzu, who is said one day to have gathered his friends to show them his most recent painting. The friends huddled round it in admiration: it was a vertical scroll painting of a mountainous landscape with a footpath that led along the bank of a stream, and then through a grove of trees to a small cottage or hut.

But when the friends turned to congratulate Wu Tao-Tzu, they realized he had vanished. Then they saw that he had stepped into the landscape of the painting, and was walking along the path and through the grove. He reached the entrance to the hut, and on its threshold he paused, turned, smiled, and then passed through the narrow doorway.

POSTSCRIPT

The day before writing the final sentences of the last chapter of this book, I received an extraordinary letter from a scholar of languages living in Qatar. For the past fifteen years, he explained to me, he had been working on a global glossary of landscape words. His fascination with the subject went back as far as he could remember. He was born in Cyrenaica, now eastern Libya, where his father trained King Idris's household cavalry. He grew up among the kopjes, vleis and veldt of rural southern Rhodesia, now Zimbabwe. He was schooled in the Dorset countryside, before beginning a period of extensive travelling in Africa and the Middle East.

It was while studying Arabic, he said, and walking the black lava fields (*harrah*), deep wadis and granite domes (*hadbah*) of the Hejaz in western Arabia, that he decided to begin gathering place-words from the Arabic dialects, before they were swept away by the rapid modernization and urbanization enabled by oil money. But Arabic's rich relations with other languages soon caused his research to ripple outwards, and his task began to grip him with the force of an obsession. He moved into neighbouring Semitic and Afro-Eurasian languages with heavy Arabic influence (Turkish, Berber, Persian, Urdu, Swahili, Maltese and Spanish). The entries for individual words grew, some of them to several pages in length, as a meshwork of cross-reference thrived between languages and usages. He turned to Sanskrit, Bengali and the many other languages of the subcontinent, then to Latin, and then the Romance, Celtic, Germanic, Nordic and Slav language families.

Then he decided to extend the temporal range of his research backwards from the present day to the first Sumerian cuneiform records of *c.* 3100 BCE: a span of more than five millennia. This required him to work with ancient and extinct languages, and reconstructed proto-languages: watching as terms sprang into being in one tongue, then tracking their passages through centuries and in cognate forms. Geographically, he journeyed across the Afro-Eurasian lands from the Atlantic coast in the west to the China Seas in the east. Topographically, he ranged from micro- to macro-scales, covering the natural features of the earth's surface (from mountains to rills); the man-made environment (cities, settlements, buildings, farms, ditches, tracks); the names of trees and plants; the names of regions and territories; terms of relative position, size and colour; and compass directions and measures of distance. Linguistically, he worked through around 140 languages, from Afrikaans to Zande by way of Comorian, Chinese, Hebrew, Tagalog and Uzbek. His hope – as he spent tens of thousands of hours in libraries and at his desk – was to show that 'the landscape is an enormous repository of language, preserving a lexicon of words as diverse, intricate and dynamic as the land itself . . . an ancient yet evolving text that tells the stories of its places and the histories of its peoples, for the land is layered in language as surely as the rocks are layered beneath its surface'.

The work became so vast in its form, he told me, so complex in its structures and so infinitely extendable in its concerns that he did not envisage ever completing it, only bringing it to a point of abandonment that might also be a point of publication – though what the physical manifestation of the book might be was hard to envisage.

'The project has,' he said, almost embarrassedly, 'something of the fabulous about it.'

Later he sent me, as an attachment to an email, the section of the glossary covering those words beginning with the letter 'B'. 'I hope the file-size can be accommodated . . .' he wrote. I double-clicked it. The document opened in Word, and I watched the page-count whirr up as my computer ascertained the extent of the text. The count hit 100 pages, then 200, then 300 . . . it settled at last on 343 pages. Three hundred and forty-three pages in eleven-point font, just for 'B'. Then I read the note preceding the first entry, '*bā* (Akkadian, jungbabylonisch lex.): *water*': 'This glossary is a work in progress. At the present time . . . it is some 3,500 pages long and contains around 50,000 separate terms or headwords.' I sat back in my seat.

It was a strange and haunting moment. It felt as if I had wandered into a story by Borges or Calvino. At the end of the second chapter of *Landmarks*, I fantasized about the existence of a 'Counter-Desecration Phrasebook that would comprehend the world', a 'glossary of enchantment for the whole earth'. I first indulged in that thought-experiment in 2007 on Lewis, when I read the Peat Glossary and imagined extending its qualities of precision, poetry and tact drastically upwards and outwards in scale. I knew it to be an impossible dream, for language is at last an untrustworthy medium, mirageous and fissile, never better than approximate in its relation to the world. Nevertheless, I resolved to begin forming my own small and partial place-word lists.

But here, now, the day before finishing the book begun by that Peat Glossary, I learnt that a world-sized Counter-Desecration Phrasebook was actually coming into being – manifested by the brilliance and diligence of this extraordinary scholar, out there in the desert, gathering and patterning a work of words that might keep us from slipping off into abstract space.

GLOSSARY X

Left blank for future place-words and the reader's own terms

GLOSSARY

GLOSSARY XI

Gift Words

Gifts

A week or so after *Landmarks* was published in the spring of 2015, the first gift word arrived. It came on an old postcard of Pendle Hill in Lancashire. The blue-ink handwriting was slightly spidery. 'Dear Robert Macfarlane,' it began, then:

> 'lighty-dark': a word to describe the light occurring at the edge of darkness after a cold clear day. Invented by me (aged 11) walking home in the beautiful, under-valued Lancashire landscape of the countryside, in the evening.

It was signed off:

> (Mrs) Margaret Cockcroft aged 96

The edge of darkness after a cold clear day . . . : a word coined in childhood in the 1930s, remembered in old age in the 2010s; a word that brought flooding back to its coiner – and rushing out at me – a moment in time and place.

In the following months, thousands more words reached me. People wrote to share place-terms that were not in my glossaries, or to respond to those that were. Letters and postcards arrived, sometimes dozens in a day, carrying not only words but also books, flowers and seeds, photographs, stones, bits of bark, stories, poems. They came from around the world – Australia, Canada, Iceland, Sweden, New Zealand, North America, South Africa, Germany, France – but mostly from Britain and Ireland. Email brought them too, as did Twitter (a word and a definition being well suited to 140 characters). They were written in several languages and numerous dialects. One was start-to-finish in Scots, and made me grin: 'Aye, ah wis fair taen wi this mairvellous "word hoard" ye hae dug up!! an faur mair valuable than ony Saxon Sutton-Hoo nonsense!'

The people who sent the words came from a wide range of backgrounds. A nurse working with long-term ICU patients. A woman whose Nazi father had flown in the notorious Condor Legion and bombed Guernica. A lollipop man who each morning discussed the weather with the parents and children he ushered safely across the road. A man who had spent 'a lifetime farming', and for whom a rich place-language had been a necessary 'part of everyday vocabulary'. A man whose family had farmed the same land on the Isle of Wight 'for more than 600 years'. A former miner who had laboured – like his father and grandfather before him – for decades in the northeastern coalfields, and who listed 'expressions peculiar to the underground world'. One envelope contained a six-page letter written in black biro on lined A4 paper, and included diagrams, pictures and many block capitals. It was signed off: 'AGED 88 & STONE DEAF!' An American poet who had translated Virgil's *Georgics* into English in their entirety described how that task had brought her to relish 'the vast and supple language that is English, so ready to register tiny discriminations of texture and color in soil, rock, water and field.' A Newfoundland artist – the well-named Marlene Creates – sent me her own 'treasury of terms for ice and snow' and was able to confirm that the old Wessex term for icicle, *clinkerbell*, had at some point made the journey to Newfoundland and survived there. The son of a farmer transcribed pages of Cheshire words and marked them with a cross-system: one cross for 'possibly still in use', two for 'known to me as a lad', three for 'known to my father in the 1920s'.

An anxiety at language death and language loss was a common theme: I heard from researchers working on such issues in Hawaii, Australia and California. Claire Hope Cummings, an environmental lawyer specializing in the land rights of indigenous people in the south-western USA, wrote to tell me of her attempts to integrate the site-specific 'landscape lexicons' of native peoples with chilly federal legalese. 'Here in Northern California', she wrote, 'place-based languages are dying out swiftly.' A correspondent from Montana offered *nele*, a word from the critically endangered Salish language, with fewer than fifty native speakers, which means 'a heavy mist falling as a gentle rain, a "grandmother" rain, healing to a deep degree: also the word for "love"'.

One day's post brought a 'weather-book' of Orcadian wind- and snow-words, 'posted from Orkney with a head of bog-cotton between the pages'; and in another envelope an eighteenth-century ballad copied out in a sloping copperplate hand from a book in the Stonyhurst School archive library, with starred footnotes to explain the dialect terms. A postcard carried a list of 'English fishermen's words for the watches of the night: *light moon flood, light moon ebb, dark moon flood, dark moon ebb*', which became a poem that tided in my mind for days afterwards. Someone passed on a word-list he had found 'on a faded piece of paper between the 100 or so sheets of an account my father left of his early years in a working class and Methodist family, in a remote Yorkshire dale'. A man sent a poem he had written for his daughter that combined place-names and bird-calls into a text that was part nonsense, part litany. Other parents sent me their children's words as fresh contributions to the language of 'Childish' I had written about in the book's last main chapter.

One correspondent reminded me that Catcleugh, a Northumberland place-name, meant 'ravine of the wild cats'; another told me of the oddly tender old Hertfordshire habit of calling the sun 'Phoebe'. A man who had been in hospital for a serious operation wrote to say he had read the glossaries while recuperating: 'The first day I was home,' he recounted, 'I was being helped by my wife to move about the house, and she called me to the dining room at the front and I slowly sat down on a chair at the window. 3 quails were dippling about on the small front garden under the trees. It was wonderful to watch as they were only feet away.' I was made aware of the vast variety of regional terms for woodlouse, among them *chuggypig* and *grammercell* (Cornwall), *chucky-pig* and *johnny-grump* (Gloucestershire), *daddy-gramfer* (Somerset), *slater* (Northern Ireland), *sow-dug* (Essex) and *sowpig* (Yorkshire). I hadn't expected such entomological burlesque. Many of the words that were sent were new to me, but instantly memorable: *yowetrummle*, literally 'ewe-tremble', Scots for the chill late-spring wind that comes in the weeks after the sheep have been sheared; or *jökulhlaup*, meaning a sudden 'subglacial flood, sometimes caused by geothermal or volcanic activity beneath a glacier'.

Again and again I was struck by the generosity shown in this sharing of words. All were freely given; not one person requested anything in return. Many of the postcards were unsigned. I was reminded of my early sense of this place-language as being ultra-specific in its reference, but also forming a kind of common ground – unenclosed and open to all-comers. I was reminded, too, of Emerson's beautiful description of language as 'a city to the building of which every person has brought a stone'.

Gifts

Of the many gifts I received, two were unforgettable. One of these came first in the form of a letter from Mary West, a woman who lived in a village close to where I had grown up in mid-Nottinghamshire. For forty years, she explained, she had been 'collecting all sorts of words and sayings, dialects . . . mostly connected with nature and the countryside'. 'It's now quite a large collection,' she continued, 'mostly on index cards . . . and housed in a wooden box . . . which I would be delighted for you to have.' And so she sent them: rehoused from the wooden box (too heavy to post) into a shoe box, secured in white tissue paper and accompanied by an alphabetized red-cloth notebook with yet more words. The index cards were separated into topics, the titles of which formed a poem of their own: 'Long-Range Forecasts', 'Graces', 'Clouds and Rainbows', 'Winds' . . . I felt improbably fortunate – impossibly grateful – to have been trusted with it all.

The other unforgettable gift was a bundle of research notebooks, passed to me by the granddaughter of a woman called Nell Young. In the summer of 1949, aged nineteen, Nell had gone out into the Gosforth area of what was then the county of Cumberland, and interviewed more than sixty dialect speakers – most of them men and most of them working the land in some way. The pages of her notebooks were thick with pencilled word-lists, diagrams, doodles, notes to self and details of speech. There were pages on the language of otter-hunting, fox-hunting, tracking, pig-killing and cheese-making. Reading the notebooks, I was drawn into the world of this young woman, four summers after the end of the war, asking earnest questions of these hard men. The outcome of her courage was a 'Glossary of West Cumberland Words', neatly handwritten in blue ink, with each word's pronunciation carefully documented in IPA.

Gift – the nature of gifts, and the gifts of nature – was one of the theoretical preoccupations of *Landmarks*, and it quickly became clear to me that I needed to find a way to give on many of the words I had been sent. So I decided to add a further glossary to the paperback edition of *Landmarks*. To reproduce the several thousand words I had been sent would have extended the book by hundreds of pages, so in the end I selected 500 of the most striking place-words – the place-*holding* words – that I had been given, from *addland* to *ʒebn-slaper*, and I gratefully print them here.

~

In May 2015, Oxford University Press revealed its 'children's word of the year' to be *hashtag*. OUP had chosen the word based on its analysis of more than 120,000 short stories by children aged between five and thirteen years, submitted to the BBC's '500 Words' competition. Taken together, these stories offered remarkable glimpses into the communal imagination of Britain's children. I read the analysis with fascination. Among the most popular characters in the stories were Wayne Rooney, Snow White, Adolf Hitler, Lionel Messi and Cinderella. Two of the most popular plots were achieving sudden Internet fame after posting a YouTube video – and finding a cure for Ebola. New words were coined: *wellysaurus*, *gloomful*, and the mutant monster mash-up *Stegasuareʒ* (which, it seemed to me, unjustly hybridized the plant-eating Stegosaurus with the flesh-biting Luis Suárez).

'Nature words' were present in the stories, but infrequently. Out of a total corpus of 53 million words, *oak* was the most popular natural term, though hardly ubiquitous (3,975 usages), then came *owl* (3,348), then *eagle* (1,855). After that were *lily* (1,535), *lair* (1,443), *countryside* (1,318), *poppy* (1,130) and *daisy* (1,061), though I presumed that *lily*, *poppy* and *daisy* were ranked highly only because they are popular girls' names, which the analysis engines had failed to distinguish as proper nouns. Down at the lower end, heading fast for extinction, were *acorn* (293 usages), *buttercup* (168), *blackbird* (167) and *conker* (155). As OUP concluded, 'the stories showed new technology to be increasingly at the centre of children's lives', and their findings confirmed to me the need to keep the language of the living world alive in the mouths and mind's eyes of young people. Technology is miraculous, but so too is nature – and this aspect of the world's wonder seems under threat of erasure in children's narratives, dreams and plots.

When I gathered and published the glossaries of *Landmarks*, I didn't imagine them as zoological display drawers, containing pinned and labelled exhibits – rather as teeming ecosystems, vivid with life. I hoped I might somehow release the vital energies of these words back out into the wider culture – though I had no preconceived notion of what this might achieve, and anyway no wish to instrumentalize this lexis in terms of its 'deliverables' or 'outcomes'. It has been one of the great surprises of *Landmarks* to watch the consequences of this release.

For the words of the glossaries have found their ways into the work of forest schools, kindergartens, environmental charities and campaign groups, and into the practice of conservationists, educators, map-makers, linguists, artists, poets, children's authors, translators, historians, architects, film-makers, psychologists, mythologists and storytellers, among others. It is not that people are suddenly speaking in dialect – 'dropping plums', as Adam Nicolson nicely puts it – but rather that the ways of seeing and the forms of relation embodied by the words have been found to be variously valuable: as sharpenings of vision, slowings of pace, deepenings of acquaintance, acts of purchase (in the sense of grip and touch, rather than procurement), brief enchantments, resistances to homogenization or exploitation, or just as acknowledgements of the immense and subtle entanglement of people and place.

I have come to realize, though, that there is one last glossary I should assemble: a dark twin to the hopeful word-lists of *Landmarks*. It will be, if I ever succeed in putting it together, a glossary of the Anthropocene – the earth epoch in which human activity has become the dominant shaping force of the environment and the climate such that it will leave a long-term signature in the strata record. A lexicon of this kind would record the particularities of the terrains and phenomena we are now bringing into being through our actions as a species. It would be a gathering of the terms that describe a heavily harnessed or drastically deranged 'nature': not a Counter-Desecration Phrasebook, then (as per the thought-experiment by Finlay MacLeod that set *Landmarks* going nearly a decade ago now), but a Desecration Phrasebook.

Such a glossary would need to detail the topographies of toxicity and dereliction that we have made, the spectacles of pollution, corruption and extinction we have induced, and the miracles of geo-engineering we have wrought. It would acknowledge human activity as a telluric force with an immense legacy. It would record, for instance, the 'trash vortex' that swirls in the gyres of the world's great oceans, or aspects of the pale hills of radioactive mine-tailings that rear above Johannesburg (gold mining as orogeny), or terms for the chambers of the deep geological repositories in which we entomb our nuclear waste. Is there a word yet for the post-natural rain that falls when a cloud is rocket-seeded with silver iodide? Or an island newly revealed by the melting of sea ice in the North-West Passage? Or the glistening tide-marks left on coastlines by oil spills? We speak memorably of a 'murmuration' of starlings, to describe vast flocks of those birds, dancing and palping in the air above reed-beds and wetlands. But we have as yet no term to denote the squalls of gulls that swirl above our landfill sites, or the high columns of red kites that turn in the air above the meat factories of the Cotswolds. These to-be-coined words would join other new-minted Anthropocene terms, including *saltscape* for the 'terrain exposed by a shrinking inland sea', *ghostroost* for a 'seabird nesting area after a die-off' and *nurdles* or *mermaids' tears* for the plastic particles that constitute a major portion of marine debris, that carry micropollutants into the marine environment in massive quantities, and that choke marine creatures up the food chain from krill all the way to albatross (in so doing leaving ghostroosts).

A glossary of this kind would also need to record our future losses. Perhaps the most extraordinary Anthropocene document I know is Cormac McCarthy's novel *The Road* (2006). *The Road* is set in a near-future North America that has been reduced to ash and rubble by an unspecified calamity. The language of nature survives in the mouths and memories of the characters – but the phenomena to which such words refer have been extinguished. Trout, grass, cranes, the colour green: all are gone. Words have been 'shorn of [their] referents'. Language has become – in the poet Paul Celan's unforgettable phrase – a series of 'word-caves', hollowed out by loss.

In late November 2015, as the Paris Climate Change talks approached, a former Director of the UN Environmental Programme, Rajendra Shende, wrote in approving but challenging response to the glossaries of *Landmarks*:

South Asia, one of the loci of poverty and milling impoverished humanity, is the living example of how along with vanishing language of environmental justice, even the landscape and landmarks too get lost. Has Robert Macfarlane included in his book vanishing words like 'archipelago of Maldives' and 'Sundarbans of

Bangladesh'? And what about phrases like 'Khumbu Glacier of
Nepal', 'Ganges Delta' and 'white tigers of Bangladesh'?

I hadn't – but these are also surely the kinds of terms and toponyms
that should enter an Anthropocene Glossary: future word-caves,
terms that will be shorn of their referents unless we shift our course.
Such a glossary might therefore help us see something of what we
have done – and something of what we have left to do. For as John
C. Sawhill puts it, 'In the end, our society will be defined not only
by what we create, but by what we refuse to destroy.'

~

The week I was finishing this new chapter – in one of the synchron-
ies that have come to characterize *Landmarks* for me – I received an
envelope postmarked 'Lancashire and South Lakes', addressed in
slightly spidery handwriting. It was from Margaret Cockcroft, to
whom I had written the previous month in thanks for her postcard. In her letter, she described some of her memories of what
she called 'a lifetime of walks – many at night, and also up hills, and
in rocky scrambles to the tops of mountains'. She regretted that old
age now made it impossible for her to be outside as freely as before,
'but the delight in countryside and walking is in the family, who help
me to walk delicately in the fields of my home county of
Lancashire'.

In the course of my letter to Margaret I had offered her a word
in thanks for her gift of *lighty-dark*. Mine was *petrichor* – literally
'stone essence' – meaning the 'pleasant distinctive smell of rain
in the air, especially strong when the first rain falls after a long
period of warm, dry weather', a word I had been sent from a

correspondent in the American desert state of Utah. In a PS to her letter, Margaret gave me another word in return – a further extension of the gift exchange:

> Sometimes a new word excites and gives rise to thought. My grandson's wife is German. She & I were by a reservoir when she said 'Look, did you see it?' I thought she said iceberg! But she'd said ice-bird, and this is the German for kingfisher, referring to the flash of blue that you might see on ice in the sun. I'll never forget this to-me-new insight into the familiar bird's name.

Later that week, cycling to work across Coe Fen on a cold morning, with my three-year-old son on the back of the bike, a bright bolt of blue and orange seared across our path, and then flickered away up the line of the lode. I braked to a halt and turned round. 'Hey – did you see it, Will?! Did you see the ice-bird?'

Robert Macfarlane, December 2015

addland border of ploughland which is ploughed last of all **Herefordshire, Radnorshire,**

adnasjur large wave or waves, coming after a succession of lesser ones **Shetland**

aff-shot cross-tide or current, often off a headland **Caithness**

aime shimmering air visible above the ground in hot weather **Caithness**

airie gentle breath of wind **Caithness**

airymouse bat **Cornwall**

aiteall fine spell between showers **Irish**

altran fine rain **Orkney**

an water that is still or quiet **Irish**

appledrain wasp **Devon**

apricity sun's warmth in winter **phenological**

assart field created by clearing scrub and woodland (assarting is the reason why ancient woods have sinuous or zigzag boundaries) **forestry**

awm steam rising from bodies of cattle **Lincolnshire**

backend autumn **Cheshire**

bairís marine phosphorescence **Irish**

bakka cliff or steep rocky shore **Shetland**

barber freezing coastal mist in calm frosty weather **Scots**

barbublin newly hatched featherless bird **Norfolk**

barf steep path **Cumbria**

beam deep, open-pit mine-working on Dartmoor **Dartmoor**

bear-brade coarse barley that is especially water-dependent when young **Lancashire**

bedding plane surface occurring in sedimentary rocks representing an event that interrupted sedimentation for some time **geological**

beequeen to climb into the heart of a huge tree **Childish**

beilichín narrow passage of water **Irish**

bell call of a red stag **venery**

bent hillside pasture **Yorkshire**

benthic zone ecological region at the lowest level of a body of water **ecological**

benzel blast of the storm **Dumfriesshire**

billinge-rain light drizzle **Lancashire**

birra land abounding with wells and springs of water **Irish**

bishy-barnaby ladybird **Suffolk**

blee open, bleak fen **Fenland**

blinder to blind with fine snow **Orkney**

blow blossom **Gloucestershire**

blue-dykie dunnock **northern England**

blustrous of a wind: blustery verging on the monstrous **Berkshire**

bobowler any sort of night-time flying insect, but especially a moth **Warwickshire**

bond-stone upright granite post marking the bound (bond) of a designated forest **Dartmoor**

booley upland grazing pasture **Northern Ireland**

booter to get a bootful of water **Northern Ireland**

borough sheltered spot out of the wind (from OE *burh*, meaning an earthwork) **Northamptonshire**

boulder-head defence-work against the sea, made up of wooden stakes **Sussex**

brant of a hill or path: steep **Lancashire**

brasfwrw big, spaced drops of rain **Welsh**

brattle thunder-clap **Co. Tyrone**

breachy brackish **Sussex**

breaclá dappled day, i.e. a day of sun and rain **Irish**

bread-and-cheese young spring shoots on a hawthorn hedge, so called because they can be eaten **Cheshire**

brew path up a steep slope **Lancashire**

brew brow of a hill **north Cheshire**

briarts first shoots of a crop in spring **Doric**

brim cold, drying wind that withers plants **Orkney**

brimbo brambles **Devon**

broadband to open and spread out beets of flax in order to dry them **Northern Ireland**

brob, brog   bushy stick used to mark the path across Morecambe Bay **south Cumbria**

Brocken spectre   magnified shadow of an observer cast against mist or cloud **mountaineering**

bullstang   dragonfly **south Cumbria**

bumbarrel   long-tailed tit **English regional**

bunny   steep-sided valley leading to the sea **New Forest**

buried moon   moon seen through vaporous haze **Northamptonshire**

burra   space that is sheltered from the wind, tucked away (such as snowdrops might grow in) **Oxfordshire**

burth   current induced by the tide that runs contrary to the main tidal stream **Caithness**

byrlymu   of rain: pouring very quickly **Welsh**

cadamán   seaweed growing on upper part of a beach **Irish**

cag-mag   very old goose **Lincolnshire**

caidhpeog   surging wave **Irish**

cambwll   whirlpool; pool in the bend of a river **Welsh**

carfax   place where four or more roads meet but do not form a cross **Sussex**

carrie   river weir, or the deep pool immediately upstream from a weir **Northern Ireland**

carrog   swift-flowing stream or torrent (usually as a place-name element) **Welsh**

catchy, skiffy	of a sky: foretelling dubious weather **Cornish**
caws	of the water of a stream: cloudy (literally 'cheese') **Welsh**
cazzardly	of weather: unsettled **Cheshire**
ceobháisteach	heavy drizzle **Irish**
chawn	crack in baked soil **Gloucestershire**
cheesybug	woodlouse **Kent**
chine	ravine in a cliff **Isle of Wight**
cilfach, cilgwyn	benignly sheltered spot **Welsh**
cladach éadálach	good beach for flotsam and jetsam **Irish**
clagfharraige	lumpy, choppy sea **Irish**
cleit	small drystone storage building **St Kilda**
clemmies	rocks **Cumbria**
clemmy	stone (of the size you might throw) **Lancashire**
clonter	rumble or thunder, as in the 'clonter of cobblestones on the bed of a stream in spate' **Cheshire**
clough	moorland ravine **northern England**
clowg	boulder on the seashore **Caithness**
coalbags	black clouds piling up in the sky in advance of a storm **Cornish**
cockscrike	dawn (literally 'cock-cry') **Cheshire**
col	utmost spot to which anything (human or creature) can be driven **Welsh**

conder eminence from which to direct boats to tell them which way the herrings have gone **Suffolk**

coose cold and unpleasant weather **Cornwall**

corof wooded precipice near a river **Welsh**

crachen poor patch of land (literally 'scab') **Welsh**

crip, crup crisp, frosty: a grass path 'crups up' when frost makes it feel crunchy underfoot **Sussex**

crittlecronks spiky, exposed roots of a tree taken down by a storm **Childish**

crompán stream; low-lying land along a stream **Irish**

cuddy hidden place for picking blackberries **Cornish**

cuisleán overgrown stream; soft, green strip of ground in a bog **Irish**

cuisne frosty vapour, cold haze **Irish**

culmen top or summit of a hill; also the upper ridge of a bird's bill **English regional, ornithological**

cumar valley or ravine with a stream **Irish**

curchas water meadow **Irish**

cwm valley **Welsh**

cyfnygau narrow passages; hardships **Welsh**

cynefin place of belonging **Welsh**

daaknane early dawn **Caithness**

danner gentle walk, stroll **Northern Ireland**

delagone twilight **Northern Ireland**

356

delph drain or watercourse flowing into a larger river **Fenland**

dendrophile person who loves trees and forests **specialist**

devil-shrieker swift **East Anglia**

diling long hollow in a pasture field **Lincolnshire**

dimple pool in a wood or dell **Derbyshire**

dimpsy trickster half-light at dawn or dusk **Devon**

dimpsy, dimsy dusk, or the darkened air brought on by poor weather, or the short period of time between daylight and dusklight: the 'cusp of duskness' (Isabel Macho) **Devon, Somerset**

díobhóg mountain stream that dries up in summer **Irish**

docky labourer's lunch **Cambridgeshire**

dog partial rainbow **south Cumbria**

doilbhcheo dark, deceptive mist **Irish**

doineann foul weather, or the stress brought about by bad weather **Irish**

domra obscuration of the sky by haze **Shetland**

dow of weather: gloomy **south Cumbria**

dowel low marsh in which water lies in wet times and winter **Sussex**

dowly of a day: dull, gloomy, misty **Lancashire**

dreeping of landscape: heavy with dew or rain, melancholic **Irish/poetic (Patrick Kavanagh)**

dringway narrow path around house **Somerset**

drix of wood: brittle rather than pliable **Cornwall**

druga small wave **Irish**

drunken-charlie grass tussocky moor grass that causes the walker to stumble with the appearance of drunkenness **Derbyshire**

dry valley valley formed by rivers when the water table was high or the ground frozen, but now abandoned by the river **geological**

dub puddle **Cumbria**

dubbing act of jumping from the sides of gills into deep rock pools (dubs) **Childish**

duirling stony beach **Irish**

dúlaoisc sea-level cave **Irish**

dumberdash short, violent shower **Cheshire**

dumbledore bumblebee **English regional**

dúshnámh underwater swimming **Irish**

éan an anró person who is out in all weathers; literally 'bird of hardship' **Irish**

eckle green woodpecker **Northamptonshire**

ecotone transition zone between two biomes, where communities meet and integrate (for example between field and forest, or lake and land) **ecological**

ees boggy floodplain **Lancashire**

eithinog covered in gorse **Welsh**

elytra hard outer wing-cases of beetles **entomological**

emmet   ant **English regional**

ershe   stubble **Hampshire**

eske   spitting rain that precedes a heavy storm
Orkney

estavelle   sinkhole from which water issues during storm
and winter flood (i.e. when the underground
drainage system exceeds its capacity) **geological**

fachlach   cracked surface of dry bog **Irish**

fardon   pillow made from the straw-stuffed stomach of
a cow **Warwickshire**

fealo   sparkle (of light on sea) **Old English**

feggy   of meadow grass: left uncut such that it
collapses to lie flat under its own weight, and
younger grass grows through it **Welsh borders**

fen-nightingale   frog **Fenland**

fiachaire   weather forecaster; literally 'raven-watcher' **Irish**

fir-candles   resin-rich splinters of pine that can be easily
burned for light **Cairngorms**

firesmoke   blending of sunrise/sunset with cloud **Childish**

flash   piece of low swampy ground **Caithness**

fleester   light shower **Orkney**

flittermouse   bat **Lancashire**

fluther   soft ground, bog **Caithness**

*fly-golding, God   ladybird **Sussex**
Almighty's Cow*

foil   tracks of deer on grass **venery**

foisty   smelling dank and subterranean **north-eastern coalfields**

fillimort, foliomort   reddish-yellow colour of dead or dying leaves **Hampshire**

foss   waterfall **northern England**

fothragfhoin   well or spring of purification **Irish**

franklins   last nights of the year on which frost can be expected, usually 19–21 May **Devon**

frass   rejectamenta left behind by insects or larvae boring into wood, fruit or leaf-matter **entomological**

fraying stock   bush, tree or other firm object used by deer to rub velvet from their antlers **venery**

frore   frozen **Sussex**

fuzzicky   of land: spongy **Cheshire**

gad   29-inch length of hazel used as a thatching spar **Sussex**

gairy   precipitous rocks **Dumfriesshire**

gall-shion   sudden fierce weather, as if it has blown in from a strange country **Irish**

gallery   path or parallel paths worn by deer in close cover **venery**

gallibaggers   top stones of walls **Somerset**

ganfer   fine, close, white, dry mist often presaging snow **Orkney**

geeve almost imperceptible fine rain that nevertheless gets you wet and cold quickly **Cornwall**

gelvernish of a wind: roaring like a smithy furnace **Cornish**

gewl to walk without looking where you are going **Herefordshire**

ghout swallet-hole, sinkhole **Somerset**

ghoyle cleft in the hills filled with gorse and bracken, and therefore largely inaccessible **Devon**

gingley land composed of soil and small loose stones **Lincolnshire**

gissle field pond fed by underground spring **English regional**

glamsy of a sky: showing dazzling parts but betokening rain **Orkney**

glar thick sticky mud **Northern Ireland**

glarry muddy **Northern Ireland**

glasreo hoar frost; literally 'green frost', because it crystallizes on grass and moss **Irish**

glat path cut out of steep sandstone **Shropshire**

gled raptor: the red or fork-tailed gled is a kite; the blue gled a hen harrier **northern England, Scotland**

gleet shining ice **Dumfriesshire**

glibbed of water: frozen such that it is rendered smooth and slippery **Northamptonshire**

gliddered   covered with a fine layer of ice **northern England**

glidders, glitters   loose stones on a hillside **northern England**

glinglish   shimmer of sunlight on water **Childish**

glisk   gleam of sunshine; glow of heat from a fire **Shetland**

glog-oil   damp hole in peaty ground **Yorkshire**

glossamer   shining filaments spun across huge areas of landscape by small spiders in autumn, usually perceptible only near dawn or dusk when the light is slant **Devon**

goaf   unsupported and dangerous region left behind a coalface **north-eastern coalfields**

gob   period of stormy weather in spring **Caithness**

goon   meadow, pasture **Cornish**

gowdspink   goldfinch **Scots**

gowk   cuckoo; also a foolish person **Northern Ireland**

gowk   cuckoo **Yorkshire**

goyallt   wooded slope in a hollow **Welsh**

gramfy-coocher   woodlouse **Somerset**

grammersow   woodlouse **Devon**

gray   slight breath of wind **Caithness**

greallach   puddly ground **Irish**

greensward   grass-covered swathe of ground **English regional**

grindle, grundle deep holloway (possible connection to 'Grendel', the monster in *Beowulf* that inhabited low-lying ground) **Suffolk**

gripped while climbing, unable to move up or down on the rockface due to fear **mountaineering**

groatie-buckies cowrie shells, reputed to bring good luck **northern Scots**

groo of a wind: to blow up **Orkney**

grownglane rumbling of a burn in spate **Caithness**

gussel strong, long-lasting wind **Orkney**

gutter indented gulleys on a deer's antler **venery**

gwlithlaw drizzle **Welsh**

gwyle gulley **Dorset**

gyland sloping piece of land; high bank **Welsh borders**

harnser heron **Norfolk**

hat narrow straight path cut through a wood **Lincolnshire**

hattle rough area of seabed showing rocks and weed **Caithness**

haughland flat alluvial land enclosed by the angles and bends of a wandering river **northern England**

hause lower neck or connecting ridge between two high points or peaks **Cumbria, Border Scots**

hazeling of a morning: warm and dry, following a dew, and therefore a good morning to sow **Bedfordshire, Hertfordshire**

heatherbleat	snipe; so called from the beating sound produced by the rush of wind through its wing feathers as it dives **Northern Ireland**
heavy	of a slope or hill: steep **north-east England**
heirs	young trees in a coppice **Hampshire**
Helm	north-easterly wind of destructive force and duration that blows down the south-west slope of the Cross Fell escarpment **Cumbria**
hendre	winter dwelling (usually as a place-name element) **Welsh**
heth	severe winter weather **Welsh**
hob-owl	large moth **Hertfordshire**
hog-gazels, hogarves	hawthorn berries **Sussex**
holly-hag	special holly woods used for fodder (especially for deer) **forestry**
hop	enclosed branch of a main valley, a blind side-valley **Cumbria**
hopliness	changes of colour along the length of a stem of grass **Childish**
horniegoggle	earwig **Scots**
hunch	very cold **east Lincolnshire**
hurdifell	steep rocky hill covered in boulders **Shetland**
hushle	strong gale **Orkney**
huvver	ridge separating different holdings of unenclosed land **Fenland**

ice-shoggle icicle **north-east England**

ile fishing ground between the shore and the tidal current **Caithness**

imlioc of land: bordering a lake **Irish**

imp scion, graft, young tree **Welsh**

in-bye meadow **Cumbria**

ing meadow, especially one bordering a river or stream **northern England**

innings land that has been enclosed from the sea **Sussex**

inselberg, monadnock isolated rock hill or outcrop rising from a plain or level ground (literally 'island mountain') **geological**

intake valley side **Cumbria**

iomramh rowing voyage at sea, or voyage story **Irish**

ironing piece small triangular island of grass left at a junction of roads **Norfolk**

jachelt of a tree or trees: grown and bent in the direction of the prevailing wind **Old Scots**

jizz overall quality or 'vibe' of a particular species of bird, usually allowing immediate identification, drawn from shape, flight, posture, size, plumage, habitat, voice and location **ornithology**

jökulhlaup subglacial outburst flood, sometimes caused by volcanic or geothermal activity underneath a glacier **glaciology**

365

karren small hollows on the surface of limestone caused by chemical weathering **geological**

katrisper strong gale **Orkney**

keelham cattle road **Yorkshire**

kesh causeway raised above a bog, or bridging old drains or streams **Northern Ireland**

kest stone-lined hedge-bank **Cumbria**

kinlit of a wind: fickle **Orkney**

kithywind whirlwind **Orkney**

lag, leg narrow marshy meadow, usually by the side of a stream **Sussex**

laine open tract of arable land at the foot of the Downs **Sussex**

lan sacred area or enclosure **Cornwall**

lanburst series of large waves **Caithness**

lasus water meadow **Sussex**

lattermath crop of grass that comes after the first mowing **south-west Wales**

laverock skylark **Scots**

leaf-brains skeletons of leaves **Childish**

leamhach bright calm patch in the sea **Irish**

leen grassy spot in a moor **Caithness**

léinseach smooth tract of water **Irish**

lentic of freshwater systems: slow-moving, almost static (ponds, lakes, marshes), from the Latin *lentus*, meaning 'sluggish' **ecological**

ligging place where a deer lies down **venery**

lighty-dark light occurring at the edge of darkness after a cold clear day **Childish/Lancashire**

linestorm fierce weather approaching in a clear berm or reef **poetic**

lipper white caps on sea-waves **Northumberland**

llwybr footpath **Welsh**

logan-stone rock balanced on top of another, such that it looks as if it could be rocked **Cornwall, Devon**

loke farm-track **Norfolk**

lonnadh rippling wave **Irish**

lonning lane, often ending at a farmhouse (possibly from 'loan', indicating the quiet place by the farm where milk and eggs would be sold to villagers) **Cumbria**

lotic of freshwater systems: fast-moving, -flowing (streams, springs, rivers, etc.), from the Latin *lotus*, meaning 'washed' **ecology**

lound sheltered from the wind **south Cumbria**

lúbloch oxbow lake; literally 'bent lake' **Irish**

lumheid-dozer pigeon (literally 'dozer-on-the-chimney-pot') **Scots**

lyring   shallow depression in tidal sandflats in which sea remains at low water **south Cumbria**

maghuisge   winter lake **Irish**

magwitching hour   dusk on the Kent marshes, especially when mist rises **Kent**

maoy, mowy   site of corn-ricks at threshing time **Cornish**

meandering   path that exists more in the imagination than in the real world **Cumbria**

meangan   of a sheep's ear-mark: branched, forked **Hebridean Gaelic**

mearin   boundary between two farms, usually marked by a fence or ditch **Northern Ireland**

meebles, mobbellunds   very small, very white, very round pebbles (a spatchcock of teeth and marbles) **Childish**

meethe, meeze   landmark used by fishermen to deduce their position at sea **Caithness**

melch   of weather: soft, gentle **Lincolnshire**

melgreaves   quicksands **south Cumbria**

merly   of clouds: gleaming **Orkney**

milkbottle   ice-slide made by children in winter conditions **Nottinghamshire**

mòirnéis   great streams of water **Irish**

monkey peas   woodlice **Kent**

moogy   foggy **Cornish**

moonbroch   halo around the moon which presages a storm **Scots** _moor grime_   wet moorland fog that slithers off the Pennines and into surrounding valleys or lowlands **Lancashire**

moss-breek   broken place on the fell where sheep rub themselves against exposed stone **Cumbria**

mungle-bungle   of ants or children: to walk in a busy line **Childish**

mytholm   meeting of waters **Yorkshire**

néaladóireacht   cloud-watching, weather-reading **Irish**

neest, noast, noost   place where a boat could be hauled from the sea and safely left, often in a hollow – natural or man-made – in a brae **Caithness**

nesh   cold **Lincolnshire, Yorkshire**

noop   fruit of the cloudberry **northern England, Scotland**

nover   high land above a steep bank or face **Sussex**

oogly   of a sky: foretelling wild weather **Cornish**

oomska   farmyard mud mixed with cow shit (from _Withnail and I_: 'You mean you've been up here in all this beastly mud and oomska without wellingtons?' asks Uncle Monty) **literary (Bruce Robinson)**

oorack   small rubbishy potato **Scots**

ootrook   backrush from a breaking wave; current setting offshore **Caithness**

overclap   clouds overclosing the earth **Dorset**

pannage   autumn pasturing of pigs on acorns or beechmast **Yorkshire** *peggle*   cowslip **Essex**

petrichor   pleasant distinctive smell of rain in the air, sometimes detectable before rain has even begun to fall, and especially strong when the first rain falls after a long period of warm, dry weather (literally 'stone essence' in Greek); also the name given to the mixture of organic compounds (terpenes, creosotes) that is rendered volatile by an increase in humidity, and that is thought to be responsible for the smell **scientific**

phoebe   the sun **Hertfordshire**

pigo   spotting rain **Welsh**

pitch   of snow: to fall **Dorset**

pitch   of snow: to accumulate, to settle **south-west England**

pixy-hunting   climbing trees in an orchard to get the last fruit, after the main crop has been harvested **Somerset**

plash   to lay and peg a young stem from a coppiced stool such that it forms a new tree **forestry**

Plato's fire   shadows dancing inside a tree hollow on a sunny day in a wood **poetic**

plodge   to wade in water **north-east England**

pluck-post   fence post or branch on which a raptor sits to pluck its prey **English regional**

polly-dishwasher   pied wagtail **Hampshire, Sussex**

pollywiggle   newt **Norfolk**

popple   common land **Yorkshire**

poppling of a sea: when waves rise and fall with quick and sudden motions **Sussex**

print-moonlight moonlight bright enough to read by **Sussex**

pudge puddle, pool or ditch **English regional, especially southern and Midlands**

purdle tumble of water in a brook **Somerset**

purdlegog top of a stile **Somerset**

puther of a fire: producing a lot of smoke **Midlands**

putherry intense stillness and humidity immediately before a thunderstorm breaks **Staffordshire**

puthery intense stillness and humidity immediately before a thunderstorm breaks **Cheshire**

quaker boggy land that looks solid enough to walk on, but quakes beneath your feet **Somerset**

queelrod bulrush **Ulster Scots**

quill spring (of water) **Sussex**

quoy area of enclosed ground **Caithness**

raddle red ochre mixed with oil, used for marking trees for felling **forestry**

radjel pile of rocks in which a fox seeks refuge: a fox-fortress **west Cornwall**

rainbod curlew **Yorkshire**

rainbowed bent double after a hard day's planting in the field ('we came home rainbowed') **north Cheshire**

ramell brushwood **Yorkshire**

ramper   raised path or road **Fenland**

ranny   shrew **Norfolk**

rassle   of a plant: to spread rapidly over an area of ground **Gloucestershire**

ream   groundwater level **Sefton**

rean   small roadside or path-side stream **Somerset**

ree   of weather: raw, cold and frosty **Caithness**

ree   spell of bad weather; also, riotous through the influence of drink **Shetland**

reel   song of the grasshopper warbler **English regional**

rew   small wood **Isle of Wight**

rhine   a ditch or lode (the Monmouth rebellion is thought to have failed on a rhine) **Somerset**

rhiw   steep hillside path, often from a farmstead or gathering point for stock **Black Mountains**

rhos   rushy pasture **Welsh**

rhosan   small area of moorland **Welsh**

roddie   small footpath **Caithness**

ronis   cairn or rocky plateau **Shetland**

roosh, rush   of a stone wall: a localized collapse whereby a little river of stones has run (rooshed, rushed) down **Cumbria**

rowet   winter grass **Hampshire**

santer   to ramble, seemingly endlessly **Northern Ireland** *scairy* bright glow of the rising sun or moon before they appear above hills **Dumfriesshire**

scarav cold, biting north-east wind **Irish regional**

scarped of land: parched, dried **Lincolnshire**

scaupy of a field: shallow in its soil **south Cumbria**

schilla loose stones on a beach **south Cumbria**

schwingmoor floating raft of sphagnum moss (literally 'swinging moorland') **ecological**

scra turf **Ulster Scots**

scrammy hawthorn in blossom **Somerset**

scree-doup cupped valley hedged in by cliffs from which debris is frequently falling **Cumbria**

scunge to explore or wander about the countryside **Northern Ireland**

scutch mark on a tree to show it should be felled **Lincolnshire/forestry**

seege sound of the sea rushing up the shore **Cornish**

seven-coloured linnet goldfinch **Shropshire**

sgrympian short, sharp shower **Welsh**

shard gap in a hedge **Wiltshire**

shaw small wood on a hillside **Sussex**

sheep-creeps, thawls, thirls holes left in drystone walls to allow the managed passage of stock animals **northern England**

shillies gravel **Cumbria**

shlud thick, heavy, clay mud **Suffolk**

shochad-storms stormy weather in April when the lapwings (shochads) are nesting **Caithness**

shoddy spent waste (including fragments of carpet) applied to hop yards as fertilizer **Worcestershire**

shon shallow bog or lochan **Caithness**

shrammed pierced to the bone by dank and bitter weather **Wiltshire**

shrie to remove thorns from a bramble stem by pulling it through a gloved hand **Cambridgeshire**

shroggs scrubby woodland **Yorkshire**

shukish of weather: unsettled **Sussex**

shurr gap left in the base of a hedge by inadequate cutting and laying **Somerset**

sile of rain: to pour heavily and persistently **Lincolnshire**

siling of rain: falling heavily **Yorkshire**

sitch brief fall and then sudden rise of a tidal river at the top of a spring tide **Devon**

skeog berry of the whitethorn **Co. Cork**

skibby light, passing shower **Orkney**

sklent breeze that helps a boat to tack to windward **Caithness**

skreever howling gale (literally 'scratcher') **Orkney**

skuther short, sharp breeze **Orkney**

slap gap in a hedge **Ulster Scots**

slattery of mud or ground: cold, wet **Cumbria**

sleech mud or sea-sand used as fertilizer **Sussex**

sligeach place abounding in shells **Irish**

slinkit wooded hollow between two fields **English regional**

slios of a sheep's ear-mark: gently sloping, on the side **Hebridean Gaelic**

slip-rift cave or chasm formed by the peeling away of one rock layer from another under the duress of gravity **geological/speleological**

slippy-curry ice-slide made by children in winter conditions **Oldham**

slograch sinkhole or sump in a bog **Irish**

slooter wet mud **Northern Ireland**

slutch squelchy, muddy ground **Lancashire**

smawthy of a day: airless and uncomfortably humid **Devon**

smigin light rain, hardly a shower **Co. Tyrone**

smit-mark painted mark on a sheep that identifies its farm **English regional**

smoog of children: to gather, crack, stack and whack bits of fallen timber in woods **Childish**

sneuk rocky point on the coastline **Northumberland**

snicket narrow path, between buildings or between a fence and a field **Yorkshire** *sniggle*   long, tangled, floating waterweed **Severn Valley**

sniggler   eel-catcher **Fenland**

sniggler   slight frost **Sussex**

snotty-gobs   yew berries **Hertfordshire**

solasach   luminous, shining **Gaelic**

solastalgia   distress caused by environmental change (climate change, pollution, mining) that alters a person's home landscape without them ever leaving it **global**

soma   of a body of water: abounding in swans **Irish**

sparver   sparrowhawk **Norfolk**

spinning-jenny   sycamore seed **northern England**

splitting the trees   of weather: fearsomely hot **Cumbria**

spoach   of an animal: to nose or quest around **English regional**

sponketts   roots of hedges clinging high on the banks of deep-cut lanes in the Weald **Sussex**

sprodder   of molehills: to scatter their earth **Worcestershire**

spuddle   to mess about in the garden **Devon**

spuggie   sparrow **English regional, especially north-east**

squad   mud **Lincolnshire**

squeech   area of wet, grassy ground near a stream **Suffolk**

squitch   couch-grass **Warwickshire**

staddle rat-proof wooden legs on which hayricks are mounted **Cornwall**

starved frozen stiff **Northamptonshire**

stealhole gap in a hedge or wall **Lancashire**

stell point in a river where salmon nets are cast, usually where a barrier narrows the flow **Cumbria**

stingle sensation of walking or running through footpaths overgrown with nettles **Childish**

stint share of grazing rights **Cumbria**

stour of a wind: to blow snow across roads and up against stone walls **Durham**

straik of snow: filling roads to fence-top height **Caithness**

strish of the sea: to fall in waves with a hushing sound upon rock or reef **literary (John Fowles)**

struttle stickleback **Suffolk**

stubbins stumps of felled trees **Nottinghamshire**

stumbles exposed tree roots on a footpath **English regional**

suant of a crop: growing evenly **Devon**

swank dell, damp hollow **Sussex**

sway deviation of an animal's footprints from the median line of passage **venery**

sweal of grass and weeds: to go limp after cutting, thus making them easier to rake up **Leicestershire**

teannaire	roaring of the sea in a cave **Irish**
teasgal	singing wind in a storm **Irish**
thin	of weather: sunny but cold **English regional**
throw	thoroughfare, public way **Sussex**
thrutch	awkward squeezing movement made in climbing **mountaineering**
tiddly-tope	wren **Devon**
tiffle	to potter aimlessly in a landscape **Suffolk**
tinka-tankas	narrow, high-walled alleyways (onomatopoeic for the echoing sound feet make when walking along them) **Warwickshire**
tonnroc	ripple-mark on water **Irish**
tresio	maximum-intensity rain **Welsh**
trink	dip or depression in tidal sandflats holding deeper water **Northumberland**
trink	small sea creek or inlet, usually under water **Caithness**
trod	faint path **Cumbria**
trunnel	road or path where in summer the leaf canopies of trees on both sides form a canopy **English regional**
tummock	knoll in a bog (i.e. 'I tried to jump across the shuck using that tummock but got a booter instead') **Northern Ireland**
tweavelet	small leaf bundles snagged around river-twigs after a flood **poetic**

twitten   alleyway or narrow path running behind or between buildings in the older parts of towns and villages **Sussex**

urchin   hedgehog **Cheshire**

uvvers   grass mown from the dykeside **Fenland**

vallum   wide ditch **Northumberland**

waller   to waddle, to move as a seal moves on land **Northumberland**

wann   gloss or gleam (especially on a raven's wing) **Old English**

want-heaves   molehills **Dorset**

water-boats   fair-weather cumulus clouds **Norfolk**

watergaw   rainbow **Scots**

weather-mooth   clear area in the sky, low on the horizon, from which the clouds appear to stream **Caithness**

whale-road   sea **Old English**

wheezer   starling **Norfolk**

whewan   wind that howls round corners **Orkney**

whins   gorse bushes **Northern Ireland**

whistle   call of a sika stag **venery**

whittle   strong gust of wind (supposedly named after Captain Whittle, whose coffin was hurled to the ground from its bearers' shoulders by such a gust) **Cheshire**

windsauker   kestrel **south Cumbria**

windypit rock fissures that emit a steamy vapour in winter **Yorkshire**

winter-proud cold **Sussex**

winterbiter having the bitterness of winter **Old English**

wintercearig cares of winter **Old English**

witchett wet through **Lancashire**

wool-o'-the-wisp wisps of wool caught on barbed wire, thorns or twigs **Cumbria**

wunnels rounded gaps in thickets where animals pass from one field to the next (a contraction of 'wild tunnels'; cf. smeuse in Glossary VII) **Childish**

xeriscape landscape in which the need for irrigation has been reduced or eliminated **agriculture, horticulture**

yelm bundle of thatching straw **agriculture, horticulture**

yowetrummle snap of cold weather just after sheep have been sheared (literally 'ewe-tremble') **Scots**

ystafell cave, chamber **Welsh**

ystrad flat-bottomed valley **Welsh**

zebn-slaper dormouse **Somerset**

GUIDE TO THE GLOSSARIES

'There's so much more to be added', Anne Campbell said of her Peat Glossary. The same is true of *Landmarks*' lexicons. In their unedited form they ran to nearly 4,500 words and terms (of which around 2,500 are present in the final glossaries), but of course even this represents only a fraction of the place-language used in these islands. The task of collecting and sorting sometimes felt endless, verging on overwhelming: there was always one more letter or email of enquiry to write, another word-list to hunt out, a further glossary to summon up from the library stacks, an additional reference to pursue. Bibliographies are wonderful places in which to wander, but also easy places in which to get lost.

So the glossaries are inevitably selective. They aspire neither to completeness (impossible), nor to evenness of coverage (near impossible), and reflect to a degree my own particular interests and affiliations (thus Gaelic and Scots are notably strong, as are the dialects of Cambridgeshire and its neighbouring counties). A good number of the words were transcribed in the nineteenth-century heyday of glossarizing and dialect research, but many come from more recent records, for I tried to lay an ear to place-language as it is used today from Shetland to Cornwall, while also seeking to curate and recover near-vanished speech. I sought to gather grit as well as pearls: landscape offers us experiences of great grace and beauty, but also of despair, hard labour and death. Thus the discomforts of *hansper* and *aingealach*, alongside the dazzle of *ammil* and *haze-fire*. I chose in the main to restrict myself to terms for aspects (both fugitive and long term) of land, sea, weather and atmosphere – rather than for animals, birds, insects, flowers and plants, on the grounds that formidable reference works already exist documenting the folk names of the flora and fauna of these islands. And I reluctantly decided not to allow place-names into the glossaries, given the immense compendia of toponyms that have already been compiled by place-name enthusiasts and societies throughout the land.

Guide to the Glossaries

I wanted to make glossaries that could be explored with ease and pleasure by their readers, and that therefore did not fankle themselves with intricacy. For this reason I have not, on the whole, supplied variant spellings for individual words; I have limited the definitions of each word to a sentence or two; I have not cross-referenced between languages and dialects; and I have not detailed dates of usage. Each glossary entry is composed of three elements: a headword; a definition; and an origin in language, region or vocabulary. I have specified either a major source language (e.g. 'Gaelic', 'Irish', 'Manx', 'Welsh'); or a particular region of dialect or sub-dialect use where known (e.g. 'Galloway' for the Galloway sub-dialect of Scots, or 'Shetland' for the Shetland dialect which amalgamates Scots, Gaelic, English and Norn/Norse); or a specialist vocabulary (e.g. 'archaeological', 'geographical', 'mountaineering', 'speleological'). Probably some of these attributions will be thought disputable or extendable; certainly these glossaries would discontent a serious-minded linguist, mongrel as they are in their origins, and mingling as they do loanwords, nonce words, neologisms and calques.

But they are not intended as scholarly to the point of definitive; rather as imaginative resources, as testimony to the vivid particularities of language and landscape, as adventures in the word-hoard – and as prompts to vision. 'Visit comes from *visum*, "to see",' writes John Stilgoe in his elegant essay-book on marsh language, *Shallow Water Dictionary* (2004):

> It and *vision* stand related. To visit means to see, not to talk, but to take notice, to take note, to actively engage the eye . . . Landscape – or seascape – that lacks vocabulary cannot be seen, cannot be accurately, usefully visited. It is not even theoretical, if theory means what the Greek word *theoria* means, a spectacle, a viewing.

What follows, then, is a partial bibliography for my 'theoretical' glossaries: a list of sources that does not (with a handful of unavoidable exceptions) include works cited in the main text, the notes or the main bibliography. Nor have I been able to include details of the countless books, poems, conversations and individual correspondences from which over the years I have gleaned single words here and there, now and then. Most of the many people who have individually contributed to the glossaries are thanked in the Acknowledgements. In the list that follows, though, I have tried to recognize a little of the vast efforts of earlier glossarians, onomasticians and toponymists, from which *Landmarks*' lexicons have so greatly benefited.

Guide to the Glossaries

Select Bibliography to the Glossaries

Angus, James Stout, *A Glossary of the Shetland Dialect* (Paisley: A. Gardner, 1914)

Armstrong, Terence, and Charles Swithinbank, *The Illustrated Glossary of Snow and Ice* (Cambridge: Scott Polar Research Institute Special Publication, 1966)

Atkinson, J. C., and Robert Backhouse Peacock, *A Glossary of the Dialect of the Hundred of Lonsdale, North and South of the Sands* (London: Asher & Co., 1869)

Baker, Anne Elizabeth, *Glossary of Northamptonshire Words and Phrases, with Examples of Their Colloquial Use, and Illustrations from Various Authors, to which are added, The Customs of the County* (London: John Russell Smith, 1854)

Batten, Ben, *Old Newlyn Speech* (Newlyn: privately printed, 1984)

Beckensall, Stan, *Place Names and Field Names of Northumberland* (London: History Press, 2006)

Blaenau Tywi History Group, *Blaenau Tywi: Names in the Landscape / Enwau yn y Tirwedd* (Llandysul: Gomer, 2014)

Bowyer, Richard, *Dictionary of Military Terms*, 3rd edn (Teddington: Peter Collin, 2007)

Campbell, Anne, *Rathad an Isein: The Bird's Road – A Lewis Moorland Glossary* (Glasgow: Faram, 2013)

Christie-Johnson, Alasdair, and Adaline Christie-Johnson, *Shetland Words* (Lerwick: Shetland Times, 2013)

Clare, John, *Poems of the Middle Period*, 'Consolidated Glossary', ed. Eric Robinson, David Powell and P. M. S. Dawson (Oxford: Clarendon Press, 1996)

Claxton, A. O. D., *The Suffolk Dialect of the 20th Century* (Ipswich: N. Adland & Co., 1968)

Connolly, Carol Anne, *An Sanasán Uisce: The Water Glossary* (Galway: privately printed, 2016)

Cooper, William Durrant, *A Glossary of the Provincialisms in Use in the County of Sussex* (Brighton: Fleet, 1836)

Cornewall Lewis, George, *A Glossary of Provincial Words Used in Herefordshire* (London: John Murray, 1839)

Cox, Richard V., *The Gaelic Place-Names of Carloway, Isle of Lewis: Their Structure and Significance* (Dublin: School of Celtic Studies, 2002)

Creates, Marlene, *Brickle, Nish and Nobby: Newfoundland Terms for Ice and Snow* (Newfoundland: Boulder Publications, 2015)

Crofts, W. M. , *The Dialect of Craven in the West Riding of the County of York, with a Copious Glossary* (London: privately printed, 1828)

Crossing, William, *Crossing's Guide to Dartmoor* (1912; Newton Abbot: Peninsula Press, 1990)

Dalzell, Tom, and Terry Victor (eds.), *The New Partridge Dictionary of Slang and Unconventional English* (London: Routledge, 2006)

Dickinson, William, *A Glossary of Words and Phrases Pertaining to the Dialect of Cumberland* (London: English Dialect Society, 1878)

Dieckhoff, Henry Cecil, *A Pronouncing Dictionary of Scottish Gaelic* (Edinburgh: Johnston, 1932)

Dinsdale, F. J., *A Glossary of Provincial Words Used in Teesdale in the County of Durham* (London: Smith, Bell, 1849)

Dolan, Terence Patrick (ed.), *A Dictionary of Hiberno-English: The Irish Use of English*, 2nd edn (Dublin: Gill & Macmillan, 2004)

Egar, S., 'Fen Provincialisms', in *Fenland Notes & Queries*, Vols. 1–4 (1889–1900)

Ekwall, Eilert, *The Place-Names of Lancashire* (Manchester: Manchester University Press, 1922)

Elmes, Simon, *Talking for Britain: A Journey Through the Voices of a Nation* (London: Penguin, 2006)

Elworthy, F. T. (ed.), *The West Somerset Word-Book* (London: Trubner & Co., 1886)

Ewart Evans, George, *The Pattern Under the Plough* (London: Faber and Faber, 1971)

———, *Where Beards Wag All: The Relevance of the Oral Tradition* (London: Faber and Faber, 1970)

Forby, Robert, *The Vocabulary of East Anglia* (London: J. B. Nichols & Son, 1830)

Gepp, Edward, *An Essex Dialect Dictionary*, 2nd edn, with addendum and biography by John S. Appleby (Wakefield: S. R. Publishers, 1969)

Gill, Walter, *Manx Dialect: Words and Phrases* (London: Arrowsmith, 1934)

Griffiths, Bill, *Fishing and Folk: Life and Dialect on the North Sea Coast* (Newcastle: Northumbria University Press, 2008)

———, *Pitmatic: The Talk of the North East Coalfield* (Newcastle: Northumbria University Press, 2007)

Huntley, Richard Webster, *A Glossary of the Cotswold* (London: J. R. Smith, 1868)

Jackson, Georgina F., *Shropshire Word-Book, a Glossary of Archaic and Provisional Words* (London: Trubner & Co., 1879)

Jakobsen, Jakob, *The Dialect and Place Names of Shetland: Two Popular Lectures* (Lerwick: T. & J. Manson, 1897)

——, *An Etymological Dictionary of the Norn Language in Shetland* (London: G. Nutt, 1928–32)

Lamb, Gregor, *The Orkney Wordbook* (Orkney: Byrgisey, 1995)

Leeds, Winifred, *Herefordshire Speech: The South-West Midland Dialect as Spoken in Herefordshire and Its Environs* (Ross-on-Wye: privately printed, 1974)

Leighton, Angela, *Spills* (Manchester: Carcanet, 2016)

Major, Alan, *A New Dictionary of Kent Dialect* (Rainham: Meresborough, 1981)

Marten, Clement, *The Devonshire Dialect* (Exeter: Clement Marten Publications, 1973)

Martin, Meriel, 'Locating the Language in the Landscape: Dialect in Exmoor National Park', unpublished MSc dissertation (London: Birkbeck College, 2013)

Marwick, Hugh, 'Notes on Weather-Words in the Orkney Dialect', in *Old-Lore Miscellany*, 9 (1921), 23–33

——, *The Orkney Norn* (Oxford: Oxford University Press, 1929)

Morris, Benjamin, 'Air Today, Gone Tomorrow: The Haar of Scotland and Local Atmospheres as Heritage "Sites" ', *International Journal of Intangible Heritage*, 8 (2013), 87–101

Murray, John, *Reading the Gaelic Landscape/Leughadh Aghaidh na Tìre* (Dunbeath: Whittles, 2014)

Newton, Michael, *Handbook of the Scottish Gaelic World* (Dublin: Four Courts Press, 1999)

Nurminen, Terhi Johanna, 'Hill-Terms in the Place-Names of Northumberland and County Durham', unpublished PhD thesis (Newcastle: Newcastle University, 2012)

O'Kane, William, *You Don't Say? The Tyrone Crystal Book of Ulster Dialect* (Dungannon: Irish World, 1991)

Owen, Hywel Wyn, and Richard Morgan, *Dictionary of the Place-Names of Wales* (Llandysul: Gomer, 2007)

Parish, W. D., *A Dictionary of the Sussex Dialect* (Lewes: Farncombe & Co., 1875)

Proctor, Eddie, 'Llanthony Priory in the Vale of Ewyas: The Landscape Impact of a Medieval Priory in the Welsh Marches', MSc dissertation (Oxford: University of Oxford, 2007), at http://www.ewyaslacy.org.uk/doc.php?d=rs_lty_0001

Guide to the Glossaries

Rackham, Oliver, *Trees and Woodland in the British Landscape* (1976; London: Phoenix, 2001)

Riach, W. A. D., *A Galloway Glossary* (Aberdeen: Association for Scottish Literary Studies, 1988)

Robertson, Thomas Alexander, *The Collected Poems of Vagaland* (Lerwick: Shetland Times, 1975)

Robinson, Mairi (ed.), *The Concise Scots Dictionary* (Aberdeen: Aberdeen University Press, 1985)

Rogers, Norman, *Wessex Dialect* (Bradford-on-Avon: Moonraker Press, 1979)

Rye, Walter, *A Glossary of Words Used in East Anglia (Being Suffolk, Essex, Norfolk)* (London: English Dialect Society, 1895)

Skelton, Richard, *Limnology* (Cumbria: Corbel Stone Press, 2012)

Sternberg, Thomas, *The Dialect and Folklore of Northamptonshire* (1851; Wakefield: S. R. Publishers, 1971)

Streever, Bill, *Cold: Adventures in the World's Frozen Places* (London: Little, Brown, 2009)

Taylor Page, F. J., *Field Guide to British Deer* (Oxford: Blackwell Science, 1971)

Todd, Loreto, *Words Apart: A Dictionary of Northern Ireland English* (Gerard's Cross: Smythe, 1990)

Trudgill, Peter, *The Dialects of England*, 2nd edn (Oxford: Blackwell, 1999)

Tudor, John R., *The Orkneys and Shetland: Their Past and Present State* (London: Stanford, 1883)

Watson, Lyall, *Heaven's Breath: A Natural History of the Wind* (New York: William Morrow, 1985)

Wilbraham, Roger, *An Attempt at a Glossary of Some Words Used in Cheshire* (London: T. Rodd, 1826)

Wilkinson, John, *Leeds Dialect, Glossary and Lore* (Leeds: privately printed, 1924)

Wilson, David, *Staffordshire Dialect Words: A Historical Survey* (Buxton: Moorland, 1974)

Some Online Resources

Anglo-Romani Dictionary: http://romani.humanities.manchester.ac.uk/anglo-romani/dictionary.html

Bosworth-Toller Anglo-Saxon Dictionary: http://bosworth.ff.cuni.cz/

Guide to the Glossaries

Defra Guidance for the Successful Reclamation of Mineral and Waste Sites: http://www.sustainableaggregates.com/library/docs/lo276_guidance-full.pdf

Dictionary of the Scots Language: http://www.dsl.ac.uk/

Dwelly's English-Gaelic Dictionary: http://www.cairnwater.co.uk/gaelicdictionary/

Electronic Dictionary of the Irish Language: http://edil.qub.ac.uk/

Forestry Commission Research Glossary: http://www.forestry.gov.uk/fr/glossary

Forests and Chases in England and Wales, c. 1000 to c. 1850; A Glossary of Terms and Definitions: http://info.sjc.ox.ac.uk/forests/glossary.htm

Geiriadur Welsh-English/English-Welsh On-line Dictionary: http://www.geiriadur.net/

Jèrriais Geography: http://members.societe-jersiaise.org/geraint/jerriais/geovoc.html

Land-Words: https://dawnpiper.wordpress.com/land-words/

National Land and Property Gazetteer Glossary: http://www.iahub.net/docs/1263829667917.pdf

Natural England SSSI Glossary: https://www.designatedsites.naturalengland.org.uk/SSSIGlossary.aspx

Official Secrets Act 1911 (with 1920 amendments in square brackets): http://www.legislation.gov.uk/ukpga/Geo5/1-2/28

Shetland Dialect Dictionary: http://www.shetlanddialect.org.uk/john-j-grahams-shetland-dictionary-intro

NOTES

List of abbreviations used in the notes

AD: Barry Lopez, *Arctic Dreams: Imagination and Desire in a Northern Landscape* (1986; London: Vintage, 2014)

AFG: Deb Wilenski with Caroline Wendling, *A Fantastical Guide: Ways into Hinchingbrooke Country Park* (Cambridge: Cambridge Curiosity and Imagination, 2013)

AL: Jacquetta Hawkes, *A Land* (1951; London: HarperCollins, 2012)

DM: Peter Davidson, *Distance and Memory* (Manchester: Carcanet, 2013)

ITC: Nan Shepherd, *In the Cairngorms* (1934; Cambridge: Galileo, 2014)

L: Richard Skelton, *Landings*, 4th edn (Cumbria: Corbel Stone Press, 2012)

LM: Nan Shepherd, *The Living Mountain* (1977; Edinburgh: Canongate, 2011)

NFWTF: Roger Deakin, *Notes from Walnut Tree Farm* (London: Hamish Hamilton, 2008)

NNL: Richard Jefferies, *Nature near London* (1883; London: HarperCollins, 2012)

NW: John Muir, *Nature Writings*, ed. William Cronon (New York: Library of America, 1997)

OED: online complete *Oxford English Dictionary*, www.oed.com

P: J. A. Baker, *The Peregrine, The Hill of Summer and Diaries: The Complete Works of J. A. Baker*, ed. John Fanshawe (1967, 1969; London: HarperCollins, 2011)

POB: Clarence Ellis, *The Pebbles on the Beach* (London: Faber and Faber, 1953)

WL: Roger Deakin, *Waterlog* (London: Chatto & Windus, 1999)

WW: Roger Deakin, *Wildwood* (London: Hamish Hamilton, 2007)

Notes

Epigraphs

Pages

vi   *'Where lies your . . . soul's star?'*: Gerard Manley Hopkins, 'On the Portrait of Two Beautiful Young People', in *The Major Works*, ed. Catherine Phillips (Oxford: Oxford University Press, 1986), p. 176.

vii   *'Scholars, I plead with you . . . the grasses?'*: Norman MacCaig, 'By the Grave-yard, Luskentyre', in *The Poems of Norman MacCaig*, ed. Ewen MacCaig (Edinburgh: Polygon, 2005), p. 431.

Chapter 1: The Word-Hoard

Pages

1   *'The hardest thing of all . . . really there'*: P, p. 33.

2   *'the quivering intensity . . . thudding into a tree'*: ibid., p. 30.

3   *'When you look back . . . the environment has changed'*: OUP head of children's dictionaries, in interview with the *Daily Telegraph*, 6 December 2008. It is worth clarifying that OUP dictionaries operate according to a central lex-icographic principle of description rather than prescription: decisions on inclusion or exclusion are based in the main on frequency of usage across a substantial corpus of texts. The *OJD* deletions are therefore chiefly symptoms of a wider cultural disengagement with nature, rather than its cause.

4   *'euphonious vocabulary . . . become part of it'*: Henry Porter, 'The Pity of a Child's Dictionary', *Observer*, 14 December 2008.

5   *'coddish'*: see Jón Kalman Stefánsson, *Heaven and Hell*, trans. Philip Roughton (London: MacLehose, 2011).

5   *'Pitmatical . . . yakka'*: see Bill Griffiths, *Pitmatic: The Talk of the North East Coalfield* (Newcastle: Northumbria University Press, 2007).

5   *'seagull voice'*: Norman MacCaig, 'Aunt Julia', in *The Poems of Norman Mac-Caig*, ed. Ewen MacCaig (Edinburgh: Polygon, 2005), p. 204.

6   *'Language is fossil poetry . . . their poetic origin'*: Ralph Waldo Emerson, 'The Poet', in *The Collected Works of Ralph Waldo Emerson, Essays: Second Series*, ed. Joseph Slater et al. (Cambridge, Mass.: Harvard University Press, 1984), p. 13.

7   *terror in the terroir*: I borrow the phrase from Joe Kennedy's fine essay 'Ter-ror in the Terroir: Resisting the Rebranding of the Countryside', *Quietus* 13 (December 2013).

7 '*hundreds of common experiences . . . no words exist*': Douglas Adams and John Lloyd, *The Meaning of Liff* (1983; London: Pan Macmillan, 2013), p. xi.

7 '*Kimmeridge (n.) . . . after a holiday*': ibid., pp. 91, 64.

8 '*the Anglo-Saxon peasant farmer . . . subtle topographical vocabulary*': Margaret Gelling, *Place-Names in the Landscape* (London: J. M. Dent, 1984), p. 7.

8 '*British Bengalis, Gujaratis . . . such vocabulary to get established*': Debjani Chatterjee, personal correspondence, 20 June 2014.

9 '*landscape is lost*': see Oliver Rackham, *The History of the Countryside* (London: J. M. Dent, 1986), and Danny Adcock, 'Water Meadows', *Caught by the River*, 16 November 2013, http://www.caughtbytheriver.net/2013/11/water-meadows/.

9 '*convivial*': see Ivan Illich, *Deschooling Society* (London: Marion Boyars, 1970) and *Tools for Conviviality* (London: Calder & Boyars, 1973).

9 '*encouraging creative relations . . . people and nature*': Jay Griffiths, *Guardian*, 10 March 2014, http://www.theguardian.com/commentisfree/2014/mar/10/michael-gove-coding-education.

10 '*People exploit . . . love what we particularly know*': Wendell Berry, *Life Is a Miracle* (Berkeley: Counterpoint Press, 2000), p. 41.

10 '*Every language is an old-growth forest of the mind*': Wade Davis, 'Dreams from Endangered Cultures', TED talk, February 2003, http://www.ted.com/talks/wade_davis_on_endangered_cultures.

10 '*I want my writing . . . each kind of tree*': *WW*, prefatory note.

11 '*Every tree . . . cannot draw every needle*': John Muir, *My First Summer in the Sierra* (New York: Houghton Mifflin, 1911), in *NW*, p. 181.

11 '*pierce . . . visible things*': Ralph Waldo Emerson, *The Complete Works of Ralph Waldo Emerson: Nature, Addresses and Lectures* (Boston: Houghton Mifflin, 1854), p. 30.

11 '*The surface of the ground . . . as to be fairly dazzling*': Muir, *My First Summer*, in *NW*, pp. 242–3.

12 '*an object in the landscape . . . beare by the compasse*': *OED*; John Smith, *A Sea Grammar* (London: I Hauiland, 1627), p. ix.

Chapter 2: A Counter-Desecration Phrasebook

Pages

17 '*Some Lewis Moorland Terms: A Peat Glossary*': a fuller version of the glossary was in due course published by Anne Campbell as *Rathad an Isein: The Bird's Road – a Lewis Moorland Glossary* (Glasgow: Faram, 2013).

Notes

17 *'A volume thick as the height . . . beyond the wit of scholars'*: Norman MacCaig, 'By the Graveyard, Luskentyre', in *The Poems of Norman MacCaig*, ed. Ewen MacCaig (Edinburgh: Polygon, 2005), p. 432.

19 *A slow capillary creep of knowledge has occurred*: as has occurred in many other languages where people have spent generations inhabiting a particular ecological niche and practising a particular life-way. The Marovo people of the Philippines, for instance, have a rich language for classifying the schooling manners of fish: the lexis includes *ukuka*, which designates 'the behaviour of groups of fish when individuals drift, circle and float as if drunk', and *sakoto*, meaning 'quiet, almost motionless resting schools of certain fish looking like a gathering of mourners'. The Tuvan language spoken by Siberian nomads is peculiarly attentive to the aural properties of the boreal landscape: *chyʐr-chyʐr* means 'the sound of treetops moving, swaying, cracking or snapping as a result of bears marking trees by clawing at them and by scratching their backs up against them'; *koyurt* is the sound of 'human feet treading deep snow'; and *hir-hir* is 'both the crackling of a campfire or the sudden rustling of a grouse's wings in the grass'. See K. David Harrison, *When Languages Die: The Extinction of the World's Languages and the Erosion of Human Knowledge* (Oxford: Oxford University Press, 2007), pp. 50, 125.

19 *'natural features . . . the steep slope of the scowling expression'*: Richard V. Cox, *The Gaelic Place-Names of Carloway, Isle of Lewis: Their Structure and Significance* (Dublin: Dublin Institute for Advanced Studies, 2002), pp. 69–85.

20 *'magnificently surcharged with names'*: Marcel Proust, *Swann's Way*, trans. C. K. Scott Moncrieff (1913; New York: Henry Holt, 1922), p. 437.

20 *'lit by the mnemonics of words'*: Finlay MacLeod (ed.), *Togail Tìr / Marking Time: The Map of the Western Isles* (Stornoway: Acair and An Lanntair, 1989), p. ii.

21 *'Cùl Leac Ghlas ri taobh . . . Gaelic Positioning System'*: Angus MacMillan, 'Machair', *Archipelago* 2 (Spring 2008), 39–40.

21 *'a modest capacity for wonder . . . made to perform'*: Keith H. Basso, *Wisdom Sits in Places: Landscape and Language Among the Western Apache* (Albuquerque: University of New Mexico Press, 1996), p. 44.

22 *'bold, visual, evocative . . . bottom of a canyon)'*: ibid., p. 23.

22 *'requires that one . . . sitting at a particular spot . . . precision'*: ibid., p. 89.

22 *'I like to. I ride that way in my mind'*: ibid., pp. 45–6.

23 *the total number of native speakers . . . now around 58,000*: according to 2011 Census results, summarized at http://www.scotlandscensus.gov.uk/news/census-2011-release-2a.

23 *'some of the place-names are forgotten or becoming incomprehensible'*: Tim Robinson, *Setting Foot on the Shores of Connemara* (Dublin: Lilliput, 1996), p. 3; see also Robinson, *Stones of Aran: Pilgrimage* (Dublin: Lilliput, 1986), pp. 13–14.

23 *'important role . . . recently'*: Cox, *Gaelic Place-Names*, p. i.

23 *'working relationship with the moorland . . . the language which accompanied that sense'*: Finlay MacLeod, 'Counter-Desecration Phrasebook Needed', *Stornoway Gazette*, 14 February 2008.

23 *We are* blasé *about place*: see Georg Simmel, 'The Metropolis and Mental Life', in *On Individuality and Social Forms* (Chicago: University of Chicago Press, 1971), p. 329. For Simmel, the *blasé* was a function in part of the numbing effect on perception that the 'shocks' of modernity had administered to the subject, and partly a function of the rise of the capitalist use-value model, which leads to what Adorno called 'a generalized equivalence of all things'.

24 *'long-cultivated knowledge . . . the knowledge mostly unrecoverable'*: Harrison, *When Languages Die*, p. 17.

24 *'Without a name made in our mouths . . . purchase in our minds or our hearts'*: Tim Dee, 'Naming Names', *Caught by the River*, 25 June 2014, http://www.caughtbytheriver.net/2014/06/naming-names-tim-dee-robert-macfarlane/.

24 *'the knowledge or belief that . . . master all things by calculation'*: Max Weber, *From Max Weber: Essays in Sociology*, trans. H. H. Gerth and C. Wright Mills (Oxford: Oxford University Press, 1946), p. 139.

24 *Weber noted the widespread reduction of 'wonder'*: I draw here on Patrick Curry's illuminating discussion of enchantment and its 'immiscible' relation to modernity, 'On Not Saving Enchantment for Modernity (Even as Religion)', in Tom Crook and Mathew Feldman (eds.), *Sacred Modernities: Rethinking Modernity in a Post-Secular Age* (London: Continuum, 2011).

25 *Our language for nature is now such that the things around us do not talk back*: writing four years before Weber, in a chapter of *Swann's Way* (1913) on place-names and place-relations, Proust made a similar distinction between the rise of the scientific and wilful, and the retreat of the unintended and enchanting: '[There are] those natural phenomena from which our comfort

or our health can derive . . . an accidental . . . benefit,' until 'the day when science takes control of them, and, producing them at will, places in our hands the power to order their appearance, withdrawn from the tutelage and independent of the consent of chance'. Proust, *Swann's Way*, p. 438.

25 *'the whole universe of beings . . . standing reserve'*: Martin Heidegger, 'The Question Concerning Technology,' in *Basic Writings*, ed. David Krell (New York: HarperCollins, 1993), p. 325.

25 *to have their own lives if they are to enrich ours*: I thank Tom Gilliver for our conversation about these matters on 3 November 2009.

25 *only that by instrumentalizing nature . . . we have largely stunned the earth out of wonder*: see Peter Larkin, 'Scarcely on the Way: The Starkness of Things in Sacral Space', http://intercapillaryspace.blogspot.com/2010/03/scarcely-on-way-starkness-of-things-in.html.

26 *'One must wait for the moment . . . something that knows we are there'*: Barry Lopez and Debra Gwartney (eds.), *Home Ground: Language for an American Landscape* (San Antonio: Trinity University Press, 2006), p. xviii.

26 *'That rivers and streams . . . nearly meet one another'*: ibid., p. 159.

26 *'a type of low brush thicket . . . shin oak (*Quercus harvardii*)'*: ibid., p. 325.

27 *'[I]t is along the banks of slow-moving creeks . . . only a second change of temperature'*: ibid., pp. 89–90.

27 *'to recall and to explore . . . slipping off into abstract space'*: ibid., p. xxiii.

28 *'the effect on the landscape resource . . . major and long-term'*: 'Lewis Wind Farm: Non-Technical Summary of the Environmental Statement', submitted by Lewis Wind Power Limited, 17 October 2004, http://www.cne-siar.gov.uk/windpower/lewiswindpower/documents/NTS%20final%20version.pdf.

29 *'a vast, dead place . . . swept by a chill wet wind'*: Ian Jack, 'Breathing Space', *Guardian*, 26 July 2006.

29 *'abominable . . . a waste and a howling wilderness'*: Daniel Defoe, *A Tour Thro' the Whole Island of Great Britain, Divided into Circuits or Journies*, 3 vols. (London: Strahan, 1724–6), vol. III, p. 74.

29 *'hideous blank . . . dreary, dismal desert'*: *Argus*, June 1858. See, for a discussion of the perception of the Australian interior as *terra nullius,* the third chapter of Roslynn Doris Haynes, *Seeking the Centre: The Australian Desert in Literature, Art and Film* (Cambridge: Cambridge University Press, 1998).

29 *'so much [of it] is unproductive wilderness'*: James Carnegy-Arbuthnott, quoted in the *Guardian*, 10 August 2013, http://www.theguardian.com/

uk-news/2013/aug/10/scotland-land-rights. Compare the July 2013 comments of the Conservative peer Lord Howell during 'Lords' Questions' that the north-east of England contains 'large and uninhabited and desolate areas' where 'there's plenty of room for fracking', 'without any kind of threat to the rural environment', http://www.telegraph. co.uk/earth/earthvideo/10211388/Lord-Howell-frack-the-desolate-North-East.html.

29 *'it is precisely what is invisible . . . a place to another'*: this is Barry Lopez's gloss on Yi Fu Tuan's arguments in his *Topophilia* (1974). See *AD*, p. 278.

29 *'Those who wish to explain to politicians . . . sounding either wet or extreme'*: MacLeod, 'Counter-Desecration Phrasebook'.

30 'An Talamh Briste, Na Feadanan Gorma . . . *or to commemorate stories'*: Anne Campbell and Jon MacLeod, *A-mach an Gleann* (Stornoway: privately published, 2007), *passim*.

31 *'Scotland small? Our multiform . . . marvellously descriptive! And incomplete!'*: Hugh MacDiarmid, 'Scotland Small?', in 'Dìreadh I', from *Complete Poems*, Vol. II (Manchester: Carcanet, 1994), p. 1,170.

31 *'What is required . . . a Counter-Desecration Phrasebook'*: MacLeod, 'Counter-Desecration Phrasebook'.

32 *'something emotive abides in the land . . . invisible to the ironist'*: Lopez and Gwartney, *Home Ground*, p. xviii.

33 *'a narrative not fully known . . . larger chains of events'*: Adam Potkay, 'Wordsworth and the Ethics of Things', *PMLA* 123:2 (2008), 394. This deep-buried meaning of the word *thing* is likely to be a residue of the Old Danish *Thing* as designating a community meeting where legal issues were disputed and settled; i.e. a parliament or a court. In such a context, the idea of a *Thing* bears within it a judicial space of uncertainty, the connotation of a matter whose resolution has yet to be determined.

33 *'galvanized against inertia . . . as our natural reticence allows us to be'*: Marianne Moore, 'Feeling and Precision', *Sewanee Review* 52:4 (October–December 1944), 499–500. I am compelled, too, by Moore's fanaticism for rhythm as a means of cognition, a kind of precision: 'it [the effect] begins far back of the beat, so that you don't see when the down beat comes. It was started such a long distance ahead, it makes it possible to be exact.'

33 *'For knowledge, add; for wisdom, take away'*: Charles Simic, quoted by Jan Zwicky in *Wisdom & Metaphor* (Kentville: Gaspereau Press, 2005), p. 74.

Notes

34 *In this respect it would inhabit . . . reciprocal perception between human and non-human*: see John Llewellyn, *The Middle Voice of Ecological Conscience* (New York: St Martin's Press, 1991).

34 *'John Locke, in the seventeenth century . . . he had perceived or imagined it'*: Jorge Luis Borges, 'Funes the Memorious', in *Labyrinths: Selected Stories and Other Writings* (New York: New Directions, 1964), p. 65.

34 *'tendered . . . alterity were itself pure gift'*: Potkay, 'Ethics of Things', 401. Potkay draws on the work of Sylvia Benso; see also Larkin, 'Scarcely on the Way'.

34 *'having language to hand'*: Zwicky, *Wisdom & Metaphor*, p. 32.

35 'Tact: 1 (a) . . . *translating Andreas Ornithoparcus)'*: *OED* online.

35 *Tact as due attention . . . as rightful tactility*: see Valentine Cunningham, *Reading After Theory* (Oxford: Wiley-Blackwell, 2001).

Chapter 3: The Living Mountain

Pages

55 *'the elementals'*: *LM*, p. 4.

55 *'heaven-appointed task . . . to the approved pattern'*: letter from Nan Shepherd to Neil Gunn, 2 April 1931, Deposit 209, Box 19, Folder 7, National Library of Scotland, Edinburgh.

56 *'I have had the same bedroom all my life!'*: Nan Shepherd, quoted in Vivienne Forrest, 'In Search of Nan Shepherd', *Leopard Magazine* (December 1986–January 1987), 17.

57 *'all movement . . . those limbs move as you look at them'*: letter from Nan Shepherd to Barbara Balmer, 15 January 1981, private collection.

57 *'library-cormorant'*: Samuel Taylor Coleridge, *Collected Letters 1785–1800*, ed. Earl Leslie Griggs (Oxford: Clarendon Press, 1966), p. 156.

58 *'a tall slim figure with a halo . . . an awe-inspiring dispatch case'*: anon., quoted in Louise Donald, 'Nan Shepherd', *Leopard Magazine* (October 1977), 21.

58 *'long lean man . . . need not cease to exhilarate'*: Nan Shepherd, quoted in ibid., 20.

58 *'dark wisdom, almost sorcery . . . giant ruffled eagle's feather'*: Erlend Clouston, personal communication, 30 April 2014.

58 'Poetry . . . *burning heart of life*': letter from Nan Shepherd to Neil Gunn, 14 March 1930, Deposit 209, Box 19, Folder 7, National Library of Scotland, Edinburgh.

59 '*possess[ed]* . . . *kind of thing that comes out of me*': letter from Nan Shepherd to Neil Gunn, 2 April 1931.

59 '*snow driving dim on the blast . . . green as ice*': *ITC*, pp. 3, 53.

59 '*does nothing, absolutely nothing, but be itself*': *LM*, p. 23.

59 '*not out of myself, but in myself*': ibid., p. 108.

59 '*Oh burnie with the glass-white . . . over stone . . .*': *ITC*, p. 1.

60 '*I've gone dumb . . . for the mere sake of making a noise*': letter from Nan Shepherd to Neil Gunn, 2 April 1931.

61 '*Dear Nan, You don't need me to tell you . . . hill & country lovers*': letter from Neil Gunn to Nan Shepherd, 30 October 1945, Deposit 209, Box 19, Folder 7, National Library of Scotland, Edinburgh.

62 '*a traffic of love*': *LM*, p. xliii.

62 '*Parochialism is universal . . . a man can fully experience*': Patrick Kavanagh, 'The Parish and the Universe', in *Collected Pruse* [*sic*] (London: Macgibbon & Kee, 1967), pp. 281–3.

63 '*irradiate the common . . . make something universal*': letter from Nan Shepherd to Neil Gunn, 2 April 1931.

64 '*lust . . . effect upon me*': *LM*, pp. 8, 9, 107.

64 '*merely to be with the mountain . . . but to be with him*': ibid., p. 15.

64 '*I am on the plateau again . . . stay up here for a while*': ibid., p. 22

64 '*The plateau is the true summit . . . eddies on the plateau surface*': ibid., p. 2.

65 '*a legendary task, which heroes, not men, accomplished*': ibid., p. 107.

65 '*thirled me for life to the mountain*': ibid., p. 107.

65 '*Birch needs rain . . . can be as good as drunk with it*': ibid., p. 53.

66 '*the coil over coil . . . leggy shadow-skeleton*': ibid., pp. 61, 52, 65.

66 '*Beech bud-sheaths . . . brightness to the dusty roads of May*': 'The Colour of Deeside', Nan Shepherd, *Deeside Field* 8 (1937), 9.

66 '*bland as silk . . . rooted far down in their immobility*': *LM*, pp. 93, 92.

66 '*I knew when I had looked . . . hardly begun to see*': ibid., p. 11.

66 '*the eye sees what it didn't . . . whose working is dimly understood*': ibid., p. 106.

67 '*snow skeleton, attached to nothing*': ibid., p. 42.

68 '*I could have sworn I saw . . . I never saw it again*': ibid., p. 2.

68 *'Such illusions . . . but steadies us again'*: ibid., p. 101.

69 *'impossible to coerce'*: ibid., p. 91.

69 *'On one toils . . . toil[s] upwards'*: ibid., pp. 10, 16.

69 *'as the earth must see itself'*: ibid., p. 11.

70 *'twisted and intertwined . . . secret of their formation'*: ibid., pp. 55, 57, 69, 33.

70 *'interlaced . . . frozen floor of a hollow'*: ibid., p. 70.

70 *'interlocks . . . hidden hollow'*: ibid., pp. 70, 106, 72.

71 *'patiently adds fact to fact'*: ibid., p. 58.

71 *'Slowly I have found my way in . . . I should know'*: ibid., p. 105.

71 *'too much . . . resumed formation and direction'*: ibid., pp. 28, 70.

71 *'The mind cannot carry away all . . . what it has carried away'*: ibid., p. 3.

71 *'strong white . . . limber'*: ibid., pp. 23, 98, 102, 51, 92.

72 *'That's the way to see the world: in our own bodies'*: Gary Snyder, *The Practice of the Wild* (San Francisco: North Point Press, 1990), p. 106.

72 *'roaring scourge . . . purple as a boozer's'*: *LM*, pp. 1, 44, 36.

72 *'boys . . . high-spirited and happy report'*: ibid., p. 39.

73 *'the body may be said to think'*: ibid., p. 105.

73 *'incarnates . . . medium for having a world'*: Maurice Merleau-Ponty, *Phenomenology of Perception*, trans. Colin Smith (New York: Humanities Press, 1962), *passim*, but see especially pp. 144–6.

74 *'something moves between me and it . . . except by recounting it'*: *LM*, p. 8.

74 *'The body is not . . . identity for the hand as much as for the eye'*: ibid., pp. 106, 103.

75 *'This is the innocence we have lost . . . all the way through'*: ibid., p. 105.

75 *'out of the body . . . soil of the earth'*: ibid., pp. 106, 92.

75 *'one has been in . . . That is all'*: ibid., p. 92.

75 *'coveted knowledge . . . pursuit of learning'*: Donald, 'Nan Shepherd', 20.

75 *'I can see the wood . . . that reverberates/illuminates'*: letters from Nan Shepherd to Barbara Balmer, 15 January and 2 February 1981, private collection.

76 *'reticent about herself . . . grace of the soul'*: Jessie Kesson, quoted in Forrest, 'In Search of Nan Shepherd', 19.

76 *'striking power . . . he said yes to life'*: Nan Shepherd, Introduction to Charles Murray, *Last Poems* (Aberdeen: Charles Murray Trust/Aberdeen University Press, 1970), p. ix.

76 *'I hope it is true for those . . . has been so good, so fulfilling'*: Nan Shepherd, quoted in Forrest, 'In Search of Nan Shepherd', 19.

77 *'a peerer into corners'*: *LM*, p. xlii.

78 'recesses': ibid., p. 9.

78 'It cannot be seen until one stands almost on its lip': ibid., p. 10.

78 'The sound of all this moving water is as integral . . . a dozen different notes at once': ibid., p. 26.

79 'journey to the source . . . and flowed away': ibid., p. 23.

79 'total mountain . . . being': ibid., p. 105.

Chapter 4: The Woods and the Water

Pages

95 'part-islanded': *WW*, p. 4.

95 'a great inland sea . . . the pleasures of living beside it': ibid.

96 'sit[s] lightly on the sea . . . like an upturned boat': ibid., p. 8.

96 'It's extraordinary what you see in an English moat': Roger Deakin, *The Garden*, BBC Radio 4.

96 'All water . . . holds memory and the space to think': *NFWTF*, p. 186.

97 'frog's-eye view': *WL*, p. 1.

97 '1. The action or fact of flowing in . . . thus flows in or is infused': *OED* online.

98 'a spring in your step': Heathcote Williams, 'It's the Plunge That Counts', *London Review of Books* 21:16, 19 August 1999.

100 'like weeds . . . spontaneous and unstoppable': *NFWTF*, p. 63.

101 'slip-shape': Alice Oswald, *Dart* (London: Faber and Faber, 2002), p. 48.

101 'Searching the map, I had seen . . . slabs of slate hollowed into baths': *WL*, p. 91.

102 'when we try to pick out anything . . . hitched to the whole world': John Muir, *My First Summer in the Sierra* (New York: Houghton Mifflin, 1911), in *NW*, p. 245.

103 'I threw myself in . . . crawled out onto the beach like a turtle': *WL*, p. 131.

104 'To enter a wood is to pass . . . paradoxically, by getting lost': *WW*, p. x.

104 'The woods and the water . . . for us to understand more thoroughly': Roger Deakin, unpublished notebook entry.

105 'fifth element': *WW*, p. ix.

105 'I am a woodlander . . . a tree is itself a river of sap': ibid., p. x.

106 'The central value of English . . . and environmental education': Roger Deakin, 'Dark Horses: Environmental Education and English Teaching', unpublished lecture delivered at the Royal Festival Hall, 21 September 1990.

107 *'The dandelion in full flower . . . is itself incomparable and unique'*: D. H. Lawrence, *Reflections on the Death of a Porcupine and Other Essays* (1925; Cambridge: Cambridge University Press, 1988), p. 358.

107 *'[r]edstarts flew from tree to tree . . . is what makes it graceful'*: *WL*, p. 91.

107 *'park-bench green . . . footballer in a striped vest'*: *NFWTF*, pp. 43, 208.

110 *'Angels are the people we care for and who care for us'*: Roger Deakin, unpublished notebook entry.

111 *'only interested in everything'*: Les Murray, quoted by Roger Deakin, *WL*, p. 3.

115 *'go on and on . . . settle for ever in one place'*: Edward Thomas, *The South Country* (London: J. M. Dent, 1909), p. 161.

115 *'I am Hansje, born and bred . . . to see the earth clarified'*: letter from Hansje te Velde to Robert Macfarlane, 15 November 2011.

Chapter 5: Hunting Life

Pages

140 *'cloud-biting anchor shape'*: *P*, p. 30.

141 *'Autumn . . . like the arch of Orion'*: ibid., p. 29.

145 *'Dear Sam . . . an infinity of sight'*: letter from J. A. Baker to Don Samuel, September/October 1945, Baker Archive, Albert Sloman Library, University of Essex.

146 *'a prickly customer' . . . 'loner' as an adult*: Doreen Baker, undated interview with David Cobham, edited transcript, Baker Archive.

146 *'Binoculars and a hawk-like vigilance . . . myopic human vision'*: *P*, p. 93.

146 *'Patching Hall Lane . . . singing lustily'*: ibid., p. 282.

147 *'Sunday May 9th . . . as a bird's throat'*: ibid. Compare Nan Shepherd: 'It is, it is, the blackbird singing! / The beat of time is in the note. / Yet its own infinite arises / From that small perishable throat.' 'Blackbird in Snow', *ITC*, p. 17.

147 *'plunged into the wet wood . . . sharing that joy'*: *P*, p. 284. When Baker came to re-describe this incident in *The Hill of Summer*, he omitted Sid from his account and implied he was alone. See ibid., pp. 204–5.

148 *'Saturday November 20th 1954 . . . revellers in the wind'*: ibid., p. 289.

148 *'Tuesday November 1st 1955 . . . autumn slum of trees'*: ibid., p. 311.

148 *'clear varnish of yellow . . . Rembrandt oil-painting'*: ibid., p. 296.

148 *'Wednesday April 23rd 1958. . . tricky and strange'*: ibid., p. 372.

149 *'glorious light . . . or a falcon, presumably'*: J. A. Baker, 'Peregrine Diaries', entry for 6 January 1957, Baker Archive.

149 *'the possibility of it's . . . flashed across my mind'*: ibid., entry for 10 January 1957, Baker Archive.

152 *'The north wind . . . pleached lattice of the hedges'*: P, p. 103.

152 *'Four short-eared owls soothed out of the gorse'*: ibid., p. 67.

152 *'Savagely he lashed himself . . . rim of the black cloud'*: ibid., p. 70.

152 *'like a small mad puritan with a banana in his mouth'*: ibid., p. 105.

152 *'glowed purple and grey like broccoli'*: ibid., p. 113.

152 *'five thousand dunlin . . . gleamed with golden chitin'*: ibid., p. 52.

153 *'the pages dance with image . . . that marshland drama'*: Kenneth Allsop, review of *The Peregrine*, *London Evening News*, 23 March 1967.

153 *'sabring fall from the sky'*: P, pp. 124–5.

153 *'A falcon peregrine . . . splinters of white wood'*: ibid., p. 49.

154 *'The peregrine lives . . . maps of black and white'*: ibid., p. 46.

154 *'rings of small black stones'*: ibid., p. 55.

154 *'into dark twiggy lines . . . blue and silver mouth'*: ibid., p. 128.

155 *'Wherever he goes . . . there be purified'*: ibid., p. 48.

155 *'Evanescent as flame . . . the white helix of the gulls'*: ibid., p. 51.

156 *'a strong feeling of proximity, identification'*: ibid., p. 126.

156 *'The body of a woodpigeon . . . We shun men'*: ibid., p. 92.

156 *'The [book's] strange and awful grip . . . hawk's feathers, skin and spirit'*: Allsop, review of *The Peregrine*, *London Evening News*.

157 *'his usual loose-limbed panache'*: P, p. 73.

157 *'the hunter becoming the thing he hunts'*: ibid., p. 92.

157 *a British raptor specialist called Derek Ratcliffe had published a landmark paper*: D. A. Ratcliffe, 'The Status of the Peregrine in Great Britain', *Bird Study* 10 (1963), 56–90. Ratcliffe's paper, among other factors, led to a control of DDT use in British agriculture, and the peregrine population saw a slow climb. In countries where pesticide use was not controlled the results were catastrophic: 2,000 breeding pairs in Finland in 1950 had been reduced to 16 pairs by 1975.

157 *'the filthy, insidious pollen of farm chemicals'*: P, p. 31.

158 *'Few winter in England . . . the ancient eyries are dying'*: ibid., pp. 108–9.

158 *'As I approached I could see . . . We cannot tear it away'*: ibid., pp. 112–13.

160 *'I hope to have the good fortune . . . Friday Feb 10th'*: undated letter from reader, Baker Archive.

Notes

Chapter 6: The Tunnel of Swords and Axes

Pages

177 'rough sea-billows . . . among them are the lost-words that I sought': see *The Kalevala*, trans. John Martin Crawford (London: G. Putnam, 1889), Runes XVI and XVII, pp. 161–80.

180 *one of which shelters a Quaker burial ground from the eighteenth century*: this plantation has been cut down since the time of writing.

182 'limned the edges of its streams . . . eaves of its woods': *L*, p. 48.

182 'seventeen thresholds that grant access to the moor': ibid., p. 133.

183 Hare-gate: *an opening in a hedge . . . winter is filled with a torrent*': ibid., pp. 195–6.

184 'Could I reconstruct . . . with which to sound the landscape': ibid., p. 149.

184 'Where before I collected fragments . . . to call upon the landscape': ibid., p. 137.

185 'Perhaps there is a glimpse . . . by virtue of their difference, their strangeness?': ibid., pp. 138–9.

186 'place-name poetry . . . beauty of certain lexicons': Autumn Richardson and Richard Skelton, *Wolf Notes* (Cumbria: Corbel Stone Press, 2010), p. 27.

187 'Ulpha is still inhabited . . . can be uncovered and celebrated': ibid., p. 9.

188 'gathered pace, taking in tributaries . . . in the Late Bronze Age)': Richard Skelton, *Limnology* (Cumbria: Corbel Stone Press, 2012), endnote.

191 'receding below the threshold . . . of all melodies': *L*, p. 126.

Chapter 7: North-Minded

Pages

209 'the malevolent north': see Margaret Atwood, *Strange Things: The Malevolent North in Canadian Literature* (Oxford: Clarendon Press, 1995).

211 'it is possible to live wisely on the land, and to live well': *AD*, p. xxviii.

211 'stand toe-to at the water's edge . . . boots in six hours': ibid., p. 252.

211 'the classic lines . . . extended, and quiet': ibid., p. xxiii.

212 'monotonic . . . plains of open water': ibid., pp. 229, xxiii.

212 'chitinous shell . . . staghorn lichen next to them': ibid., p. 254.

212 *'the grace of accuracy'*: Robert Lowell, 'Epilogue', in *Robert Lowell: Collected Poems*, ed. Frank Bidart (London: Faber and Faber, 2003), p. 838.

213 *'removed and exceptional part of Scotland'*: *DM*, p. 8.

214 *'a pencil-stripe of light . . . relentless daylight over Norway'*: ibid., p. 60.

214 *'green silence . . . the returning cold'*: ibid., pp. 63, 18, 21.

214 *'A little stone jetty . . . extraordinary water'*: ibid., p. 38.

215 *'noticed everything . . . put away for the winter'*: ibid., p. 73.

215 *'[f]ine gradations . . . runs the length of the room'*: ibid., p. 71.

217 *'to capture the moment, lost and yet preserved forever'*: ibid., p. 7.

217 *'which dies even as . . . catch its likeness'*: ibid., p. 147.

217 *'conservatorie'*: Thomas Browne, *Urne-Buriall* (1658), in *Religio Medici and Urne-Buriall*, ed. Stephen Greenblatt and Ramie Targoff (New York: NYRB Classics, 2012), p. 114.

217 *'the predatory loss that shadows all human pleasure'*: *DM*, p. 14.

217 *'basalt rocks bordering the Baltic . . . the high sun on the sea'*: ibid., p. 6.

218 *'black dog flickers . . . edge of the lawns'*: ibid., p. 65.

218 *'We have gathered things . . . the place where we live'*: ibid., p. 24.

218 *'moony silver . . . the bright sky into itself'*: ibid., p. 66.

218 *'breaks forward into the sunlight . . . light into itself'*: ibid., p. 74.

218 *'hold the dimming sky . . . islands in the archipelago'*: ibid., pp. 64, 70.

219 *'All the years I have been writing . . . laughing, painting out of doors'*: ibid., p. 40

220 *'In a winter-hammered landscape . . . ignorance falling away from us'*: Barry Lopez, *About This Life: Journeys on the Threshold of Memory* (1998; London: Harvill, 1999), p. 122, and *AD*, p. xxviii.

220 *'The sharpness of the morning frost . . . magnifying lens'*: *DM*, p. 165.

220 *'depthlessly clear'*: *AD*, p. xxiv.

Chapter 8: Bastard Countryside

Pages

231 *'drosscape'*: see Alan Berger, *Drosscape: Wasting Land in Urban America* (New York: Princeton Architectural Press, 2007).

231 *'edgeland'*: see Marion Shoard, 'Edgelands', in *Remaking the Landscape*, ed. Jennifer Jenkins (London: Profile, 2002), pp. 117–46.

231 *'crapola'*: Philip Guston, quoted in Philip Roth, *Shop Talk* (New York: Houghton Mifflin Harcourt, 2001), p. 135.

231 *'bastard countryside . . . the noise of humankind'*: the passage was added by Victor Hugo to the 1861 edition of *Les Misérables*. I use the translation given by T. J. Clark in 'The View from Notre-Dame', in *The Nineteenth-Century Visual Culture Reader* (London: Routledge, 2004), p. 179.

231 *'the messy limbo . . . outer-Outer London'*: Kenneth Allsop, *Adventure Lit Their Star: The Story of an Immigrant Bird* (1949; London: Penguin, 1972), p. 9.

232 *'asphalt . . . noose'*: Iain Sinclair, *London Orbital* (London: Granta, 2002), pp. 17, 140.

232 *'frontier line to civilisation'*: Richard Jefferies, Preface to *Wild Life in a Southern County* (1879; Toller Fratrum: Little Toller, 2011), p. 15.

233 *'Why, we must have been blind . . . but we saw them not!'*: Walter Besant, *The Eulogy of Richard Jefferies* (1888; London: Chatto & Windus, 1905), p. 167. Besant, it should be noted, was not wholly approving of Jefferies, considering his talent narrow and certainly confined to non-fiction.

234 *'broke most radically with . . . human history'*: Eric Hobsbawm, *Industry and Empire* (London: Penguin, 1967), p. 15.

234 *'Wilderness! . . . I have never forgotten it'*: Charles Dickens, *Nicholas Nickleby* (1839), ed. Jill Muller (New York: Spark, 2005), p. 439.

234 *'London looks so large . . . so barren and so wild'*: Charles Dickens, *Little Dorrit* (1857), ed. Harvey Peter Sucksmith (Oxford: Oxford World's Classics, 2008), p. 131.

234 *'unseen influence . . . under the calm oaks'*: *NNL*, p. ix.

235 *'quitting the suburb'*: ibid., p. 85.

235 *'rubbish heaps . . . garden flowers about the metropolis'*: ibid., pp. 90, 154.

235 *'coloured . . . like a continuous garden'*: ibid., p. 169.

235 *'very large cinder and dust heap . . . any stray morsels of food'*: ibid., pp. 87–8.

236 *'berry year . . . eight in a stalk'*: ibid., p. 119.

236 *'put forth green buds . . . flowers not sown in order'*: ibid., pp. 130, 133.

236 *'fully two thousand . . . their very wings seem to flap together'*: ibid., p. 129.

238 *'It would be very easy . . . method of knowing'*: ibid., p. ix.

239 *'Everyone must find their own locality . . . you find yours yonder'*: ibid.

239 *'keep[ing] an eye . . . as it really is'*: ibid., pp. xi, 11.

239 *'bluebells . . . unseen, except by rabbits'*: ibid., p. 23.

239 *'The landscapes I have in mind . . . regarded as invisible'*: Paul Nash, *Outline: An Autobiography* (London: Faber and Faber, 1959), p. 229.

239 *'pastoral crooks . . . many who do not are unnoticed'*: *NNL*, pp. 42, 75, 76.

240 '*Even trees which have some semblance . . . their outline changes*': ibid., p. 15.

240 '*walk all round [a] meadow . . . scheme of colour is perceivable*': ibid., p. 13.

240 '*wavelets . . . so unwind the pattern*': ibid., p. 110.

241 '*This changing of focus . . . reference to me, the looker*': *LM*, pp. 10–11.

241 '*the leaves are enlarging . . . the tinted petals uncurling*': *NNL*, p. 5.

241 '*a thousand thousand buds . . . even to number them*': Richard Jefferies, 'Hours of Spring', in *Field and Hedgerow* (London: Longmans, Green & Co., 1889), p. 8.

241 '*Sparrows crowd every hedge . . . there must be thousands*': *NNL*, p. 27.

241 '*astonished and delighted . . . in the most secluded country*': ibid., p. 28.

242 '*There are about sixty wild flowers . . . vetches, and yellow vetch*': ibid., p. 38.

243 '*great green book . . . are quite forgotten*': ibid., pp. 151–2.

243 '*Before it is too late . . . like Mars, but glowing still*': *P*, p. 32.

243 '*The heart . . . longs for the beautiful*': Jefferies, 'Hours of Spring', p. 9.

244 '*[T]he goldfinches . . . continue to proceed*': Richard Jefferies, *The Hills and the Vale* (1909; Cambridge: Cambridge University Press, 2011), p. 293.

244 '*The earth is all in all to me . . . thought's self within*': Jefferies, 'Hours of Spring', pp. 8–9.

244 '*I am not a part of nature . . . the rain without*': Edward Thomas, *The Icknield Way* (1913; London: Constable, 1916), p. 281.

245 '*delicate grasses . . . into the dust*': *NNL*, pp. 6, 117.

245 '*white granular powder*': Rachel Carson, *Silent Spring* (1962; New York: Houghton Mifflin, 2002), p. 3.

245 '*The dust of London . . . the inanimate things around us*': *NNL*, p. 171.

245 '*dust . . . which falls on a ledge*': Richard Jefferies, *The Story of My Heart* (1883; London: Longmans & Co., 1907), p. 1.

245 '*immense City*': *NNL*, p. 20.

245 '*the atmosphere of London . . . out into the cornfields*': ibid., p. 41.

246 '*the aurora of dark vapour . . . presage, gloom, tragedy*': ibid., p. 147.

246 '*in course of time I shall find out . . . there never was any earth*': Richard Jefferies, 'My Old Village', in *Field and Hedgerow*, p. 329.

246 '*decisively worsened . . . possessed of an animate threat*': Simon Grimble, *Landscape, Writing and 'The Condition of England': 1878–1914, Ruskin to Modernism* (Edwin Mellon: Lewiston, Queenston, Lampeter, 2004), p. 54.

247   '*The old men say their fathers . . . cut himself a path*': Richard Jefferies, *After London; Or, Wild England* (1885; Oxford: Oxford World's Classics, 1983), p. 1.

247   '*the deserted and utterly extinct city of London*': ibid., p. 129.

248   '*old red brick wall . . . bunches of wall grasses flourish*': *NNL*, p. 65.

248   '*the great nature . . . closely to the metropolis*': ibid., p. 82.

Chapter 9: Stone-Books

Pages

263   '*fragment of gabbro . . . quartz-veined grit*': *POB*, p. 96.

263   '*What is a pebble? . . . we must examine it more closely*': ibid., pp. 13, 53.

263   '*wax-like lustre . . . difficult to describe*': ibid., pp. 68–9.

264   '*Gneiss (pronounced "nice") . . . schistos, meaning "easily split"*': ibid., p. 59.

264   '*the rudiments of wave action . . . the smoothing of pebbles*': ibid., p. 15.

264   '*frozen into its underside*': ibid., p. 42.

264   '*Collectors of pebbles are rare*': ibid., p. 11.

265   '*combed the beaches . . . glittering collections*': ibid., p. 12.

265   '*All I know is that . . . and eat pebbles*': Vladimir Nabokov, interview with Alvin Toffler, *Playboy* (January 1964).

266   '*I have used the findings . . . purposes altogether unscientific*': *AL*, p. vii.

266   '*creatures of the land*': ibid., p. 181.

266   '*The image I have sought to evoke . . . all in one piece*': ibid., p. vii.

266   '*an uncommon type of book . . . recognized categories*': typescript contained in the 'Readers' Union' file, Jacquetta Hawkes Archive, University of Bradford. The text was written by Hawkes to accompany the 1953 Readers' Union edition of *A Land*.

267   '*There is . . . a passion of love and hate*': Harold Nicolson, 'Sermon in Stones', review of *A Land*, *Observer*, 3 June 1951.

267   '*something of their imaginative range . . . tragically overdue*': H. J. Massingham, 'Sermons in Stones', review of *A Land*, *Spectator*, 1 June 1951.

268   '*highly emotional pitch . . . mystery of its manifestations*': Hawkes, 'Readers' Union', Hawkes Archive.

268   '*an absurdly tender age . . . trees in our emotional lives*': ibid.

269   '*only the most severely technical . . . more imaginative purposes*': Jacquetta Hawkes, handwritten response to Beacon Press's request for background material for a 1991 reissue of *A Land*, Jacquetta Hawkes Archive, University

of Bradford (a typed and amended version was sent to Beacon on 8 March 1991).

269 *'ice without and fire within . . . also to nature and the land'*: Nicolas Hawkes, interview with Robert Macfarlane, 4 April 2011.

270 *'When I have been working . . . agreeably conscious of my body'*: *AL*, p. 1.

270 *'fine silhouettes of the leaves . . . only orbit that was open to it'*: ibid., pp. 1–5.

271 *'does not come to an end with its rock and its soil'*: *LM*, p. 41.

271 *'There I lie on the plateau . . . the total mountain'*: ibid., p. 105.

271 *'sweet short turf . . . felt the wondrous present'*: Richard Jefferies, *The Story of My Heart* (1883; London: Longmans & Co., 1907), p. 20.

271 *'I imagine . . . all the particles of the universe'*: *AL*, p. 30.

272 *'every being is united . . . simplest forms of contemporary life'*: ibid., p. 32.

272 *'inside this delicate membrane . . . history of life'*: ibid., p. 31.

272 *'Consciousness must surely be traced back to the rocks'*: ibid., p. 30.

272 *'the simple reaction . . . herring in Cretaceous slime'*: ibid., p. 203.

272 *'affinity with rock . . . Blue Lias'*: ibid., pp. 100, 99.

272 *'Rodin pursued the idea . . . rather as always a part of it'*: ibid., p. 99.

273 *'It is hardly possible . . . which these thoughts bring to me'*: ibid., pp. 98–9.

273 *'just . . . escape[d] disaster'*: Jacquetta Hawkes, Introduction to 1978 edition of *A Land* (London: David and Charles, 1978), p. 1.

273 *'has to be told in words . . . the senses must be fed'*: *AL*, p. 36.

273 *'a continual whipping . . . dead march of the intellect'*: ibid., p. 37.

273 *'the glow of desert suns . . . the once boiling granite'*: ibid., pp. 60, 14.

273 *'the [Neanderthal] skeleton . . . fresh with chalk-dust'*: Christine Finn, introduction to *Jacquetta Hawkes: Archaeo-Poet (1910–96)*, at http://humanitieslab.stanford.edu/53/58.

274 *'Jurassic water snails . . . praise their God'*: *AL*, p. 70.

274 *'Stand at Moreton-in-the-Marsh . . . from desolation to desolation'*: ibid., p. 91.

275 *'our composed Britain'*: ibid., p. 45.

275 *'speak of insecurity . . . known to us as the British Isles'*: ibid., pp. 16, 24.

275 *'blessed heritage of farmers . . . radar and jet propulsion'*: Iain Sinclair, 'The Festival of Britain', *Guardian*, 22 April 2011.

276 *'regional difference . . . restoration of their country'*: *AL*, pp. 100, 201.

276 *'for a faint but palpable . . . mountain regions'*: ibid., pp. 218–23.

276 *'the land under him . . . with a fierce longing'*: T. H. White, *The Book of Merlyn* (Texas: University of Texas Press, 1977), pp. 109–12.

276 *'sense of community . . . parson, shepherd and clerk'*: J. B. Priestley, *Postscripts* (London: William Heinemann, 1940), p. 12.

276 *'the racial stock'*: *AL*, p. 180.

277 *'for months . . . Yours faithfully, Henry Williamson'*: letter from Henry Williamson to Jacquetta Hawkes, 1 February 1952, Jacquetta Hawkes Archive, University of Bradford.

278 *'a rock . . . full of fossils . . . stone to speak'*: *AL*, p. 98.

278 *'When we concentrate on . . . not of the now'*: Vladimir Nabokov, *Transparent Things* (1972; London: Penguin, 2012), p. 7.

Chapter 10: The Black Locust and the Silver Pine

Pages

289 *'I am a poetico- . . . ornith-natural, etc.!'*: John Muir to Robert Underwood Johnson, quoted in Terry Gifford, *Reconnecting with John Muir: Essays in Post-Pastoral Practice* (Athens: University of Georgia Press, 2006), p. 42.

290 *'The world is big . . . good look at it before it gets dark'*: John Muir, *John of the Mountains: The Unpublished Journals of John Muir*, ed. Linnie Marsh Wolfe (Madison: University of Wisconsin Press, 1979), p. 313.

290 *'Everybody needs beauty as well as bread'*: John Muir, *The Yosemite* (1912), in *John Muir: The Eight Wilderness-Discovery Books* (Diadem: London, 1992), p. 714.

290 *'The clearest way . . . a forest wilderness'*: Muir, *John of the Mountains*, p. 313.

290 *'Writing . . . is like the life of a glacier; one eternal grind'*: John Muir, letter to Sarah Muir Galloway, 17 April 1876, reprinted in *John Muir: His Life and Letters and Other Writings*, ed. Terry Gifford (London: Baton Wicks, 1996), p. 221.

291 *'an infinite storm of beauty'*: John Muir, *Travels in Alaska* (Boston and New York: Houghton Mifflin, 1915), in *John Muir: The Eight Wilderness-Discovery Books*, p. 724.

291 *'Wildness is a necessity . . . but as fountains of life'*: John Muir, *Our National Parks* (Boston and New York: Houghton Mifflin, 1901), p. 1.

292 *'glorious . . . conversion'*: John Muir, *My First Summer in the Sierra* (Boston and New York: Houghton Mifflin, 1911), in *NW*, p. 161.

292 *'This fine lesson charmed me . . . meadows in wild enthusiasm'*: John Muir, *The Story of My Boyhood and Youth* (Boston and New York: Houghton Mifflin, 1913), in *NW*, pp. 138–9.

293   *'opened to . . . inner beauty'*: ibid., p. 139.

293   *'old bondage days'*: Muir, *My First Summer*, in *NW*, p. 161.

293   *'"But where do you want to go? . . . any place that is wild," I said'*: Muir, *The Yosemite*, in *John Muir: The Eight Wilderness-Discovery Books*, p. 613.

293   *'gradually higher . . . best places we came to'*: Muir, *My First Summer*, in *NW*, p. 153.

293   *'We are now in the mountains . . . we seem to have been so always'*: ibid., p. 161.

294   *'Most people are* on *the world . . . touching but separate'*: Muir, *John of the Mountains*, p. 320.

294   *'One's body seems homogeneous throughout, sound as a crystal'*: Muir, *My First Summer*, in *NW*, p. 228.

294   *'Squirrelville, Sequoia Co. . . . they are in* me-ee-ee': letter from John Muir to Mrs Ezra Carr, *c.* 1870 (dating uncertain), in *John Muir: His Life and Letters*, p. 140.

294   *'indeed . . . the tree-lover's paradise'*: Muir, *My First Summer*, in *NW*, p. 209.

294   *'silky gray carpet . . . three inches high'*: ibid., p. 281.

295   *'forest kings . . . 300 feet in height'*: John Muir, *The Mountains of California* (New York: Century, 1894), in *NW*, pp. 436, 424.

295   *'knowledge . . . time in the almanac sense'*: Muir, *Mountains of California*, in *NW*, p. 403.

295   *'silvery luster . . . satiny'*: Muir, *My First Summer*, in *NW*, pp. 251, 249.

295   *'wind-history . . . storm story'*: ibid., pp. 185, 235.

295   *'beneath the interlacing arches . . . paw out oval hollows'*: Muir, *Mountains of California*, in *NW*, p. 445.

295   *'lithe, brushy top . . . continuous blaze of white sun-fire'*: ibid., pp. 467–70.

296   *'broad gray summit . . . a beautiful shrubby species'*: Muir, *My First Summer*, in *NW*, pp. 241–2.

297   *'becomes so adhesive . . . no small geological significance'*: ibid., p. 227.

297   *'as trackless as the sky'*: ibid., p. 185.

297   *'the wild gala-day of the north wind'*: Muir, *Mountains of California*, in *NW*, p. 340.

297   *'fiery, peppery, full of brag . . . sting the onlooker'*: Muir, *My First Summer*, in *NW*, p. 193.

297   *'cloudland . . . hills and domes of cloud'*: ibid., p. 185.

297   *'How fine the weather is! . . . peace to every living thing!'*: ibid., p. 172.

298 '*showy and fragrant*': ibid., p. 163.

298 '*I was swished down . . . been more gloriously exciting!*': Muir, *The Yosemite*, in *John Muir: The Eight Wilderness-Discovery Books*, p. 638.

299 '*fastens a hard, durable crust . . . night on the mountain-top*': Muir, *Mountains of California*, in *NW*, p. 351.

299 '*scalding gas jets*': Muir, 'Snow-Storm on Mount Shasta', in *NW*, p. 644.

299 '*The strange, wild thrilling motion . . . escape being shattered*': Muir, *The Yosemite*, in *John Muir: The Eight Wilderness-Discovery Books*, p. 643.

300 '*a vast undulated wave*': John Muir, 'Mountain Sculpture', *Overland Monthly* 12 (1874–5), 393.

300 '*knife-blade . . . smooth cobblestones*': Muir, *Mountains of California*, in *NW*, pp. 545–6.

300 '*destruction of the forests . . . falling before fire and the ax*': ibid., p. 547.

301 '*rosiny logs . . . sunbeams of centuries of summers*': Muir, *My First Summer*, in *NW*, pp. 202–3.

301 '*Few are altogether deaf . . . forest preservation would vanish*': John Muir, 'The National Parks and Forest Reservations', speech given at a meeting of the Sierra Club on 23 November 1895 and published in *Sierra Club Bulletin* 1:7 (January 1896), 282–3.

302 '*A lot of activists expect . . . they only germinate after fire*': Rebecca Solnit, *Hope in the Dark* (Edinburgh: Canongate, 2005), pp. 85–6, 93.

Chapter 11: Childish

Pages

315 '*As you sit on the hillside . . . look like a door, opens*': Stephen Graham, *The Gentle Art of Tramping* (1927; London: Thomas Nelson, 1938), p. 63.

315 '*Between every two pines is a door leading to a new life*': the phrase does not occur in Muir's published works; he handwrote it on a page of his copy of the first volume of Emerson's *Prose Works*. See for an account of the pursuit of the source of this elusive quotation: http://www.oberlin.edu/physics/dstyer/Muir/QuotableJohnMuir.html.

316 '*It had gone again . . . that the house was gone*': Susan Cooper, *The Dark Is Rising* (London: Chatto & Windus, 1973), pp. 30–31.

317 '*Children have many more . . . terms to translate them*': Henry James, Preface to *What Maisie Knew* (1897; London: Penguin, 1966), p. 9.

Notes

318   'the hundred languages of children': Loris Malaguzzi, in *The Hundred Languages of Children*, ed. Carolyn Edward (New Jersey: Norwood, 1993), p. vi.

319   'It was cold when we began . . . nobody seemed to mind': *AFG*, p. 4.

320   'the real and fantastical place that the park was becoming': ibid.

320   'with imagination and with daring . . . connect one place to another': ibid., p. 5.

320   'a place of possibility . . . ordinary and the fantastic': ibid.

320   'yellow at the edges . . . pink forest': ibid., pp. 8, 11.

321   'of newly made mud': ibid., p. 12.

321   'secret water . . . continuous, touchable surface': ibid., pp. 20–21.

322   'After one of his shipwreckings . . . It was quite soft': Tim Dee, 'Naming Names' *Caught by the River*, 25 June 2014, http://www.caughtbytheriver. net/2014/06/naming-names-tim-dee-robert-macfarlane/.

323   'shelter day-dreaming . . . topophilia': Gaston Bachelard, *The Poetics of Space*, trans. M. Jolas (1958; Boston: Beacon Press, 1994), p. 6.

324   'The children out in the woods . . . they're extinct': Chris Packham, quoted in 'Let Children Trespass and Start Fires', *Daily Telegraph*, 20 May 2014.

324   'returning the results to London . . . patterns of land use': Denis Cosgrove, *Geography and Vision: Seeing, Imagining and Representing the Word* (London: Tauris, 2008), p. 166.

324   'use the green lanes . . . lonely gates for horseriders': William Howitt, *The Rural Life of England* (London: Longmans, 1838), p. 43.

324   'bustle . . . school-children upon bypaths': Robert Louis Stevenson, *Essays of Travel* (London: Chatto & Windus, 1905), p. 127.

325   'the sandlots and creek beds . . . of literature itself?': Michael Chabon, 'Manhood for Amateurs: The Wilderness of Childhood', *New York Review of Books*, 16 July 2009.

325   'A door, a door . . . with his whole body': *AFG*, p. 20.

325   'the travelling to reach . . . somewhere else too': ibid., pp. 15, 16.

325   'Childhood is a branch of cartography': Chabon, 'Manhood for Amateurs'.

326   'map of maps . . . map of the mind's adventures': *AFG*, pp. 34, 36.

326   'weaved words and ways together': ibid., p. 28.

326   'honeyfurs': ibid., p. 29.

326   'My name is Kian . . . I was born in space and Mars': ibid., p. 28.

327   'This is the mountain . . . just climb up here': ibid., p. 35.

327   'hold infinite possibilities . . . an invisible door': ibid., pp. 38, 25.

SELECT BIBLIOGRAPHY

Landmarks is itself a bibliography of a kind, so I do not intend (on the whole) to list here books that have already been mentioned. Details of those can be found in the main text or the notes. Rather, what follows should be taken as a partial map of the tributaries and outflows of that main current: a selection of the books, poems, plays, songs, films, music, blogs, sound-works and essays that have influenced *Landmarks*, or to which *Landmarks* has led me, but that have remained uncited to this point. I have asterisked those works that have been particularly important.

On Children and Nature

Griffiths, Jay, *Kith* (London: Hamish Hamilton, 2013)
Nabhan, Gary Paul, and Stephen Trimble, *The Geography of Childhood* (Boston: Beacon Press, 1994)

On Creaturely Life

Herzog, Werner (dir.), *Grizzly Man* (2005)
Hines, Barry, *A Kestrel for a Knave* (London: Penguin, 1968)
Hughes, Ted, *The Hawk in the Rain* (London: Faber and Faber, 1957)
Santner, Eric, *On Creaturely Life* (Chicago: Chicago University Press, 2006)
*Simms, Colin, *Goshawk Lives* (London: Form Books, 1995)
*————, *Gyrfalcon Poems* (Exeter: Shearsman, 2007)
————, *Otters and Martens* (Exeter: Shearsman, 2006)
White, T. H., *The Goshawk* (1951; New York: NYRB Classics, 2007)

Select Bibliography

On Close Attention

Blythe, Ronald, *At the Yeoman's House* (London: Enitharmon, 2013)

Borodale, Sean, *Bee Journal* (London: Jonathan Cape, 2012)

Browne, Thomas, *The Major Works* (London: Penguin, 1977)

Clare, John, *Major Works*, ed. Eric Robinson (Oxford: Oxford University Press, 2008)

Clark, Thomas A., *Yellow and Blue* (Manchester: Carcanet, 2014)

Dee, Tim, *Four Fields* (London: Jonathan Cape, 2013)

Lane, Cathy, *The Hebrides Suite* (Hanau and Frankfurt: Gruenrekorder, 2013)

Larkin, Peter, 'Being Seen for Seeing: A Tribute to R. F. Langley's Journals', available here: http://intercapillaryspace.blogspot.com/2008/08/being-seen-for-seeing-tribute-to-r-f.html

———, *Leaves of a Field* (Exeter: Shearsman, 2006)

*Lopez, Barry, *About This Life: Journeys on the Threshold of Memory* (New York: Knopf, 1998)

———, *Crossing Open Ground* (New York: Scribner, 1988)

Mabey, Richard, *The Common Ground* (London: Hutchinson, 1980)

Morgan, Ann Haven, *The Field Book of Ponds and Streams* (New York: G. P. Putnam's Sons, 1930)

Murdoch, Iris, *Existentialists and Mystics* (London: Penguin, 1997)

Oswald, Alice, *Woods Etc.* (London: Faber and Faber, 2005)

*Robinson, Tim, *Connemara: Listening to the Wind* (Dublin: Penguin Ireland, 2006)

———, *Connemara: A Little Gaelic Kingdom* (Dublin: Penguin Ireland, 2011)

———, *Connemara: The Last Pool of Darkness* (Dublin: Penguin Ireland, 2008)

Sinclair, Iain, *The Edge of the Orison* (London: Penguin, 2005)

*Skelton, Richard, *SKURA* [complete musical works and accompanying text] (Cumbria: Corbel Stone Press, 2012)

Ward, Colin, *The Allotment: Its Landscape and Culture* (Nottingham: Five Leaves, 1997)

On Language and Landscape

Basso, Keith, '"Speaking with Names": Language and Landscape Among the Western Apache', *Cultural Anthropology* 3:2 (1988), 99–130

Select Bibliography

Billeter, Jean-François, *The Chinese Art of Writing* (New York: Rizzoli, 1995)

*Bonnefoy, Yves, *Beginning and End of the Snow/Début et Fin de la Neige*, trans. Emily Grosholz (Lewisburg: Bucknell University Press, 2012)

*Clark, Thomas A., *The Hundred Thousand Places* (Manchester: Carcanet, 2009)

DeSilvey, Caitlin, Simon Naylor and Colin Sackett (eds.), *Anticipatory History* (Axminster: Uniformbooks, 2011)

Evans, Gareth, and Di Robson (eds.), *Towards Re-Enchantment: Place and Its Meanings* (London: ArtEvents, 2010)

Finlay, Alec, and Ken Cockburn, *The Road North*, see: http://www.theroadnorth. co.uk/

Friel, Brian, *Translations* (1980; London: Faber and Faber, 2012)

Goodwin, Mark, sound-enhanced poetry, at https://soundcloud.com/ kramawoodgin

Gorman, Rody, *Sweeney: An Intertonguing* (forthcoming)

Groom, Nick, *The Seasons* (London: Atlantic, 2013)

Kinsella, John, *Disclosed Poetics* (Manchester: Manchester University Press, 2007)

Leonard, Stephen, *The Polar North: Ways of Speaking, Ways of Belonging* (London: Francis Boutle, 2014)

Marsden, Philip, *Rising Ground: A Search for the Spirit of Place* (London: Granta, 2014)

Meloy, Ellen, *Eating Stone* (New York: Pantheon, 2005)

Mengham, Rod, 'Grimspound', in *Contourlines*, ed. Neil Wenborn (Cromer: Salt, 2009)

Proulx, E. Annie, 'Big Skies, Empty Places', *New Yorker*, 25 December 2000

Ray, Andrew, *Some Landscapes* blog, http://some-landscapes.blogspot.co.uk/

*Robinson, Tim, *My Time in Space* (Dublin: Lilliput, 2001)

Spirn, Anne Whiston, *The Language of Landscape* (New Haven, Conn.: Yale University Press, 1998)

Thomson, Derick, *Meall Garbh: The Rugged Mountain* (Glasgow: Gairm, 1995)

On Metaphor

Curry, Patrick, 'Radical Metaphor', in *Earthlines* (August 2013), 35–8

Donoghue, Denis, *Metaphor* (Cambridge, Mass.: Harvard University Press, 2014)

Johnson, Mark, and George Lakoff, *Metaphors We Live By* (1980; Chicago: University of Chicago Press, 2003)

Select Bibliography

On Naming and Knowing

*AR, *Wolf Notes* (Cumbria: Corbel Stone Press, 2010)

Bailly, Jean-Christophe, *Le Dépaysement* (Paris: Éditions du Seuil, 2011)

Carter, Paul, *The Road to Botany Bay: An Essay in Spatial History* (London: Faber and Faber, 1987)

Chatterjee, Debjani (ed.), *Daughters of a Riverine Land* (Sheffield: Bengali Women's Support Group, 2003)

———, *Words Spit and Splinter* (Bradford: Redbeck Press, 2009)

*Clifford, Sue, and Angela King, *England in Particular* (London: Hodder & Stoughton, 2006)

Cocker, Mark, and Richard Mabey, *Birds Britannica* (London: Chatto & Windus, 2005)

Heaney, Seamus, *The Haw Lantern* (London: Faber and Faber, 1987)

———, *North* (London: Faber and Faber, 1975)

Hoban, Russell, *Riddley Walker* (London: Jonathan Cape, 1980)

Grigson, Geoffrey, *The Englishman's Flora* (London: Phoenix House, 1955)

*Mabey, Richard, *Flora Britannica* (London: Chatto & Windus, 1996)

Michaels, Anne, *Fugitive Pieces* (1996; London: Bloomsbury, 1997)

Robertson, Robin, and Alasdair Roberts, 'Leaving St Kilda', in *Hirta Songs* (Southend: Stone Tape, 2013)

Self, Will, *The Book of Dave* (London: Viking, 2006)

Solnit, Rebecca, *Infinite City: A San Francisco Atlas* (San Francisco: University of California Press, 2010)

Stewart, George, *Names on the Land: A Historical Account of Place-Naming in the United States* (1945; New York: NYRB Classics, 2008)

*Stilgoe, John R., *Shallow Water Dictionary* (New York: Princeton Architectural Press, 2004)

Turner, Nancy J., *Ancient Pathways, Ancestral Knowledge*, 2 vols. (Montreal: McGill-Queen's University Press, 2014)

On Thinking with Landscape

*Abram, David, *The Spell of the Sensuous* (New York: Pantheon, 1996)

Dillard, Annie, *Pilgrim at Tinker Creek* (New York: Harper's Magazine Press, 1974)

———, *Teaching a Stone to Talk* (New York: Harper & Row, 1982)

Select Bibliography

*Leopold, Aldo, *A Sand County Almanac & Other Writings on Ecology and Conservation*, ed. Curt Meine (New York: Library Classics, 2013)

Schama, Simon, *Landscape and Memory* (New York: Vintage, 1995)

Wylie, John, 'Landscape, Absence and the Geographies of Love', *Transactions of the Institute of British Geographers* 34 (2009), 275–89

On Wonder

Daston, Lorraine, and Katherine Park, *Wonder and the Orders of Nature* (Cambridge, Mass.: MIT Press, 2001)

Descartes, René, *The Passions of the Soul* (1649), in *Meditations and Other Metaphysical Writings*, trans. Desmond M. Clarke (London: Penguin, 1998)

*Fisher, Philip, *Wonder, the Rainbow, and the Aesthetics of Rare Experience* (Cambridge, Mass.: Harvard University Press, 2003)

Henderson, Caspar, *The Book of Barely Imagined Beings* (London: Granta, 2012)

———, *A New Map of Wonders* (London: Granta, forthcoming)

Hoffman, Julian, *The Small Heart of Things* (Athens, Ga: University of Georgia Press, 2013)

Mauries, Patrick, *Cabinets of Curiosities* (London: Thames & Hudson, 2011)

Warner, Marina, *Signs and Wonders* (London: Chatto & Windus, 2003)

ACKNOWLEDGEMENTS

I thank first, and profoundly, those among the living who have inspired this book, and who are written about here: Anne Campbell, Peter Davidson, Simon Fitzwilliam-Hall, Barry Lopez, Finlay MacLeod, Autumn Richardson, Richard Skelton and Deb Wilenski. The Peat Glossary (the glossary that began *Landmarks*) was compiled by Catriona Campbell, Kenneth Campbell, Ruairidh MacIlleathain, Donald Morrison and Mary Smith, as well as by Anne and Finlay. 'A Counter-Desecration Phrasebook' (the chapter that began *Landmarks*) was initially encouraged by the writer and editor Gareth Evans, one of the most intellectually generous people it has been my luck to know.

The jaw-dropping global glossary about which I write in the Postscript is the work of Simon Fitzwilliam-Hall. Its full name as a project-in-progress is 'Language in the Landscape: A Multilingual Glossary of Topographical Terms and Place-Name Elements in the Afro-Eurasian Lands' (or 'The Topoglossary' for short). Simon can be contacted on ahfhall@yahoo.co.uk.

Landmarks could never have reached the page without the expertise of Philip Sidney, who turned the glossaries from a helter-skelter welter of words into a navigable delta of categories and subcategories. He was, throughout, painstaking, patient, dedicated, imaginative, sharp-sighted – and good-humoured, even when the going got seriously *stuggy*. Julith Jedamus close-read the first draft with typical acuity and attention; she has now crucially shaped three of my books. Simon Prosser has been editorially brilliant, a fine friend, and solid as a *klett* in terms of support. Jessica Woollard, as ever, has been staunch and subtle as agent, friend and reader. At Penguin I have been fortunate enough to work with Richard Bravery, Emma Brown, Anna Kelly, Claire Mason, Anna Ridley and Celeste Ward-Best, and to be copy-edited by the lynx-eyed Caroline Pretty. It remains a huge privilege to collaborate with Stanley Donwood. Jonathan Gibbs's woodcuts for the glossaries are rich and strange.

Acknowledgements

The relations of language and landscape have fascinated me for as long as I can remember, but I am hardly the first to be drawn to the subject. The bibliography details some of the texts and music that have informed *Landmarks*, but I would note here that I have been influenced and guided especially by Tim Robinson (the *Stones of Aran* diptych and the *Connemara* trilogy); Richard Mabey (*Flora Britannica*); Sue Clifford and Angela King's *England in Particular* (which shows that celebratory particularism is quite distinct from triumphant nationalism), as well as the wider activities and publications of Common Ground (co-founded by Sue and Angela with Roger Deakin); the research and writing of the great place-name scholar Margaret Gelling; the ninety-year-long labours of the English Place-Name Society; Barry Lopez and Debra Gwartney's *Home Ground*; the extraordinary work of the poets Bill Griffiths and Katrina Porteous in researching and celebrating the language of the north-east of England, both in verse and academic writing; and the ongoing writing and music of Richard Skelton and Autumn Richardson. I thank also the photographer Dominick Tyler: Dom and I first discovered our common passion for this terrain in 2007–8; and then five years later realized we were both writing books on the subject. Dom's *Uncommon Ground* (London: Faber and Faber, 2015) contains his exceptional photographs of a hundred land features, as well as his accounts of seeking them out up and down the country. His online crowd-sourced glossary of place-terms, 'The Landreader', can be seen and contributed to at: http://www.thelandreader.com/.

The compilation of my glossaries proceeded slowly for a decade or so, before reaching its blizzard phase during the past eighteen months. I have met with such kindness in that time; so many people have shared words with me. I thank in particular (as well as those named above and in the book): Ben Cartwright, Amy Cutler, Gavin Francis, Melissa Harrison, Henry Hitchings, Amy Gear, Caroline and Kurt Jackson, Stuart Kelly, Chamu Kuppuswamy, Rosamund Macfarlane, Matthew Oates, 'Dawn Piper', Jane Stevenson, Winifred Stevenson and Ken Worpole. Bob Jellicoe has been a constant source of ideas and language: his tape recordings of Suffolk longshoremen, made nearly half a century ago, constitute a precious trove of East Anglian coastal culture. Meriel Martin's recent research into Exmoor dialect, and the questions of language for landscape more broadly, has been exemplary; my thanks to Meriel for allowing me to *fossick* freely in the extensive glossaries she gathered.

In addition, for their contributions to the glossaries, I am grateful to Bill Adams, Sean Borodale, Nick Bullock, Alex Buxton, Horatio Clare, Rachel Cooke, Adrian Cooper, Mark Goodwin, Rody Gorman, Nick Groom, Alexandra Harris, Geraint

Acknowledgements

Jennings, Mari Jones, Roger Jones, Pat Law, Liz Lloyd, Cathlin Macaulay, John Macfarlane, Malachi McIntosh, Roy McMillan, Leo Mellor, Benjamin Morris, Kate Norbury, Darryl Ogier, Liz Ogilvie, Jules Pretty, Fiona Reynolds, Rob St John, James Smith, Jos Smith, Ian Stephen, Sarah Thomas, Malachy Tulloch and Stephen Watts.

For other kinds of help, support, thought and encouragement, thanks to Myles Archibald, Will Atkins, Jeff Barrett, Terence Blacker, James Canton, Debjani Chatterjee, Mike Collier, Patrick Curry, William Dalrymple, Rufus Deakin, Steve Dilworth, Naomi Geraghty, Alison Hastie, Michael Hurley, Robert Hyde, Grace Jackson, Joe Kennedy, Peter Larkin, Hayden Lorimer, Victoria McArthur, Andrew McNeillie, Duncan Minshull, George Monbiot, Helen Mort, Andrew Ray, Graham Riach, Di Robson, Titus and Jasmin Rowlandson, Chris and Jan Schramm, Stephen Taylor, Rosy Thornton, Robin Turner, Andrew Walsh, Marina Warner, Kirk Watson, Roderick Watson, Caroline Wendling, Simon Williams, Kabe Wilson, David Woodman and Mark Wormald.

Many hundreds of people contributed to the 'gift glossary' that features in this paperback edition. I have been unable individually to thank many of those who wrote, and indeed unable to identify all of them. I'd like here, therefore, to express my deep gratitude and acknowledgements to all who have made contact since the publication of *Landmarks*, and especially those who have offered or otherwise given words, including (but by no means limited to) the following: Felicity Alexander, June Ames, Tom Andrewes, Dennis Andrews, James Stout Angus, Claire Annabel, Ben Anson, Wendy Argent, Anne Armitage, N. J. Austin, Caro Baker, Teresa Baker, Sarah Banbery, June Barber, Noenoe Barney-Campbell, Stephen Barran, M. A. Bartle, Andrew Bartley, Ben Batten, Ginny Battson, Catherine Bennett, Charles Bennett, David Betteridge, Alan Bigg, John Birkett, Elaine Bishop, John The Boat, Katie Bond, Helen Bowman, Clive Bowring, Colin Brazier, Barney Brown, Caroline Brown, Victoria Bull, Tom Bullough, Anne Burke, Miriam Butler, Christine Butterworth, Alex Buxton, Marjorie Byers, Ann Carr, Kenneth Carson, Katherine Carter, Nicola Chambury, Chris Chapman, Jean Chapple, David Chun, John Clare, Elisabeth Claridge, Alan Cleaver, Margaret Cockcroft, David Collison, Matthew Commin, Carol Anne Connolly, Geoff Cooper, Chris Cornford, Joe Cornish, Peter Court-Hampton, Mary Cox, Christine Craig, Marlene Creates, Philip Crocker, Claire Cummings, Martin Davies, Bob Delaney, Lorna Delanoy, Brian Dillon, Bronwen Dinneen, R. S. Dobson, Mike Dodd, Mark Dolan, Lawrie Donnison, Veronica Duggan, Andrew Dunning, Andrew

Acknowledgements

Eastaugh, Elisabeth Eddy-Mulcahy, Toby Edwards, Ed Elliott, Liz Else, Oliver Facey, Ruth Facey, Jamie Fenton, Anne Fielding Smith, Graeme Fife, Keith Foster, Sara Fox, Alan Garner, Rodger Garratt, Peter Gater, Valerie Gibbs, Jim Gilchrist, Anne Gill, Harry Gilonis, Marian Glasscoe, Chris Gomersall, Jenny Goodhand, Glen Graham, Richard Graves, Doug Greenwood, Tanya Gregson, Naomi Griffiths, Hugo Gye, @haggardhawks, Viv Hancock, Tim Hannigan, Richard Hanwell, George Harding, Meriel Harrison, Michael Haslam, Kathryn Hatcher, Susan Hathcock, Jonathan Hayman, Deborah Hayter, Seamus Heaney, Kay Hedges, Max Hemmings, David Hetherington, Chris Hext, Clare Hicks, Simon Hodgkinson, Sarah Hollis, Graham Holmwood, Jeremy Hooker, Sarah Hosking, Catherine Hughes, Alan Hunter, J. S. Hurst, Simon Ings, Brian Jackman, Bobby Magic Jaeger, Minu Hunter Jaeger, Tim Jeanes, Bob Jellicoe, Christine Jennings, Colin Johnson, Ian Johnson, Kimberly Johnson, Melvyn Jones, Olwen Jones, Irma Kellett, Michael Kerr, Vicki Kynas, Joseph Lalor, Stephen Lees, W. J. Legge, Angela Leighton, Catherine Leonard, Edna Leonard, Brian Le Messurier, Iris Lerpiniere, Ann Lloyd, E. Lonsdale, Andrew Lothian, Peter Lowe, Jemma Lowin, Diana Ludwik, John Macfarlane, Rosamund Macfarlane, Isabel Macho, Hazel McIntosh, Andrew McKillop, Elinor McLean, Geoff Manaugh, Vereen Marcer, Myles Marchington, Fiona Marlow, Cathy Matheson, Roger Mattam, Stephen Mayhew, Geoffrey Mead, Naomi Michael, China Mieville, Mary Millar, Jim Miller, Peter Mitchell, Alistair Moffat, Pippa Morgan, Hilde Morris, Ben Myers, Duncan Nagle, T. P. Nash, Ken Neville-Davies, Vicky Nield, A. Norgate, Doris Norton, G. A. Noy, R. M. Nuttall, Marigold Oakley, Jayne O'Connell, Lorna O'Leary, Marion Oughton, Ross Packman, Michael Parker, Wendy Patch, Roy Pearse, Vicky Pearson, Margaret Peart, Donald Peck, Lisa Pickard, Clausdirk Pollner, Katrina Porteous, Eddie Procter, Charles Rangeley-Wilson, James Rebanks, Dan Renton, Graham Riach, Bernard Richards, Keith Richards, Martin Riley, Claire Rogers, Patrick Russell, Michael Scarborough, V. Schroder, Bernard Sheridan, Ian Short, Elisabeth Shuker, Angela Silkstone, Colin Simms, Dave Sissons, Richard Skelton, Jane Smith, Roger H. Smith, Caroline Spatchett, Brian Spencer, Robbie Stamp, Dave Stanley, Julian Stenhouse, Nigel Stephenson, Paul Stewart, Val Stockley, Felix Tandon, Harvey Taylor, Helena Thomas, Janet Thomas, Richard Thomas, Carol Thorne, Agnes Treherne, Mike Trevorrow, Adrian Tuck, Dave Tyson, Chris Vere, Tim Walker, Wendy-Jane Walton, Jacob Watcham, Alan Waters, Elizabeth Watt, Tim Weaver, Andy Wedge, Mary West, Jean Willis, Clare Wilson, Henry Wilson, Rab Wilson, Lucy Wishart, Brian Wood, Josephine Woods, Antony Woodward, Judith Yarrow and

Acknowledgements

Nell Young. The National Trust has been hugely helpful in seeking and gathering in words from its millions of members, and I wish to thank Helen Beer, Mike Collins, Anna Lea and Sally Palmer for all their interest and support.

I am indebted to various institutions, chief among them Emmanuel College, Cambridge, where I am fortunate enough to hold a teaching fellowship; and the Faculty of English, Cambridge, where I hold a senior lectureship. Conversations with my students (notable among them Tom Gilliver, Anna Main, Charles Rousseau, Napper Tandy and Lewis Wynn) were vital to the development of *Landmarks* – as was the award of a Philip Leverhulme Prize by the Leverhulme Trust. The Trust's trust in me, and its support – logistical and financial – of the book's writing, has been outstanding. I am grateful also to the Cambridge University Library and the London Library.

For permission to quote from the published and unpublished work of J. A. Baker, I thank the Baker Estate and Myles Archibald at HarperCollins. Nigel Cochrane and Sandy Macmillen at the Albert Sloman Library, University of Essex, made my time in the Baker Archive both possible and pleasurable. John Fanshawe and Mark Cocker's efforts in bringing Baker's archive to Essex, transcribing and editing the journals, and extending our knowledge of Baker's life and world, have been immense. John also expertly read my Baker chapter.

For permission to quote from the published and unpublished work of Jacquetta Hawkes, I am grateful to Nicolas Hawkes, as well as to Christine Finn for her permission to quote from her unpublished biography of Jacquetta Hawkes, and to Special Collections, University of Bradford Library, for access to the Jacquetta Hawkes Archive and for permission to reproduce unpublished material.

For permission to quote from the poetry of Norman MacCaig, I am grateful to the MacCaig Estate, and to Neville Moir at Polygon.

For permission to quote from the poetry of Hugh MacDiarmid, I am grateful to Carcanet Press.

For permission to quote from the work of Nan Shepherd and from his own memories of Nan, and for other kinds of support, I am grateful to her literary executor, Erlend Clouston. I am grateful also to the Trustees of the National Library of Scotland and to Dairmid Gunn for permission to quote from Neil Gunn's letters, and to George Mackie for permission to quote from Nan's letters to Barbara Balmer.

I sometimes wonder if I will ever find a subject other than landscape to write about, having done so for fifteen years – but soon after always conclude that it is unlikely, given that the terrain is infinite in its interest and unfathomable in its

Acknowledgements

complexities. I have been circling the books and ideas at the core of *Landmarks* for years now; some of the chapters here have now been close to a decade in their thinking and revising. I am grateful to all those editors who have enabled and encouraged me along the way, among them Lisa Allardice, Myles Archibald, Jamie Byng, Nick Davies, Charlotte Knight, Julia Koppitz, Paul Laity, Norah Perkins, Susanna Rustin and Helen Tookey. Notably (as above), 'A Counter-Desecration Phrasebook' found its first expression in *Towards Re-Enchantment: Place and Its Meanings*, ed. Gareth Evans and Di Robson (London: ArtEvents, 2010), and 'The Living Mountain' began as a long essay prefacing the 2011 Canongate reissue of Nan Shepherd's masterpiece of the same name. Fragments of 'Hunting Life' have their origin in my 2005 Introduction to the NYRB Classics reissue of Baker's *The Peregrine*, and some paragraphs of 'The Black Locust and the Silver Pine' were part of an Introduction to a 2006 edition of Muir's *My First Summer in the Sierra*. 'Bastard Countryside' and 'Stone-Books' both began in 2011 as essays for the Collins Nature Library on Jefferies and Hawkes respectively. I have written and spoken on Lopez and Deakin in numerous different places and at numerous different times.

Finally, above all and for ever, love and thanks to Julia, Lily, Tom and Will.

INDEX

Index

Index

He just wanted a decent book to read ...

Not too much to ask, is it? It was in 1935 when Allen Lane, Managing Director of Bodley Head Publishers, stood on a platform at Exeter railway station looking for something good to read on his journey back to London. His choice was limited to popular magazines and poor-quality paperbacks – the same choice faced every day by the vast majority of readers, few of whom could afford hardbacks. Lane's disappointment and subsequent anger at the range of books generally available led him to found a company – and change the world.

'We believed in the existence in this country of a vast reading public for intelligent books at a low price, and staked everything on it'
Sir Allen Lane, 1902–1970, founder of Penguin Books

The quality paperback had arrived – and not just in bookshops. Lane was adamant that his Penguins should appear in chain stores and tobacconists, and should cost no more than a packet of cigarettes.

Reading habits (and cigarette prices) have changed since 1935, but Penguin still believes in publishing the best books for everybody to enjoy. We still believe that good design costs no more than bad design, and we still believe that quality books published passionately and responsibly make the world a better place.

So wherever you see the little bird – whether it's on a piece of prize-winning literary fiction or a celebrity autobiography, political tour de force or historical masterpiece, a serial-killer thriller, reference book, world classic or a piece of pure escapism – you can bet that it represents the very best that the genre has to offer.

Whatever you like to read – trust Penguin.